Where to Nest

Kristen Van Nest

RISING ACTION

Cover Illustration © **Nat Mack**
Cover Photography © **Robyn Von Swank**
Distributed by **Blackstone Publishing**

ISBN: 978-1-990253-57-7
Ebook: 978-1-990253-62-1

TRV010000 TRAVEL | Essays & Travelogues
BIO026000   BIOGRAPHY & AUTOBIOGRAPHY Personal Memoirs
TRV026000 TRAVEL | Special Interest | General

#WhereToNest

Follow Rising Action on our socials!
Twitter: @RAPubCollective
Instagram: @risingactionpublishingco
Tiktok: @risingactionpublishingco

To the love of my life, my cat Nala

This memoir is the author's story. The memories and experiences are from her recollection and may not reflect the experiences of those featured in the book.

Where to Nest

PROLOGUE

My mom and I sat in the parking lot of LaGuardia Airport in New York City. Despite having planned for this moment for months, my nerves were still getting the best of me.

"Do you have the drugs?" I asked my mom. "From my cavity filling?" I know it's not normal to get anti-anxiety drugs when you are having routine dental work, but I have a phobia of needles. My dentist was likely a little lenient with my prescription because she loved interrogating me during my annual exams, eagerly waiting for my travel stories while both her hands were shoved in my mouth. She tried to set me up with her son once, whom I'd never met but had seen a million times in the pictures in her office–him, his sister, and their dog, all in matching white shirts and khakis in front of a stone-gray photo lab backdrop.

"What was it like in Luxembourg?" she'd ask me.

"It was kind of like an adult Disneyland in that—*grgrlgrl*," I'd attempted to respond, cut off by her gloved hands entering my mouth.

My mom opened her car's glove compartment. She pulled out the anti-anxiety meds and passed them over.

I went to put them in my mouth, then stopped. "Sorry if it makes you uncomfortable."

"It's okay. This is a special circumstance," my mom said.

"Thanks." I popped the pill in my mouth. "Hopefully it will start working after I've gone through security." The pills were step one on my anti-anxiety checklist to take away the stress of moving to China.

What was waiting for me in China? Nothing, really. Having never visited Asia, I had only a few acquaintances there, didn't speak Mandarin, and didn't even have a job or place to live. My plan was to move there, find a job, and live there for who knows how long. All I knew was that I had wanted to move to Asia to work in international marketing, and friends of friends had told me that Shanghai had a similar feel to New York City, where I currently lived.

As I sat in the window seat on the Chinese airline that I had chosen to save forty dollars, an Asian woman in her forties barreled towards me. With a huge smile on her face, she documented every angle of the plane with her phone. As she settled in, she took more pictures: the front of the inside of the plane, the side, and then one with me in the background! Holding her camera out so I could see what she'd taken, she showed me a picture of... myself. Giving her a thumbs up, she grinned. My pill had kicked in, so nothing could faze me.

Step two of my anti-anxiety plan: *Beyoncé*. What better to help me remain confident than listening, on repeat, to someone who is an actual goddess.

Step three of my plan: mondo vino! This was one of my last chances to have American wine, but why not try Chinese wine? As I took a sip, it was a little grainier than its European counterparts.[1] More importantly, it had alcohol in it (not normally on anxiety medication, I didn't know you shouldn't mix it with alcohol, whoops!). I drank it in, letting it dye my mouth cannibal red. It looked like I ate the blueberry girl from *Willy Wonka and the Chocolate Factory.*

My seatmate was doing her own self-care: a sheet face mask. As I peered over, we made eye contact through her mask slits. A smile crept up between the corners of the mouth hole. I glanced away.

Suddenly, a bunch of men jumped from their seats and started yelling. Frantically, I looked around. *Was there a fire?* No, it was the flight attendant selling duty-free cigarettes. Previously, while living in Europe, I remembered seeing Europeans leave the airport with huge packs of duty-free ones. Here, there seemed to be a bidding war on the plane. The men rushed the flight attendant. Had the Marlboro man, alone on his horse, slowly meandering through the plains, known that one day this would be happening because of him?

The sudden commotion made my uneasiness grow. The plane's carpet had that distinct 1990s look: that pure chaos pattern designed specifically to hide anything—even child's vomit at a Chuck E. Cheese. Wondering if this plane had been on this earth longer than me, I peered at the tiny, communal television a few rows ahead. Was that—I squinted—Chuck Norris? This felt like a stereotype, but a Chuck Norris karate film truly was playing. The Marlboro man, Chuck Norris ... was this really 2013? At least this movie couldn't make me cry. My seatmate had settled into the next phase of her trip: playing Candy Crush for the next five hours.

It was time for step four of my anti-anxiety plan: reading *All the Rules: Time-Tested Secrets for Capturing the Heart of Mr. Right* by Ellen Fein. My friend's sister was a matchmaker and swore by it. She had advice like,

"Giving a hand-job isn't cheating" and "A line of coke is cheaper than a Red Bull." She knew how to live life to its fullest and wasn't that why I was moving to Shanghai? The year before, I'd returned to New York City after a wild experience abroad and felt a sudden disconnect from my closest friends from high school. We no longer had much in common.

"I love EDM concerts. I take Molly and go on the craziest trips every weekend," a friend would say.

"My last crazy trip was spending Oktoberfest living with a go-go dancer in Munich," I would say as an attempt to relate, but then everyone would stare at me blankly. My experiences abroad made me awkward, and I couldn't fit back into the culture from which I came. I didn't even own a pair of boat shoes.

I knew from the book that I had to wait four hours before texting a guy back for the first time and then thirty minutes in between every text after that, so I was ready to find love ... as well as hopefully a job and a place to live. In reality, I wouldn't have sex for a whole year after following all the rules in that damn book. No man would live up to their stringent guidelines, and I have always been an A student, following directions neurotically, which in this case meant a vagina as dry as your mouth when you have a hangover.

Nervously packing all my belongings back into my carry-on backpack, I waited to step off the plane. It was 7:51 p.m. in Shanghai and 7:51 a.m. Eastern Standard Time. This was the dreaded moment: leaving my flight to find out how to make Shanghai my new home. If any moment was going to give me anxiety, it was stepping off of a plane into a completely unknown country.

Off the flight, the clean cream walls found in pretty much any inter-national airport greeted me. Adrenaline pumped through my veins, and

I bit my lip. Surprisingly, it felt better than an orgasm. Every cell in my body felt alive. It was the greatest high I'd ever experienced. I was living in a country that I knew nothing about where I would start a new life. I felt free. My whole body vibrated with excitement.

Then, a new fear hit me: had I peaked? Will I ever feel an adrenaline rush like this again?

Maybe I should consider how my addiction to traveling started.

CHAPTER 1: AMERICANS IN PARIS

Untethering from My Childhood Ball and Chain

New Canaan, Connecticut, United States—In 1647, Pieter Van Nest, a small-town farmer from the Netherlands, left his familiar, agricultural hometown to board a ship to New Amsterdam, now New York City. He had no idea what lay ahead but chose to take this great risk and set up a new life in the New World, which at that point was pretty much a forest and some large rocks. Essentially, he was Tom Hanks in *Castaway* if Tom *chose* to be stranded. Today, the Van Nest neighborhood in the Bronx is named after his former farm and everyone living there has access to bodegas.

The Dutch translation of our last name, "Van Nest," means "from Nest," which is the Americanized version of Ness, the farm town in Holland we come from. While where I'm from is instilled in my name, so adventure is in my blood. Like Pieter, I've spent my life searching for a place to belong, including visiting Thailand during a government coup, eating chicken hearts in Shenzhen (it tastes like chicken, but gummier), and this one time I'm pretty sure I got foot and mouth disease walking through dirty typhoon water in Shanghai. My journey started when I was sixteen.

"I just think spending your summer in Paris would be better than spending your summer with that friend of yours," my grandmother explained, handing me a bunch of pamphlets about summer programs abroad. With her pearl necklace and glamorous Grace Kelly blond hair, she was determined to have me spend my summer in the Old World.

The friend, Patricia, and I were less affluent than the other kids in our town, one of the wealthiest towns in the U.S.: New Canaan, Connecticut. The coolest thing about my hometown was that Chloe Sevigny used to smoke cigarettes behind our gas station and yet never managed to burn the entire suburb to the ground. The second coolest thing was that Chloe Sevigny had the opportunity to burn it to the ground.

My grandparents bought my family's tiny apartment, my mom paying them rent each month, so we could attend the *good* public schools. By that I mean, when the homecoming king, because he was part of the football team, couldn't do the homecoming queen and king halftime performance, his father, the Chairman and CEO of a publicly traded airline, came out as his stand-in. On a motor vehicle ladder, he and the homecoming queen—in their crowns—crossed the field, waving at the crowd. As another example of how much money the school had, it took five years for people to realize a pair of lunch ladies—who were sisters—had embezzled over $500k. That's around $2,000 in lunch money a week, which is kind of badass. Gym class also included yoga by candle-light.

"You live in an apartment?" one of my rich friends once asked, crin-kling her nose, after giving me a ride from our high school in her BMW SUV. Friends were never invited over to my house because while they had life-size Barbies, the newest PlayStation games, and pet horses, I had the usual stuff: a handful of regular-size, secondhand Barbies, a Tamagotchi, and a pet snapping turtle, Snappy, that I'd caught in the local river and fed worms in my bathtub.

Playdates felt like a trip to a Disney castle; I'd wander into a friend's home and admire their spiral staircase, primary bedroom bathroom with four sinks (why would you even need this?), walk-in closet, or private movie theater. Like Disneyland, these homes always felt a little sterile: they'd been designed by the contractor to maximize their profit and normally had little furniture because most of the family's money went to the mortgage. Or in the case of my friend whose Dad was a Russian oligarch, because they didn't have enough time to pack their furniture when fleeing Russia after finding out there was a hit on him by Putin. Needless to say, I was so jealous of their mansions. My apartment was so small there was no place to avoid the screams of my parents fighting over money.

"Don't put your elbows on the table," my step-grandfather would scold me at Thanksgiving dinner. "Wealthy people have a code of man-ners, and to be one of them, you have to show you know their rules." This was drilled into my head even as I struggled to fit in with my rich friends. *I must hide that I'm different.* For this reason, every piece of my personality was shaped around how to get ahead in life, not what made me happy. Focused on achieving the American dream, I idolized living in a giant generic box with an outlandish mortgage, having a loving husband and kids, and maybe even have enough money left over to get a hot tub and two to three sinks in the master bathroom, because even when I'm filthy rich, four sinks would be excessive.

Other than Patricia, my friend group was all nerds. In most teen movies, the nerds are a small group of outcasts who would finagle their way into parties or do crazy things at band camp. If my friends became a music group, our band name would be "Born to Be Mild." We never got invited to any parties where actual alcohol was served. While most high school kids were drinking 40s and having unprotected sex, we were watching *13 Going on 30* in someone's basement. At that point, I would have done *anything* to drink a warm Mike's Hard Lemonade in someone's damp backyard shed. I'd also made out with only one guy. It was during a game of manhunt. After waiting in a pile of damp leaves next to each other for about an hour, he finally made his move, and we kissed . . . but our tongues felt like two bats fighting in a cave. Later, we'd find out that no one came searching for us because the birthday girl had a panic attack and had been rushed to the hospital.

I should also note that I've always been obsessed with cats. I have a photo from the eighth grade of me holding my cat, Meow Meow, a gorgeous chocolate Burmese, while dressed in cat pyjamas, sitting on cat-covered sheets. While my parents were getting divorced, Meow Meow was my everything. As they screamed, I'd hug little Meow Meow close as he desperately tried to escape my arms.

No one wants to fuck the Cat Girl. So, when I left my town and met people who knew nothing about me, my prospects of hooking up went up. Maybe, with experience abroad, I would transform from a Cat Girl to a sexy and sophisticated Cat Woman.

"When I was around your age, I lived in Paris with my soon-to-be first husband, and it was magical," my grandmother emphasized. "I'll match every dollar you make at your catering job if you want to go." She shoved a picture of Notre Dame on one of the brochures at me, very convinced that I shouldn't spend the summer with Patricia.

That summer, while Patricia was sadly getting hooked on PCP, oxycodone, and other drugs, and my nerd friends played Frisbee in the park, I danced on tables at Place de la Bastille, sipped wine from plastic cups with friends from all over the world in front of the Eiffel Tower, and audibly cried watching *The Notebook* on a Transcontinental flight next to a friendly Corsican father and his two highly-concerned pre-teen daughters.[2]

While my grandmother helped me avoid a drug addiction, I became addicted to something else, something that would give me a high and drive me away from home. Nothing made me feel more alive than the adrenaline rush of trying to fit into and finding my way out of unique and awkward situations. In fact, I'd spend my entire twenties wandering the globe, searching for that *je ne sais quoi*, before ending up in L.A. as a comedian. Also, don't worry; according to Instagram, Patricia is now a nurse in Austin, Texas—a very lucrative career.

After that month in Paris, I decided that I wanted to spend the following summer, before senior year, in Switzerland. Having saved up enough catering money, I was able to afford to go to a language school there while living with a host family. I was seventeen and making moves, not only by traveling. Determined, I set a goal to get a boyfriend before college and sent Sam, a guy I had a crush on, a suggestive postcard.

I really enjoyed getting to know you better at the firepit before I left. Your rendition of 'Wonderwall' still stays with me. It was so beautiful. I hope we can get to know each other more when I get back.

From a few towns over, Sam knew nothing about my cat obsession. His town was much like mine, except that all the women went to the same hairdresser, so their blond hair looked identical down to the hue. Within a week of my return, we were an item. His black straightened hair brushed to the side in a long bang, and his pale skin made him look like a vampire unable to be in sunlight. He was constantly playing Magic: The Gathering but refused to let me come to any of his competitions because he said it wouldn't be a turn-on watching him battle it out in a basement.

He wore a ripped black T-shirt and a studded, choker necklace daily because he "didn't want to look like a rich asshole," which is how I intentionally dressed, in prominent Ralph Lauren polo shirts with double popped collars (I had bought them on sale on eBay). As an aspiring rich person, I considered this a neutral look that would help me fit into the old-money society of New York City's adjacent suburbia. After all, my grandfather always reminded me how important networking with my wealthy classmates was in order to have future job prospects. What job was that, as a high schooler? Who knows? But my business self-help books always said your business success relies more on your decisions than your circumstances.

Sam lived in a big house with a lush lawn and gravel driveway. Like most, it was a huge box, very generic, but maximizing interior floor space so a developer could sell it quickly. They had a white golden retriever and a russet golden retriever. His mother was the sweetest housewife, who'd secretly smoke cigarettes when she thought that everyone else had gone to bed. A few times, Sam found her crying behind the house. When asked why, she explained that her home country of Slovenia was at war, and bombs had gone off in her hometown that day. At the time, I admired how strong she was, hiding her feelings from her own family to spare them the pain. I had to learn to do this to be the woman that I thought I wanted to be.

I envied their big house, seemingly perfect family, and outdoor speakers that looked like rocks. They had *everything* from the SkyMall catalog: an antique globe table that opened to reveal a full bar set, plastic eyes and mustaches that you could place on a tree to make it look like it had a face, and a paper towel stand with not one—but four—USB ports in its base. Every single person in their family could charge their phone in the exact same place at the exact same time. Wasn't that the American dream?

Since I thought that we were going to get married, I'd try to use my career-focused attitude to win over his difficult father.

"Any chance you could look over my résumé?" Résumé in hand in the doorway, I trapped him in his home office, where his fraternity paddle hung on the wall. He only drank his coffee black "because he's a man," believed his brother was "bisexual" because that was easier than admitting he was gay, and would frequently finish off two bottles of wine a night and black out on his sofa in his cowboy boots. He worked from home, so I have no idea why he needed to wear his boots at all.

Upon reflection, his dad probably didn't really like me, a woman, trying to connect with him through my drive to be a future breadwinner. While most of my friends were raised by type-A moms who went to college to get an M-R-S degree (find a Mr. to be a Mrs.) and saw it as their full-time job to raise a family and be respectable, better-than-their-neighbors members of the community, my family was different.

My mom had always encouraged me to make my own money. When she was eleven, her father passed away from cancer, leaving my stay-at-home grandmother with three kids and bills to pay. Determined, my grandmother sold the fixer-upper brownstone in New York City that my grandparents had bought together and moved into a small rental. My grandmother didn't have a college degree or a job, as it wasn't the norm for women to work back then, but she had mouths to feed. From this, all the women in my family raised me to make my own money. It was risky to rely on others.

I hoped that Sam would find my ambition sexy. After all, he never wanted to be like his dad, even though his entire identity seemed to revolve around his father's approval. We were in love. Once in college, I even convinced him to study abroad in Paris with me. Is there anything more romantic than sipping wine in red berets at a café outside the Louvre? Bad news: he tried to break up with me a week before we left.

"I want to be single on this trip," Sam told me.

My jaw dropped. "We're both going to be in Paris for the whole semester, living a few blocks from each other, and you want to break up now?!" After two years of him going to college in Seattle and me going to college in D.C., I had planned this whole romantic semester in Paris for the two of us.

"I just feel like I need to, like, find myself," he said. "And I need to learn French, so I shouldn't hang out with other foreigners." Maybe he only wanted to go to Paris because it was legal to drink there.

"I'm fluent in French, so we can practice together, and I'll live down the street from you!" I pleaded. My business self-help books always said a good sales pitch focuses on winning over someone's emotions, not only providing a good rationale.

"Remember all the fun times we had driving to get fried chicken during lunch break? Or eating steak and eggs over an open fire after camping each year for our anniversary? Or eating Copper River salmon in Seattle after a long hike?" Honestly, we'd eaten a lot of great food together. Maybe in Paris, we could make new memories involving niçoise salad and escargot.

"You're right, I forgot about those, my bad," he responded. "We *should* stay together." The next night, he used his fake ID to buy me a six-pack of The Pike Brewing Company beer, one I fell in love with on a trip to visit him in Seattle. I wondered how many men in history have thought a six-pack was a good solution to anything. This didn't seem like an acceptable apology, but I was hanging onto him by a thread, so I let it go. Like all my friends, I had learned that achieving the American dream meant marrying a rich man, and I wasn't ready to let go of mine. Yes, I wanted to make my own money and have my own career, but I also expected a man to pay the check and support our family. After all, he was perfect. He could play the bongos!

In Paris, Sam and I both lived in the 8th Arrondissement with wealthy host families. Being in their home felt like being in Versailles. I was jealous of their high ceilings, crown molding, and nuclear family. It was a world away from my single mom's tiny apartment, and I was determined to have this for my own family someday. Through my hard work, sweat, and Sam's inheritance, we'd get there.

Walking from my host family's home to his was a straight shot down Rue de Courcelles, a wide cobblestone street. I walked past Parc Monceau, a frequent subject of Claude Monet. Its black gate with gold arrowheads, overflowing with flowers and Parisians in Nike tracksuits, glowed in the sunset. Next, I passed the Art Deco Hotel de Banville, named after a famous poet and ranked one of the most romantic in Paris. What a magical place to be in love.

After dinner with my own host family, I often headed over there to stay the night, as he had a private, one-bedroom *chambre de bonne*. These were old maids' quarters for affluent Parisian families.

"And you didn't come home last night," my host mother would say in French. I'd smile and look confused, pretending that I suddenly didn't understand what she was saying. If I had a boyfriend down the street and ended up moving in there, she wouldn't be able to make any more money renting out her extra room to exchange students. She was that French mix of refined and messy. She had perfect hair, slippers, and dressed like she'd just painted a masterpiece and finished off a pack of thin cigarettes.

"We like you more than the other host students we've had. They all studied the arts, but you study international affairs. We can talk to you about the news!" she admitted one day. George Washington University charged their normal tuition regardless of what program you chose to study abroad and then pocketed the difference, so I chose the most expensive one. My program specialized in the arts, with weekly outings to live shows, operas, and museums. At the time, I honestly had no idea that I would ever be performing on a stage, but I loved every moment.

Back then, I thought that I had to choose wealth or a career in the arts. In my town, the belief was that following a creative path was never a "career." It was positioned as a fool's errand and to follow it, you would have to accept that you'd never be able to afford a mortgage or a family. Since my mom was a struggling painter, I saw this play out firsthand. Despite creating beautiful paintings, the time it took to create them versus how much she got paid was less than minimum wage. Soon, she had to give up her art altogether. After my parents' divorce, like my grandmother, my mother had bills to pay and mouths to feed.

"Art is in your bones," my grandmother had always told me, a photographer herself. I ignored my sparkle. I didn't want to end up broke, unable to provide for a family. With this experience, I forced myself to focus on a successful business career and squashed any thoughts at ever pursuing my creativity. Within business, because I loved travel, I set my eyes on becoming an international businesswoman.

Being successful at business to rise up from the difficulties I'd experienced growing up became my obsession. So much so that I graduated from college in only three years, to save on my student loans, but still ended up with $120k in debt. In my hometown, the parents of my friends always said when we entered their homes, "Kristen, it's so impressive you graduated in three years ... And Sam, I heard you're still doing Magic: The Gathering tournaments, how lovely!" I was working my ass off because I didn't have money to fall back on. This made my understanding of the world very different from many of my classmates'.

"Where are your cold towels?" I'd ask a friend at a high school party one night. Growing up, we couldn't afford A/C, so on hot summer nights, my mom would put cold washcloths on our heads before bed to keep us cool. After all, the four seasons are sweaty pits, sweater weather, cold everything, and horny.

"Cold towels?"

"You know ... to stay cool."

"Or we could just turn on the A/C?" Their faces crinkled. This hadn't even crossed my mind as an option.

Sam would finish the full four years, and his parents would pay for his education. He was thoroughly embarrassed one night years earlier when his dad drove their Maserati home drunk from a party and sloppily announced, "You go to any college you want; I'll pay for it all!" I dreamed one day, I'd be able to do the same. Maybe the real American dream was being like a Kennedy: having enough money to hit someone with your car and get away with it.

Sam's host family hated him because he couldn't speak French.

"When I don't understand him, the father yells louder in French," he complained, his lips stained with the vin de table we drank from a plastic bottle before taking a bite of the baguette, saucisson, and goat cheese sandwiches I had made for us to eat in Parc Monceau.

"Do you want to practice now?" I offered. Once we both learned, we could speak French in front of our future children one day, so they'd be bilingual.

"No, I don't want to."

My mind drifted. "I'm worried about finding a job. All the on-campus interviews are happening right now, and here I am in Paris," I lamented. I had tried to do a video interview with Reuters, but my host family's internet kept cutting out.

"My ideal career is like the Magic: The Gathering legend, Paulo Vitor Damo da Rosa, where you don't even need a job, you're like so good, you can live off your winnings. That way, I can have stability, but like, still pursue my love of music," Sam said. As a good partner, I wanted to encourage his creativity, but he'd never seen the hardship I'd seen in my family.

Sam looked around the park. "I think I want to get a tattoo of a tree, you know, so I never forget nature when I'm working a corporate job." How do you forget nature? You can walk outside literally anywhere in the world and it's there. Have you ever wondered if an ex was brooding or just dumb?

"When I get back, I'll have one semester left to try to find something, hopefully in New York. Then when you graduate, you can come up and join me," I said, ignoring the picturesque scenery, my mind consumed with the path ahead. As we sipped our wine in the park, I fantasized about my future with Sam—us sitting just where Monet's subjects would have sat decades before, having a picnic splashed in sunlight. While I matriculated into French culture, Sam didn't.

"You sure you don't want to practice French?" I asked him on a regular basis.

"I'm so tired of speaking French. I don't understand anything in my classes."

"Can you just learn ten words?" I retorted, frustrated. Why didn't he want to learn about another culture? How would we become citizens of the world if he didn't at least try? It started to sink in that not everyone wanted to incorporate other cultures into their lives. Yes, croissants were great, but some people just wanted to stick to everything bagels. Don't get me wrong, they're amazing, but sometimes I wanted a stick of butter in my bread, too. Traveling was all about eating bread in new and exciting places.

For Christmas, we decided to do a tour around eastern Europe. Before the trip, I saw a pretty wool dress in the shop window. On an extremely tight budget, I didn't do any shopping in Paris, but the dress was in a box labeled 7€.

"How do you like my new dress?" I asked Sam as we put on our bags to head out on our trip.

"You don't look good in dresses," he said, standing there in his favorite *Radiohead* shirt, ripped from years of wear.

"What? That's such a mean thing to say!"

"I'm helping you. Now you know you don't look good in them, so you'll only buy pants," he said.

"Is it my legs?"

"I don't know, you don't look good."

On our flight, I looked out the window, processing what he had said to me. Making me feel bad about how I looked didn't really seem like it was helping me. If he loved me, why would he say something so hurtful? If we were going to be together forever, I guess it was better to know what he liked and didn't like so I could be the best partner I could possibly be. That's what all the housewives in my hometown did. All the media at the time talked about how "women can have it all:" a family *and* a career. That's what I wanted: a happy husband and a successful career to help give my future children everything they needed.

I thought back to his mother, hiding in the shadows in their backyard, out of sight from her family, crying about her hometown being bombed to rubble. Didn't being a strong woman mean hiding your feelings? If this flight were to go down suddenly, I would be instructed to put on my mask before assisting others. Why are women always supposed to put their own needs last in every other situation that isn't a deadly disaster? You had to bury those feelings really deep.

In Prague, I'd found us a great deal in a four-star hotel, probably because we were visiting in the dead of winter. On Christmas, they served us champagne for breakfast.

"Chin! Chin!" Clinking glasses, we guzzled our free champagne and returned for more. We didn't want to pay for Wi-Fi in the room, so after breakfast, we waited to use the lobby computer next to a big Christmas tree and a Nespresso machine with a picture of George Clooney on it to message our families. The man before us was on a porn site; we all have our own ways of celebrating the holidays.

For dinner, Sam's family paid for us to eat at a nice restaurant. We went to Prague Castle and ate under heat lamps on the terrace, overlooking the city. The stars sparkled, I looked at the man I loved, and he looked back at me. I held his hand as we walked down the cobbled steps of the castle because I loved him—and didn't want to slip on black ice.

Back at the hotel room, I lit a red candle, and we opened a bottle of absinthe, hoping to see the green fairy.

"You can't hold your liquor," Sam said as he mixed Sprite into my absinthe. Having heard that van Gogh may have chopped his ear off because of absinthe, I was totally fine having a smaller portion.

Once I finished my glass, I headed to get more. Sam went to use the bathroom. As I picked up the bottle, I discovered it was empty.

"Sam, where's the absinthe?"

There was a thud.

Rushing to the bathroom, I slid to a halt when I saw red was splattered everywhere and Sam was on the floor.

"Oh my God, what happened? Are you bleeding?!"

He looked around. "The red is candle wax. I knocked over a candle and slipped on the wet floor near the bath!" Apparently, hallucinating wasn't the only way absinthe could hurt you.

"You're drunk; let's go to bed."

Getting into bed, I tucked Sam in and turned off the lights. This wasn't the romantic end of Christmas Day abroad with the one I loved I had hoped for. The bed suddenly felt wet.

"Oh God, did you pee?" Sam accused me.

"No, I'm not the one who blacked out. You peed! And you're always the one who pees!" This wasn't the first time he'd peed while drunk. He had a habit of not only sleepwalking but sleep urinating. There were a few times where we'd been at our hometown friend's parties, and I had woken up in the middle of the night to him peeing in the corner or standing over the bed urinating while still asleep. This had never resulted in a major fight, although I guess it should have? If I'd broken up with him the first time, I wouldn't even be in this predicament.

When Meatloaf sang his famous lyrics in "I Would do Anything for Love (But I Won't do That)" was he referring to not being willing to live a life where at any point you could be peacefully slumbering and wake up to someone peeing on you. In hindsight, since Sam was the only person I'd ever dated, I had no idea that getting peed on was extremely bizarre and out of the ordinary. And if you love someone, aren't you supposed to unconditionally accept all their flaws? Why had no one ever written a love song about how yellow showers bring May flowers?

Pee is sterile and 75% water, which gave me solace. In fact, if you're trapped in the desert, you can drink your own urine up to three times before it becomes dangerously saturated.[3] I'd learned this from reading *National Geographic* after convincing my dad to sign up for a year subscription. Did I want the magazine because of my love of travel? Not at that age. It was because if he bought it through the Scholastic Book Fair, I had just enough points to buy a bright blue, blow-up chair to sit in uncomfortably until it instantly went out of style.

It's sad how much I let Sam get away with over the four years we dated. I also didn't really know what a "healthy" relationship was. How can you tell if you're in something as sweet as a cronut or as toxic as nail polish remover? Everyone in my family was divorced, and sometimes it felt like my parents loved hating each other more than they loved me.

"I'm calling the police!" my mom yelled at my father while I sat in my room at age ten, trying to build a romantic story arc between my Barbies to block out the sound. Barbie had discovered that Ken was a cheater, but she also had feelings for his alluring brother, played by my Prince Eric from *The Little Mermaid*, who, as the eldest of the two brothers, happened to be heir to the throne. All the other girls wanted to be with Eric because he was the prince, but Barbie didn't care, she had her horses. She didn't need him, but in the end, they would fall in love. Sadly, Barbie never married Eric because within the hour, my house was filled with police, my dad was swept away, and my parents were soon divorced.

"Your family spent so much money on lawyers fighting each other in court they could have paid for your college," my aunt told me years later.

While my dad said they went to court over a hundred times and my mom said only a dozen times, regardless of the real number, my dad claimed it resulted in him losing his job. Since he spent so much money on divorce attorneys, he filed for bankruptcy. My mother had to take on the lion's share of caring for us on an elementary and middle school art teacher salary. My parents lost so much, and so did my brother and I. When bad things happened at home when I was older and dating Sam, I'd head over to his house and cry in his arms. His family would kindly let me stay for dinner, but I couldn't sleep over. Sam explained that it's not only that his parents were concerned we'd have sex and I'd get pregnant, but one of their yard workers was injured when a ladder fell over after being knocked over by their dog. His parents told Sam that because of this, they were getting sued, and if I got pregnant on their land, I might sue them, too. Clearly, my low economic status, unstable family situation, mid-2000s baby pink lipstick, blue eyeshadow, and persistent questions, such as, "Based on your forty years of professional experience, what are your top three tips for finding a job?" did not make me wifey material. In the romantic scene in *The Lady and The Tramp* where they eat spaghetti, chewing on the same piece until they touch noses, I never imagined that I would be the Tramp.

With no roadmap of what a loving relationship could be, I was clueless, and poured my love into anyone who would take it, even if that was a cat who despised me or a young man who thought loving *My Chemical Romance* made him unique.

"You always get too drunk; I can't believe this," Sam yelled at me, still accusing me of peeing in our bed. Yes, I got too drunk sometimes, but I didn't think I was that bad compared to most people in college? I wasn't the reason we were lying in a hotel bed filled with pee. Finding a dry spot, I tried to fall asleep. It wasn't worth arguing with someone blacking out. In the morning, he admitted it was him, but I didn't act mad. Being mad wouldn't make anything better. It was an accident. Relationships are about hard work and being there for each other no matter what. Right? I read somewhere that when things get tough, you just need to try even harder, never give up. Or, as put by a woman about to get broken, "I can fix him."

When we got back to Paris, we'd have one last night with his host family before flying back to the U.S.

"Your French is so good!" the father said to me. Sam slumped in his chair.

A year later, I'd have my dream job as a marketing consultant in New York. Having returned from an important business trip, I ran a bath. When a message popped up from Sam, I smiled. We video chatted for at least an hour every night.

"I have a headache, but the trip went well. How'd the career advice call with your dad go?" I asked. He was having trouble getting any leads for jobs for when he graduated.

"I can't do this anymore. The idea of waiting for you at the altar terrifies me. You want this corporate life, you're applying for the Fulbright and want to travel, and I honestly want to own a collectibles shop, play Magic: The Gathering on my back porch, and live in the Rocky Mountains." He word-vomited as he broke up with me over video chat after four years together. Having poured everything I had into him, this crushed me. I had followed all my business books! So devastated, I lost fifteen pounds and looked like a skeleton. We were high school sweethearts—soulmates. We were supposed to spend the rest of our lives together. We both liked Subway Italian combo sandwiches, for Christ's sake!

Relationships are between two people—you can't make someone love you. Perhaps my business books didn't apply here. While I was working so hard, Sam was pissing away our relationship—literally. In hindsight, it also makes me really sad that there was a point in my life where I thought someone who put me down all the time, and, who occasionally peed on me—was the best I could ever get. That relationship was a sort of rock bottom. Having had that low sense of self-worth makes me so angry at my younger self and at the world for creating cultural environments where women think they are lucky to have a man who treats them like crap. Everyone deserves better than that and yet, somehow, we end up in these moments where we feel trapped until we realize we can escape to something better. It's also made me realize how much I've grown since then. My future life and home should be overflowing with love. Maybe even have a little felt sign outside the door with white lettering saying: "Make love, not urine <3."

CHAPTER 2: OKTOBERFEST

Never Drink a Beer Smaller than Your Head

One year later, on a train in between Paris, France and Munich, Germany—"I really enjoyed your stay, and I'd like you to be my girlfriend," I read in French, having to scroll through text after text on my cheap, tiny screen non-smartphone I'd bought for my trip.

"Fuck," I said a bit too loudly, considering I was in a tiny train car. "Desolée," I said in French to another passenger who gave me a stern look.

At this point in my life, I'd never rejected someone. When I met Fabien the year prior while studying abroad, there was light chemistry, so when I received a Fulbright Scholarship to live in Luxembourg for a year, I reached back out to visit him in Paris for a week before heading to Oktoberfest in Munich. My week living with him and his mother was like something out of a romance novel, except for the one time we were hooking up and I made eye contact with Jesus's lifeless eyes as he hung from the cross on the wall above Fabien's bed. There is nothing that kills the mood, like seeing your Lord and Savior watching you commit a sin.

While I had a lovely time, I wasn't sure I was ready for a relationship. A lot had happened since I'd last seen Fabien. When Sam and I broke up, I was devastated and still living at home with my mom, commuting into my branding consulting job in New York City. My plan was to continue to live with my mom to save money until Sam graduated, and then he and I could get an apartment together. The money I made was money for *us*, not for *me*—you could never start too early on building a nest egg for your family.

I thought working in branding consulting was my dream job. After all, I had a job where work would pay me to travel! I got to do cool things like fly to Cleveland to try everything on the Taco Bell breakfast menu and then listen to focus groups say things like, "Any brand that partners with Taco Bell is whoring itself out," only to burst out laughing.

"Not in front of the client!" my boss would say, kicking me under the table.

In my free time, I hung out with a sweet girl from Vermont named Sarah, who happened to move to New York at the same time as me, also knowing no one. Determined to see every aspect of the city, we drank every weekend and most weeknights. When she and I weren't going out, I was going on what I liked to call "practice dates."

A bit rusty on the dating front, I decided to say yes to every guy I matched with on Tinder. Dating in New York was choosing not to have kids and instead adopting an exciting man-child project, which will suck up all your energy and ask you to help pay his rent. This was self-inflicted torture. There's definitely someone trapped on a loop in hell right now where every day is having to make small talk with a man who worships

Louis CK. On one of these practice dates, we met at a dark wine bar where every time he touched my arm, I cringed.

"Could you see him?" Sarah asked when I told her of the experience.

"Not really, it was dark. The bar was trying to be moody."

"Yeah, I think maybe you're not attracted to him."

"I'm not?" I sat back in my chair. Aren't we supposed to like people for their personalities? I felt bad overlooking someone because I didn't find them attractive. I was an equal opportunity dater—and had no idea what I liked.

"I mean, if he was nice, but you didn't really want to kiss him, and you recoiled when he touched you ..."

"Ohhhh." It all made sense now. My body was telling me what my overthinking brain wasn't ready to admit. So focused on what these men were like on paper and if we could mold a life together, I hadn't thought about whether I even found them sexy. Living solely for the future, I didn't take the time to consider any of my own wants and needs.

Basically, I was on overdrive, and I had been all through college as well. I chose to take on $120k worth of student loan debt while I was seventeen, without a fully formed brain, making $10 an hour catering. That meant that if I wanted to save money to avoid ending up like my parents, I had to pay off my student loans, which were the equivalent of a second rent payment every month, and budget very carefully.

College for me was a race to find a job that paid well enough to cover those loans. While my classmates were barely passing their classes and sleeping with whoever they pleased, I was on a highly optimized work schedule with regimented partying thrown in at specific times: I'd wake up at 6 a.m. to study before my 8 a.m. class. After that, I'd head to my internship at an investment bank, work there for a few hours, and head back to take more classes. On weekends, I'd pregame with my girls starting at 9 p.m., head over to the bars in Georgetown, drink shots for approximately three hours, then my phone alarm would go off, and to save money, I'd take the flats out of my copious purse, and walk the forty-five minutes back to campus holding my heels. I'd then shower—because you don't need to be sober to shower (pro tip: don't try to shave your legs drunk)—so I could be up by ten and back in the library studying. To graduate a year early, I took additional classes each semester and summer courses that I had to fit in after my internships.

Fast forward to the current point in my life. At twenty-two, I had pretty much been running on survival mode with no time to enjoy my life or simply breathe. My busy college schedule had paid off. Getting my "dream job," I moved to New York and was living that fancy young professional life where in meetings I asked groundbreaking questions like, "Is your brand more of a Hershey bar or a Lindt chocolate?"

"I have never been paid that much money in my entire life," my mom said when I got the job offer. When the partner at our firm bought us sushi with gold flakes on it, I felt as if I'd won the lottery. Such opulence wasn't for people like me.

Having grown up with pretty much no disposable income, I was scared to spend that money. After visiting my family, I would fill a suitcase with food from Costco and wheel that thing for an hour and a half making multiple transfers between trains back to Brooklyn, individually wrap each piece of chicken, and shove it in the freezer. I was *not* paying New York City grocery prices. While my coworkers would spend what seemed like hours debating where they'd go for lunch (was it a $25 salad or $35 Mongolian BBQ?), I'd eat my meal prep lunch at my desk. I still took the metro home at two a.m., walking the last twenty minutes in the empty Brooklyn streets, this time in my heels, to save the twenty dollars it would cost to take a taxi. This level of frugality meant I had a decent savings account. That, in addition to the small stipend awarded by the government for living expenses as a Fulbright Scholar, meant I could go to Luxembourg for a year.

"You have to go," Sarah said. She was right. Even so, it was scary to fathom being unemployed for a year. Could I afford it? Would I ever be able to eat gold-foiled sushi again?!

"But what if I can't get a job when I get back? Companies care about loyalty, and a gap in your résumé doesn't look good." This had been drilled into my head. Having only been at my first job for a year, I was concerned that quitting so quickly would be the kiss of death for my career.

"This is a once-in-a-lifetime opportunity." She was not going to negotiate. She also loved traveling and was not letting me pass this up.

At that point, I didn't really know who I was. My favorite color? Periwinkle, because it was my grandmother's favorite. My favorite drink? Dark beer, because my college boyfriend always ordered a dark beer, so I'd get the same. My favorite food? In high school, I took a special evening class where people from my town (the "rich town") shared a classroom with kids from another town (the "poor town"). The teachers in the less affluent town's district organized it so that there could be cultural exchange between differing socioeconomic classes within our County, but Patricia and I took it so we could try to get invited to more parties. On the first day, they blindfolded us and led us into a room to meet people from the other town. The goal was to try to highlight how we create biases based on how others look.

"What's your favorite food?" I asked the stranger.

"Pizza," a guy with a gruff voice said. "What's your favorite food?"

"Caviar," I said. Was that true? Who knows, but it seemed like something a rich kid would say and my entire identity in high school through college was to try to chameleon my way into fitting in with the affluent class. All of my thoughts, likes, and dislikes, were based around trying to social climb and fit in as opposed to what truly made me happy. An empty glass, you could fill me with whatever you liked. My entire identity was designed to morph into what others wanted, when what I really needed was to be filled with experiences to make me myself.

With no idea who I was and a terrible case of burnout, I decided to say yes to the Fulbright grant I'd applied to a year ago when I was in a completely different headspace. Then, I'd assumed I'd never get it but, YOLO, might as well apply.

While that trip started with two types of penetration—mine with my French crush and Jesus with stakes through his bloody hands and feet—everything was great with Fabien. He was a history major, so we jumped in his family's tiny car and headed to Versailles. There, he chased me through the back garden, taking photos of me and adding a commentary in his sexy French accent, "They had big orgies back here. You might come around a bush and see the King fucking someone." Our Presidents seemed extremely boring compared to this. I couldn't picture George W. Bush in the White House Rose Garden participating in an orgy.

As we wandered through the palace, he leaned in and whispered each little historical detail in French. The old me would have designed her entire life around this type of existence, but the new me wasn't sure I was ready to commit to anything until I knew myself better. On the train to Oktoberfest, I had to decide. Did I want to keep dating him and live this romantic dream or not? Maybe my dream of having bilingual children could still happen.

The train started to slow. In a country I'd never been to before, I would soon meet the stranger from the internet that I had agreed to stay with.

Munich's Central Station looks like a Cracker Jack box with a high, flat ceiling with striped paneling and overhead lighting.

"Kristen?" A tall girl in her late teens with a ski jump nose, long, thin limbs, knee-length brown hair, and a heart-shaped hairline approached me. Most importantly, would she kill me? As she came towards me, I flinched, but realized that it was to give me a hug, not dig her teeth into my flesh. When she pulled away, I saw that she had such a big smile that it would put the Cheshire cat to shame.

Luckily, I'd developed a strategy to find "safe" people to stay with on Couch Surfing, a free website where you could connect with locals offering to host people. First off, I would only stay with women, and I'd read their bios to make sure they didn't have anything like, "What's your social security number and mother's maiden name?" or "Listen, you're gonna LOVE being my sister wife!" or "Have you ever tasted human feet?" Then, I'd read all the reviews and check that everyone who had written them also had a number of reviews, so I could assume they were real people. Ida had a couple of reviews saying she was nice and fun to party with.

After taking the train, we arrived on a narrow cobblestone street, entering her small house with vines growing up the sides.

"This is the bathroom," she said after showing me up a narrow staircase. She pushed open the door, and a row of bras with diamonds, spikes, and more lined the side of her bathtub, hung there to dry. "Oh sorry!" she said, scooping up the bras.

That's odd. How do you wear a bra like that under a T-shirt? With so many rhinestones, it would look like you were born with a hundred nipples. Or the red one with lace sticking out all over would look like you had a family of snakes living on my tits. But maybe she only wore thick sweaters. A thick sweater can hide everything. Whenever I felt a low level of confidence, which was often back then, I'd slip on a thick wool one and it'd feel like a warm—albeit often scratchy—hug.

"And this is my room. I thought we could share the bed, or I could get a blow-up bed."

"Sharing is fine," I said. In her mother's home, it felt safe enough to share a bed with a stranger. That night, we met up with her friend and headed to the tents.

"You can borrow my dirndl," she said before we left, slipping into a blue checkered one with little embroidered red flowers.

"A diddy?"

"A traditional German dress. All the girls wear them to Oktoberfest." The one she handed me was a little more conservative, cherry red with a floral pattern and a white off-the-shoulder top with lace cuffs. Likely she wore it when she was younger, but I was honored to be included in the tradition. She put on a cute heart necklace, and I watched her do her makeup in the mirror. She seemed so confident. Why do I dress cute? To hide that my personality type is "feral animal looking for love and cheese."

When we arrived at Oktoberfest, it consisted of a huge field with an adjacent fair and a wide green alleyway lined with humongous tents, each with their own crest. It felt very much like Medieval Times or an adult playground. Down the center of the row were wooden food stalls with gingerbread house cookie cutter roofs with white trim.

"Each beer house has its own tent," Ida said, pointing to the crest on the tent closest to us.

At one of the tents, the big wood doors were open, but a bouncer stood watch and a rope hung across the doorway.

"We're full," he said to a group of young gentlemen.

"They're full, so we can't get in," I said with a shrug. Ida played with her necklace, somehow adjusting the length within seconds so it hung just above her boobs. Like magic, it made me want to look at them more than anything. Who knew a necklace's length could perform such tricks. Noting this, I now constantly adjust the length of my necklaces for maximum effect.

"Can we come in?" she asked, pulling her shoulders back and accentuating her cleavage.

He unlatched the rope, letting us in. She seemed like the kind of person who could get anyone to do whatever she needed. I envied this confidence.

The tent was filled with tables surrounded by long benches, but no one was sitting at them. They were all standing on them with huge beer steins in hand. We found a spot and climbed up. An older, rougher-looking woman in a dirndl, somehow holding ten beer mugs the size of my head, delicately balanced on top of each other, walked around the room.

"Ein Prosit der Gemütlichkeit ..." everyone sang in unison, followed by, "Eins, zwei, drei ..."

"Those women, they train to hold all the beers like that and then will work Oktoberfest for years." It was fascinating to me that balancing beers could be a sought-after skill, promising years of seasonal work with great tips!

For ten Euros each, we bought a huge mug and joined in the party. Everyone sang song after song as a live band played. I didn't know the German words, so I just moved my mug back and forth like a pirate and swayed with my newfound friends. I was trying to fit in, but not with any sort of goal—to social climb, to convince someone to hire, or mold myself to what someone else wanted from me. I was being myself, terrible singing voice and American accent included. I felt, dare I say it ... free.

"Ein Prosit der Gemütlichkeit ..." the band started to sing again. Didn't they just play this song? I didn't know what it meant or any of the words, but I had just heard it only a few minutes before.

"Eins, zwei, drei!" Ida shouted. "Now, you take a sip."

Holding my beer to my lips, its cold frothiness felt good, as I was sweltering from body heat.

"Now say, 'Oi, oi, oi!'" she said in unison with everyone else in the room.

"What is this song?" I asked, yelling over the crowd.

"It's 'Ein Prosit,' which means, 'I Salute You.'" She smiled, listening to the lyrics before she translated. "It's a song saluting our cozy time together and how good the time that we have with friends is." She took a sip of her beer then leaned back in. "Since everyone takes a sip during the chorus, the band is paid extra every time they play it. They play it as many times as they can."

"Makes sense." I nodded. I had always heard that Germans were good businesspeople.

We stayed in the tent for a while, before heading to another, this time slipping under the rope when the bouncer was away. At the end of the night, the tents closed, and we headed to a club.

The club, located in a basement, was loud, but we sat at a table with free drinks that Ida had talked our way into.

She leaned in. "I'm a go-go dancer, but don't tell my friend; she doesn't know."

"A go-go dancer?"

"Oh, you know, I dress up in all gold and dance in a cage at corporate parties and things like that."

Staring at her blankly, I processed this information. "Big companies have parties with girls in cages?"

"Yeah, you know, just fun dancing really." She said it so nonchalantly, as if every major company had a budget to buy cake for the office on someone's birthday, maybe a quick team building offsite, and most importantly, have girls in cages. Why spend money on anti-harassment training when you could simply lock up all your female workers?

As a guy grabbed her hand to dance, I sat in the booth processing all the information I knew about Ida, mainly that her mom is a government official whose daughter is secretly a go-go dancer. Am I in a political crime drama? Also, Ida is now one of the coolest people I had ever met. She knew who she was, what she wanted, and didn't care what others thought. Why wasn't I doing this? Yes, I looked like the dead girl at the beginning of every episode of *Law & Order*, but I hadn't died yet! Allowing myself to be freer meant having fun *not* to network, but purely for the sake of enjoying myself.

In our taxi on the way home, she turned to me. "You know I wasn't always like this. I was studying abroad in Australia and in the middle of the trip, I got the news my dad had died. He had a heart attack. I flew back immediately and was so depressed. I was so heavy from gaining weight, for the funeral we had to buy a new black dress last minute since I didn't fit in any of mine. I had terrible acne because I stopped showering. I had to shake everyone's hand, but all I wanted to do was stay at home and cry."

"I'm sorry you had to go through that."

"I learned that life is short. We need to use our time wisely."

As we walked the last few blocks up the cobblestone hill from our taxi, I watched her cute figure sway in the night breeze. She was so young yet had been through so much, and she seemed so happy. That's what I was most jealous of: how happy she seemed. I wanted that. Spending so much time preparing for the future, I hadn't focused on enjoying the present.

The next morning, I waved goodbye to her and her mother. It would be my last day at Oktoberfest, and I'd be spending it with my high school friend's distant cousin whose family owned a meat stall.

In the middle of the main row at Oktoberfest, I surveyed the area, the name of their meat stand written on a piece of paper. A stall with a cookie cutter roof looked like it had the right German lettering.

"Hi, I'm Julia's friend."

The older gentleman in the stall squinted at me and then said something to his son.

"Julia is my friend from high school, she said she wrote to you. I am here visiting."

They spoke to each other and then both their faces lit up.

"Yes! Yes!" the older man said, "Uh, do you eat meat?"

"I love meat!" Why is it called cured meat? Because it will cure your depression if you eat enough of it off a wood board.

"Uh." The older man gestured to his son, and they scurried behind the shop, opening up the various compartments of their stand. The son came out. Heavyset and tall, he looked like a linebacker, except for his cookie cutter, lace-trimmed, store apron. Underneath his shirt had the shape of a skull weaved into a spider web. He rushed down and took my backpack.

"We keep in store," he said, placing the backpack safely in the stall. His dad motioned to me and spoke in German and then handed his son two pieces of white bread with a huge slab of meat inside. His son then handed it to me.

Biting in, it was the fattiest meat I had ever eaten, like if you took bacon but made it two inches thick. It wasn't smoked or charred; it felt more stewed, so the fat was a thick gelatin. My body is not a temple. It's a McDonald's at 3 a.m. in a college town. This was delicious, and I was fully embracing pleasure.

"Thank you!" I said through bites.

"You like?" his dad asked.

"It's delicious." This trip was at least teaching me that I could never be vegan.

"You more meat on you," his dad said before laughing, pointing at my figure.

As I finished my sandwich, we waved goodbye to the father, and the son took me to the "Festvelt Tradition" tent. This was where old people, children, and couples usually hung out at Oktoberfest, or at least this was the gist of what I could get out of his broken English. He only knew a few words in English, and I spoke zero German.

"You sport?" he asked.

"I was captain of the Junior Varsity Volleyball team in high school," I said way too proudly for what it was.

He blinked at me.

"Umm ..." I made the hand gesture of doing a volley.

"Yes!" His eyes lit up.

"Do you play sports?"

"Handball."

Now, it was my turn to stare. What is handball?

He motioned throwing something.

I still stared.

He thought for a moment and then made a more dramatized attempt at throwing something.

Nope.

He continued to struggle. With the language barrier, I doubted he would ever manage to explain a new sport to me. The number of times bros have tried to explain football to me in English while we're watching it, and I still have no idea ... the cards were stacked against him.

"Um ..." He thought for a moment. "Hobbies?"

"I read business self-help books?" I didn't really have any hobbies because I had been so focused on trying to have a career that hobbies had felt like a waste of time. "Maybe day drinking?"

"I motorcycle," he said, grinning, "In a gang." Damn, this guy was hardcore. He played sports *and* was in a gang.

This was how our conversations went for most of the day, which was a bit awkward but still enjoyable. I felt like one of the seals at the zoo. Every single thing I did was like a new, exciting experience for him. He had amethyst eyes and long babylike eyelashes that would flutter in excitement. After all, it was his first time seeing an American girl eat a gingerbread cookie shaped like a heart, drink a beer the size of a bowling ball, or eat one last lard sandwich before he took me to the train.

Using his huge physique, he helped me lift my giant living-in-Europe-for-a-year bag from my train station locker into the upper compartment of my train car. On the platform, he looked at me through the glass window.

"I love you! You rock!" he screamed.

Oh my. Did he actually love me? No, I just think he didn't know how to say anything a little less than that and his excitement seemed dialed up to an eleven at all times. As the train pulled away, I waved at this large ball of joy.

Sitting back in my seat, I was exhausted from the festivities but also apprehensive of what was next. Soon I would arrive in Luxembourg where I'd be living for the next year by myself. This was the start of a new chapter for me, one that no one from home could relate to or provide guidance on. Who would I be at the end of this year and who was I now? Why did everyone keep telling me to watch *Taken* before I left?

At Oktoberfest, I'd met so many different kinds of people, and the thing that really resonated with me was their happiness, confidence, and authenticity. Having spent so much of my life pretending to fit in with my peers, I hadn't really shaped myself. Thankfully, I had this year to figure out what kind of beer I like (ones the size of my head), what foods I like (meat ones, but with more meat than fat, the ratio is important), and what kind of people I like. That meant less of a focus on men and making other people happy.

The housewives in my hometown focused so much on being "perfect." A friend had told me about the mother of one of the boys in our grade. She came down with a fever but was too stubborn to admit she needed help taking care of her four sons. Instead of getting a nanny while her husband was at work, she locked all the elementary school boys in her room, took some sleeping pills, and drifted off to sleep as they cried around her. Luckily, her mother-in-law arrived unexpectedly and came to help. My hometown taught women to be ashamed of asking for help. An ideal mother could do everything—cook, clean, care-give—on her own. There had to be other options for who I could become rather than the examples I had growing up. While running from that future life, I wasn't sure what I wanted instead.

Looking back at my phone, it was time to respond to Fabien. I had started my trip with an alluring, intelligent man waiting for me on the other side of the Atlantic, but I was running away from a traditional life. If I chose to move forward with him, I was giving into the old me. I needed space to discover the new me.

"I really like you as a person and hope we can hang out again on my trip, but I need to be single right now," I texted Fabien in French. To that, his texts started pouring in, to the point my little Nokia looked like it was about to have a heart attack it was buzzing so hard.

It didn't matter; I was doing this for me.

Chapter 3: New Year, New You

Berlin, Berghain, and Bauhaus

Three months later, Berlin, Germany—New York and Berlin had that same winter cold that digs through a wool coat and burrows into your bones. The summer before I quit my job for the Fulbright Scholarship, I was working in New York City. The company had recently bought an office in Berlin and had sent Greta, an employee from the office there, to stay the summer working for a client. We became close friends, and we also hung out with Dino, a gay South African writer in his late thirties and his friend Maria, a first-generation Guatemalan who grew up on Staten Island. Greta invited everyone to come for New Year's in Berlin.

She lived in the Neukölln borough of Berlin, which appeared to have a lot of kebab shops and felt a bit hipster. Her apartment had the beautiful molding and off-white paint I'd grown accustomed to in Paris. I'd only seen this faded eggshell, thick textured paint in Europe. It was like they clung to their history, which also explained why I'd been told multiple times, "America doesn't have an history, it's only been around for 200 years!" Looking at the current political landscape, we managed to muck things up in record time.

The theme of the New Year's party was the 1920s because, as Greta explained, Berlin was going through a rebirth phase and becoming the trendy, new place to live as it had been in the 1920s and 1980s. I was also going through a rebirth: one where if you stripped away my work, wealth, and social status, who I was at my core without those silly things we sometimes wrap our identity around.

"All the artists moved to the East Side after World War II," Greta explained. "The rent was cheap so first the artists came and then the businessmen followed."

Bending her head, she snorted a line of coke off a mirrored table, and her sister took a line after. In fact, everyone at this party seemed to be doing coke. This was the most I'd ever seen, and I had never tried it myself.

At that point, I had only smoked weed a few times. At first, I hadn't gotten high at all, I think because I wasn't inhaling properly. Once I figured out how to inhale, there were a couple of times when I'd completely blacked out. Striving to be an overachiever at everything it was likely from inhaling too well to the point where I had zero oxygen.

"You ruined the night," Sam would say, having to take me home and put me to bed after I'd collapsed in a forest, unconscious and unresponsive after taking a hit.

Other than weed, my only experience with drugs was when I stayed with a girl in Hamburg a few weeks prior who had three boyfriends: one she would marry someday, one who was fun for now, and one she'd send topless photos. Did I mention she was a kindergarten teacher? My travels were teaching me that the conservative rules I'd been taught in school, for example, that marijuana was a gateway drug to heroin and abstinence was the only way to not get pregnant, were not factually accurate. In fact, a lot of people have found happiness in between these extremes. The question was: where did I want to *fit* in all of this.

My host in Hamburg let me stay in her roommate's room, who was out of town. A clear hippie, the roommate's bed was a mattress on the floor with bedposts made of shoddily nailed-together logs draped in red cotton and pink mesh fabric. Scared it would collapse on me in the middle of the night, I got even more scared when I woke up and noticed this weird science project. There was a little thermometer sticking out of a moist Tupperware box. Inside the box, there was some dirt and then something red and white growing out of it.

"Is that a ... magic mushroom?!" I'd only ever seen them in psychedelic music videos and 1960s documentaries, but this was it. *I'm living in a drug den!* I thought to myself. *What if this place gets raided?! Are they going to take my passport away? They'll think I'm a drug mule and throw me in jail?! Then I'll definitely lose my Fulbright! Is this what Taken was about?*

Other than that, I hadn't been around drugs a lot.

"You want any?" My Berlin host asked, pointing to a pile of coke, trying to be polite. I thought for a moment. If I had one snort, would I become a drug addict? To be fair, when I was four, my mom bought me a four-pound bucket of jellybeans from Costco and I'd eaten the entire thing in less than 24 hours. Also, knowing my obsession with efficiency, a drug that could make me do more things faster, might be my kryptonite.

At that point in my life, I had no idea how addiction worked or what caused it.

"I'm good, but thank you."

"Kristen!" Maria called, entering the room. Maria and Dino bounded over to give me a hug. We hadn't seen each other since the summer.

"Want any?" Greta said.

"I'll take some," Dino said.

"I'll have a little," Maria said.

Since I had already left Luxembourg when I heard we were supposed to wear white for this party, I wrapped myself in a sheet and Greta's roommate gave me a gold crown to wear. It felt more like Rome in the 620s than Berlin in the present day, but at least I matched the coke.

At midnight, we rushed to the roof. With the entire city shooting off fireworks, the sky was on fire in every direction. My heart pounded in my chest, a rush of adrenaline as I felt alive in a way I hadn't in a very long time. Being focused on work, my future—I hadn't felt present in a very long time. My assumption was that I had to focus on work, no drugs, and minimal partying to be "successful," but looking around me, everyone here paid their bills, many as very successful managers, and a bit of coke on New Year's hadn't crushed their dreams.

A beam of sparkling light shot up from the night below, making me hunch down to dodge the sparks. Greta's roommate, a cigarette gingerly bobbing out of the edge of her mouth, stuck a firework's long wooden base into a champagne bottle, lighting its fuse. The fireworks blasted off into the sky above us, its white beams spread out like delicate, cascading gem droplets.

I tried not to think about all the people back in the U.S. who blew off a limb each year trying to shoot fireworks. Was that a problem here, too?

The night air was cold, especially since I was only wearing a sheet, but adrenaline warmed me. I loved it here.

We headed downstairs for the Bleigiessen. Literally translated to "lead pouring," this is when you melt a bit of metal on a spoon over a candle. Then, you dump the wet metal into a glass of water and from the shape it makes as it dries, it can predict what the rest of your year will be like. For example, if it looks like a ball, then good fortune will roll your way. If it looks like an eggplant, you will be blessed with lots of great you know what. Okay, I made that one up.

"We want to have kids soon," one of Greta's friends told me as Greta crouched over, holding the spoon over the fire. His wife did a line of coke.

Nodding, I sat quietly, unsure how to continue this conversation. Looking over, I saw Greta reading the sheet of symbols closely, presumably trying to interpret her fortune. I would have preferred to participate in that conversation, but it was, unfortunately, entirely in German.

"I need to head to bed, long day of travel and all." I smiled, excusing myself. I might not be ready to try coke, but there was one thing that I knew I loved: sleep. As I closed my eyes, I felt grateful for the chance to spend a week in Berlin, having these experiences.

The next morning, I woke before everyone. As I lay in bed, it felt good to be around old friends. Since moving to Luxembourg, I had been a bit lonely. Esch-Sur-Alzette, where I lived in student housing, was one of Luxembourg's larger cities, weighing in at thirty thousand people. It was a mining town, and the most exciting thing to do in the area was to go to the park and look at tiny deer in a cage. Neither a student nor a miner, I felt quite isolated and on my own path. Who was my crowd? I probably needed to figure out who I was first.

In the afternoon, the others started to wake. Greta's new fling kindly brought her a breakfast tray consisting of a bowl of cereal and a neatly laid out line of coke. They say chivalry is dead.

"Want some?" Greta asked, snorting the line. My New York friends shook their heads, lightly shuffling their weight. Apparently, this was too much, even for them.

Having slept late, we headed to Berghain, the most famous club in Berlin, mainly because it's impossible to get in. In fact, the guard at the front door is nicknamed "Hitler" and to be called that in Germany shows how psychotic he is. Everyone lines up and waits for hours only to get a nod "yes" or "no." There were rumors that even Elon Musk couldn't get in.[4] I didn't want the confidence of Elon; I wanted the confidence of my high school bully now in my DMs trying to sell me an MLM scheme.

"I got us tickets," Greta said.

"How?" Dino asked.

"I fucked the bouncer."

"Oh," I said, not expecting this. It was so kind of her to do this for our trip, but none of us had asked her to. I'd always thought good hospitality was putting fresh sheets on the bed or leaving out some nice, scented hand soaps, but fucking a bouncer? The etiquette book my grandmother bought me mentioned in what order to use silverware and to send a thank you card after a party, but it had nothing about that.

Once at the front of the line, we showed our tickets. Greta gave a tall bald man with a mustache a big hug, and we were in. As we waited to check our coats, a man in briefs and a harness told another friend he'd been there since eight a.m., was heading home to shower, and would head back. I don't think I could party that long. The only thing I'd ever done for that long was binge *Murder, She Wrote*.

We meandered through the rooms of the club. The first was a downstairs den. It looked kind of like a wine cave, but instead of being filled with bottles of expensive, vintage collectibles, I was surrounded by gay men wearing only cock rings and military boots. It was so muggy there that we headed upstairs. As I slipped through the sweaty dancing bodies, I was surprised at how little this bothered me. Was I ready to strip naked? Definitely not, but everyone enjoying themselves didn't seem to be hurting anyone.

The main room had a high ceiling, maybe five or six stories with all the walls painted black. Loud techno music played as people in leather with black fishnets and feathers danced.

"I fucked the bouncer up there," Greta said, pointing to a little black platform three stories up.

"Nice," I said, nodding my head in approval. *I wonder if anyone in the mile high club has ever died of vertigo?*

To the side of the main floor was a long bar. We grabbed vodka sodas and Club Maté, a caffeinated, non-alcoholic soft drink made with the South American yerba maté plant. We'd been downing these like water for energy. The American equivalent would be vodka and Red Bull, but this seemed more organic.

"They never check your shoes," Greta said, pulling drugs out of her black boots. Wanting to roll, everyone except for me took Molly, washing it down with Club Maté.

"I'll be Mom tonight!" I joked. No one seemed to be bothered by my choice to abstain—the sign of good friends. My biggest concern was that

I'd get tired. If Greta would fuck a bouncer for me, I could definitely stay awake for her, so we could keep the party going.

As the night progressed, we headed to another part of the club, where there was an additional bar.

"Dino, come here, I will show you," Greta said as we passed a dark hallway. "There are sex rooms back here." Starting to follow them back there, Greta stopped me. "Not you." She knew this was a bit much for me. Instead, I headed to the bathroom. A group of people burst out of the stall, presumably having done blow. I never understand how guys get in bar fights because all women do is make friends in the bathroom. Maybe they should plug in a PS5 above the urinals to get the guys hanging out in there. I am simply trying to solve the problem of male loneliness. Inside, the stall was covered in graffiti and reeked like sewage. As I gingerly tried to hover my ass over the toilet seat to avoid touching it, I looked around, wondering where you could sanitarily do blow in this bathroom.

As I balanced myself, something wet dripped on my back. The entire ceiling was covered in condensation, presumably from everyone's body heat. I finished peeing and ran out of there like Forrest Gump, trying to not touch anything.

"Are you okay?" A stranger asked as I sprinted by.

"I'm fine!" I shouted back, my hands pointy in my runner stride.

By the end of the night, we found a sofa in a back room, and all sat together, my friends slowly coming off their high. We leaned our heads on each other, discussing all the funny things that had happened. It felt good sitting with this group, a simple joy in being in each other's company ... until another nasty-smelling liquid started dripping on us from a pipe above.

The next day, everyone slept in again and stayed in that night, but I had to meet up with this cute guy's sister. Introduced by a friend in Luxembourg, Jack and I immediately hit it off, and hearing that I was soon heading to Berlin, he suggested I contact his sister who lived there. They grew up on the Upper East Side. This meant they had had an entire city at their fingertips by the age of thirteen and thus knew how to masterfully use their privilege to talk themselves in and out of anything.

His sister Dorothy greeted me in a towel. She had a big poof of curly, caramel hair down to her belly button.

"I thought we'd go to a movie premiere tonight. It's 1920s themed."

"Sure!"

"I think we have to dress like the 20s."

"I only have this," I said, looking down at my jeans and flouncy black top. Her gorgeous apartment was a huge one-bedroom with the same trim and old yellowing paint as my friend's. With a leather sofa, high ceilings, and designer books on the coffee table, it felt like an adult's apartment. Whoever she was subletting from had impeccable taste.

"I think it's fine," she said, looking through her closet. As she did so, her towel started to fall, flashing me her bush before she repositioned it. I blinked rapidly. I was trying to push myself to enjoy new experiences, but Berlin was wild. There didn't seem to be any rules here. You could flash someone within fifteen minutes of meeting them.

Before we headed to the movies, we met a business associate of hers for dinner. He was the head of a startup and despite mentioning he had a wife and kids, was eye-fucking Dorothy who bit her lip as she spoke. To say I was a third wheel was an understatement. At first, I tried to be part of the conversation, interjecting here and there, trying to dampen the uncomfortable tension, but then I gave up. Something was up between them.

Finally, at the premier, she and I realized it was an actual premier, as in there was a red carpet, and everyone else was dressed to the nines in 1920s attire with beaded flapper gowns, feathers in their hair, and jewelry that would cost multiple years' worth of my current government stipend. They glared at Dorothy and me, both in jeans and fifteen years younger than most of the people in the room. We were two Americans who clearly didn't appreciate that this was their big, fun, dress-up night. Once in the theater, the film, *The Artist*, turned out to be a black-and-white silent film. Dorothy started to doze off in between me and the startup founder.

"Excuse me," she said, getting up and exiting the theater. Having assumed she was going to the bathroom, I was surprised when it was only me and the founder still sitting with the empty seat in between us at the end of the film. As a shy person with anxiety, this was my nightmare.

Sorry, Dorothy texted me as I rode alone in the taxi with this strange man, *I was embarrassed that I was falling asleep, so I left.*

After attempting awkward small talk, I insisted that he drop me off at the nearest train. All of this was very bizarre, but I found Dorothy kind of fascinating, much in the way you can't look away from a trainwreck.

I spent the next few days with my friends, the highlight being a party in an abandoned warehouse where we danced on top of a Trabant (a small car only manufactured in East Germany under the communist regime) until its roof caved in. The lowlight was Greta's very alternative roommate giving me a weird Berlin-style haircut with bangs that ended just below my eyes.

It should have been a red flag when the tatted-up hairdresser looked at me and growled in his thick German accent, "I want to shave your head."

Looking at myself in a mirror at a shop across the street from the barber, I cried. I looked like Princess Peach and had to spend the next couple of months straightening these ill-placed curtains, since, if I didn't, I looked like David Bowie in *Labyrinth*.

"Wasn't she kind of crazy?" Greta asked when I told her that I was going to a dinner party at Dorothy's.

"I really dig her brother," I said. It was rare I could chat so deeply with someone about economic development, but more importantly, he was pretty. I wanted to go partially to continue my quest to hook up with her brother, but also because I found her unhinged in a way that kept me curious. She seemed to thrive in all the environments I hated, like getting hit on by colleagues, being bored in the movie theater, and wearing the wrong thing to a party. While I shriveled like a raisin, she blossomed like an aerated glass of wine.

She answered the door in an oversized, cotton button-down cinched at her waist. She had this immaculate balance of put-together and hot mess.

"I love writing because I have something I can show my parents," she said to her colleague, another writer.

"Yes, it feels so good having something on paper—our legacy," her coworker said. I tilted my head, listening intently. Working in marketing, everything I did was behind the scenes, helping rich companies become richer. Was this something I wanted to continue doing when my Fulbright was over?

Shortly after, the founder guy from the other night joined us, as well as a good-looking guy, a German who had a nose that always seemed to be pointing up, and two meatheads—both who had shaved heads and wore white tank tops to show off their thick muscles. One of the meatheads had a huge line of fresh Frankenstein-like stitches up his forearm.

"At Berghain, I fell down the stairs onto a broken bottle," he explained. That club was where memories were made.

As Dorothy's coworkers started to leave, one of the meatheads teased, "Those people are so boring. The kind who stay up late playing chess and drinking burgundy." They could be out in the world, ripping their arms open on broken glass!

"Your cleavage is showing," the nice-looking guy said, leaning towards me. I think he was trying to flirt with me, but I was over it. Having recently finished reading a book on pickup artists, I learned there are men who would pay a man who dresses up like a magician to teach them how to talk to women. His tips included things like "negging", a tactic of offering negative feedback to emotionally manipulate someone into feeling inferior so they might sleep with you. While hoping to educate myself on how to avoid these types of men, I learned that men will do anything instead of going to therapy. The attractive guy then moved on to Dorothy, who happily flipped her hair and batted her eyelashes.

When it was just the five of us, she suggested we head into her bedroom to chat, so we sat on the edge of her bed, and all put underwear on our heads to make things less serious now that the intellectuals had left. The fetching guy and Dorothy looked like they wanted to jump each other's bones, so the snarky-looking German, the founder, and I excused ourselves.

After a bit, the injured meathead and the founder gave up waiting and left. As he took his coat off the hook, the founder murmured angrily, discouraged that the girl he wanted to apparently cheat on his wife with was not interested.

"What happened?" the snarky German asked as Dorothy plopped down on the sofa with us.

She giggled. "I didn't want to have sex with him."

"But you got some sugar?"

"We went down on each other."

"At least you gave him something other than blue balls," he said.

We discussed American politics. In other parts of the world, following the American media cycle was like watching reality TV. It reminded them that things could be worse. Gun nuts, anti-choice purists, people who wear cheese hats—we were a Netflix documentary, and no one knew how many seasons it would go.

"I'm getting tired. Can we continue this discussion in bed?" Dorothy asked, yawning. I had loved having such interesting conversations with so many foreigners with such different backgrounds.

In bed, we slowly started to doze off, so Dorothy turned off the lights. Lying at the edge of the bed, facing outwards, I started to fall asleep. A hand snaked around my waist, then slowly moved to the edge of my pants. I pushed it off and heard a rustling behind me. *That was strange.* My eyes started to close. My head was spinning from drinking too much, having lost about a year's worth of brain cells on this trip.

The pair of them whispered behind me, and one of them unhooked my bra. Annoyed, I pushed the guy's arms away. Then I felt another hand snake around and massage my breast. This time, I looked down and could see the hand's black nail polish in the dark.

It was Dorothy!

I took a deep breath. I wanted to fuck her *brother*! I guess he didn't mention that we had flirted. Did I want to have a threesome? I had never fathomed I'd be in a situation where this was an option. Being taught abstinence-only in high school, the only way we learned about condoms was by watching *Philadelphia*, where Tom Hanks' character died of AIDS. Having had hardly any sex with anyone but my high school sweetheart Sam—whose mother was staunchly anti-choice and whose best friend was my gynecologist—I was terrified of getting an STI. The main reason I didn't want to have a threesome: what do I do with my hands? Not even knowing where to put my hands when taking a picture, what about when you have two bodies to please? It was really intimidating and more stressful than enjoyable having to factor in the number of hands and holes. I felt like a kid playing that game where you have to fit the blocks in the holes in which they fit, but which hand fit in what hole?

Pushing her off, that seemed to convince them I was not down. Did I leave then? It was super late at night, and I had no idea how late the trains run in Berlin or if I'd be able to find a taxi. Would a taxi be too expensive? Where was I relative to my friend's up-and-coming neighborhood? Having decided to stay, I pretended to be asleep even though I heard them hooking up behind me.

"Can I put my arm around you?" the German asked me later in the night.

"Sure." Snuggling was always nice. After a while, he had both arms around me. Since they were the ones who had hooked up, I wondered how Dorothy felt. My mother had always told me never to have two friends over at the same time for a playdate because someone would feel left out. That seemed to apply to threesomes as well.

In the morning, my phone vibrated. It was a text from Greta.

Are you alright?

Coming home now, I texted. With the other two still asleep, I grabbed my things and left.

"I think they wanted to have a threesome with me last night," I told my friends as I arrived back at Greta's apartment.

"*What?*"

"They said they wanted to chat in bed, and I didn't realize that was code for threesome."

My friends stared at me and then burst out laughing in unison. "What did you do?"

"I just rolled over and pretended I didn't hear them."

"Oh my God." Maria grimaced. "Why didn't you leave?"

"I was tired and didn't know if the trains were still running!" What can I say, I love sleeping.

On my last day in Berlin, all my New York friends left in the morning, and I decided to go to the Holocaust Memorial.

"I feel kind of bad that we were here all week and never made it to any museums," Maria said as she packed her bag.

Walking around the Bauhaus architecture of the city on my own, I was definitely no longer in my small conservative town. Did I regret not participating in a threesome or tripping on Molly? Not really. Those didn't seem like my vibe. Even so, I was grateful for those around me and that regardless of what anyone else thought of their choices, they did what made them happy. Not everyone wants a wedding ring; some people prefer a cock ring. As I navigated who I wanted to be, I realized that I wanted friends who respected my comfort zone. I also liked being surrounded by people who push for adventure and for something more, something better—a yearning for unique experiences. Finally, I was grateful for the opportunity to take the time to learn what I liked and didn't like. A first step towards discovering myself.

CHAPTER 4: OCCUPY WALL STREET

Am I in a Toxic Relationship with Uncle Sam?

Two weeks later, Utrecht, the Netherlands—As tiny countries sandwiched between two super powers—France and Germany—which have been fighting each other on and off for centuries—Belgium, Luxembourg, and the Netherlands have found themselves stuck in frequent geopolitical turbulence. More directly speaking, World War I and World War II fucking sucked for everyone involved. Due to these major political issues, these three countries joined together to create the Benelux region. Soon this snowballed into, "Hey, do you also think war sucks?" among other things, and as more and more countries joined in, the European Union was formed.

Today, Luxembourg leverages this role for its own power. For example, despite being a tiny country, the head of the European Commission was a Luxembourgian politician. Before that, he was the EU's Finance Minister, which is a great position to have if you're a country that helps individuals and corporations avoid paying tax. Luxembourg was basically setting the policy to regulate itself. From an internal perspective, this was smart policy: setting laws that helped the Luxembourgian people.

My Fulbright Scholarship's topic of research was on nation branding or how countries brand themselves to attract business, politics, and tourism. For this project, I presented my findings to the national government's communications working group, the *Service Information et Presse*, after interviewing the ministers of various government divisions and the Mayor of the City of Luxembourg. In a larger country, there is no way I would have had the level of access to top government officials that I did. I was grateful for it and took the project seriously.

While in Berlin, in between visiting sex clubs, I had secured an invitation from the German government's nation branding division to interview their communication officials on how they branded Germany.

"You know we have a little bit of a dark history," a kind woman in a navy suit with a thick German accent said. Only someone in government PR would make this understatement of the century. "So, we try to stay away from nationalism. You know, our country flag and so on, since this was very big when—" this was when she broke into a whisper "—the Nazis were in charge." How do you make pro-government slogans when your government used to be Nazis?

She explained that they branded themselves "Germany: Land of Ideas." They'd built monuments to showcase at sports games or popups not of political figures, but of things like giant Baier Pharmaceutical pills, new luxury car models, or their soccer team. In Europe, Germany had a stereotyped reputation for being the most productive and industrial country—an engine of the EU economy, and they chose to showcase this over the nationalism that laced their dark past.

Shortly after my stay in Berlin, I convinced the US embassy in Luxembourg to write a letter on my behalf to get a discount rate to attend a conference on nation branding in Utrecht in the Netherlands.

At the conference in Utrecht, I met doctorate students writing theses on how countries brand themselves. Hoping the next phase of my career would be in nation-branding, I could have networked at this event. Unfortunately, I had to show up late the second day because, in my excitement, I had forgotten to pack professional pants and had to wait until H&M opened that morning. It was then that the founder of the conference screamed at me, "You know, everyone else paid full price, so please don't tell anyone you got a discount." I hadn't realized that I'd strong-armed him into letting me come. A letter from a US embassy was something he could definitely not refuse, especially since his nation-branding practice relied on governments to hire him, and we all know the US has the fattest pockets of them all. If there's anything that I'd learned from negotiating between my parents during their divorce, it was the importance of leverage, and while unintentional, I had laid my secondhand, brown suede kitten heels with a bow on top right on his bare neck.

Aside from that, at this conference, I had a blast. It was sitting through lecture after lecture in a building that looked more like a church than a conference hall. I was praying at the temple of nerd-dom.

On the last day, one of the nation-branding professors from Utrecht took us around the city. In one of the main squares, we came across an Occupy Wall Street camp. Through my travels, I'd already experienced similar protest sites in Dusseldorf, Hamburg, Berlin, and London, but this one was different. There were no shoddy, brightly-colored tents with "Treat animals with respect!" or "I've walked enough to know the world is flat" spray painted on them. Instead, the entire camp was full of clean, huge, thick green canvas tents. The open tent in the center had people standing with smiles, drinking out of thermoses.

"Why are all the tents the same?" I asked the professor, completely perplexed.

"The government handed them out. The military apparently had extra. Are you okay?"

At this point, I was blinking rapidly and stumbled backwards a bit in shock. "You're telling me the government helped them? Like they're here to protest the government, but the government still helped them out?" I gasped.

"Yeah, they looked like they were freezing out here, so the military came and handed out tents and equipment."

To me, this was unfathomable. The US government has a huge military budget, and yet people are living under bridges. These people were out here protesting the Dutch government and the government still made sure they were warm. Isn't this what every government should do? Imagine if part of the military budget went to helping the homeless, veterans, or families. When we think of belonging, shouldn't we all live in a country that generally cares about our well-being?

Growing up, whenever my parents went to the security deposit box to take out silver coins, I knew we were about to go through a rough patch. After playing soccer, running in the field in my hot pink "Flaming Flamingos" team shirt, then inhaling a bunch of sliced oranges, we'd head over to the bank.

My cleats would sully the local branch's generic gray carpet with chunks of grass and dirt. A clerk would come to meet us, and as I held my mom or dad's hand, depending on the day, they would lead us through the double doors into the vault. My parents would sign something, and then they'd use a key to open the outer safety deposit box and pull out a thin inner box. What was in all the other boxes on the wall—maybe a family heirloom, the missing blue diamond from the *Titanic*, or perhaps the Arc of the Covenant and if this banker opened the wrong one, spirits would come out and eat my soul?

Sitting at a table in the vault, whichever parent I was with would delicately pull back the black velvet to reveal some jewelry, maybe an old watch that used to be worth something but looked like a piece of junk, and then slowly pull something out from deeper within the box. Un-taping the top of the plastic tube, they would pour out the silver coins and count them. This was the rainy-day fund, the one that they promised themselves they'd never touch, but they were at rock bottom with bills to pay and mouths to feed.

Today, I still have silver coins. My dad gave them to me to "barter with when the Russians attack our power grid," but I think he really took comfort in knowing that if I am having a rainy day, like my parents did when I was growing up, I could sell them.

These Occupy Wall Street protestors were here to bring awareness to how the income gap today was worse than during the French Revolution.[5] That meant it was harder than ever to "make it." The "American Dream" is pulling yourself up by your bootstraps, from rags to riches. There is this pride around "Anyone can make it in America," but I wouldn't wish that on anyone. Why is that something to be proud of? Why force people to struggle if they don't have to? Shouldn't the government take care of their people? The Fulbright Scholarship that I was traveling on felt like a relic to a better America, one that invested in its people.

At that time, I had hardly any money in my savings and every penny was going to travel. I yearned for the wealth all my friends in high school and college had. Money meant freedom and security. It meant opportunity to spend it on whatever you like. What did I want to spend it on? Did I want to grow up and have a family in the suburbs like my friends? Isn't that what you're supposed to want? While traveling through Europe, I'd had a chance to see that not everyone wanted *that*. There were so many other ways to live, but which fit the me I was becoming?

CHAPTER 5: SWITZERLAND

Nearly Murdered by a Lover

Six weeks later, Zurich, Switzerland—The time had finally come. Having met him a few months earlier at a party in Luxembourg, and his sister having tried to bang me in a threesome in Berlin, I had my turn to make love to the man with whom I was infatuated. I was going to spend my weekend with Dorothy Van de Zump's brother: Jack.

Jack looked like a Kennedy. He had gone to Cambridge with a good friend of mine in Luxembourg. He had come to visit my friend and as two New Englanders abroad, we had hit it off immediately. I'd been messaging him ever since.

Why could I not stop thinking about him? Jack's plaid pants he'd had custom-made in India, popped collar polo, thick lips, and haircut were enticing. As a self-proclaimed Connecti-cunt, at that point in my life, I was a sucker for all things preppy, and this man and I were cut from the same cloth that is East Coast snob-ciety. He was everything that a girl from my hometown had been trained to want: he worked in banking, so he made a ton of money, and he also came from a family with a ton of money. Sadly, a lot of my attraction to him at the time was mainly because he was rich, went to Cambridge, and was wearing Vineyard Vines. He'd also already created a life abroad and I was looking for inspiration for what to do after my Fulbright. Plus, I didn't have any guys I was into in Luxembourg, after all it is the second smallest country in the EU, leaving a ton of free space in my brain, my heart, and my vagina to lust over this gentleman who I hardly knew.

My body tingled for the entire train ride over from Luxembourg to Zurich, where he lived. There is no one more unhinged than a horny person. Go alone to a stranger's house? Why not! Before he finished work, I wandered the cobblestone streets alone, fantasizing about him. The city was old and pristine, with ancient rock fountains flowing with fresh glacier water that you could drink directly from their spouts. It was cold, nestled in the mountains, with a big lake next to the city. The ambiance made me feel like a princess ready to finally see her prince (that she had been quietly obsessing over for months).

When he got off work, he arrived in corduroy mustard-colored pants thick enough to have been woven from the Beast's fur. HOT.

"I washed the sheets. My bed is yours for the weekend," he said as we arrived at his place. His sheets were white, just like his sister's—the last stranger's bed I'd been in. We dropped off my bags, and he took me for a tour of the city. He seemed nervous as he speed-walked ahead of me, rapid fire describing different buildings. I understood; I was nervous, too.

For dinner, he took me to a restaurant that had been remodeled from a factory that used to make sails. As someone from New England, this was so sexy. As a child, I had visited Mystic Seaport, the whaling museum on Martha's Vineyard, and saw the seventeenth-century ships that brought my ancestors to the new world dotting the coast. On these trips, we camped because we couldn't afford a hotel and were no longer allowed to stay at my dad's apartment.

The last time we had stayed there, my brother and I made a little heart shape out of small rocks in the grass. We thought it was cute, but his landlady didn't feel the same after her weedwhacker propelled them at full speed into her shins, creating large gashes. From then on, his landlord found a legal loophole to ban us from staying there. Unable to afford a hotel, my dad took us camping all over Connecticut during his weekend visitation. It was fun to learn so much about our local history. However, it was less fun studying flashcards for my AP History exam by flashlight in a tent. On Mondays, we'd have to wake up at 4 a.m. and drive back to my hometown to go to school. Sometimes, this involved not having been able to shower because a family of raccoons had moved into the campsite's public restroom. I found myself barely able to stay awake from the lack of sleep, feeling my eyes flutter closed during important exams. It was also difficult trying to "be cool," fit in, or even develop friendships, when every other weekend I found myself at a campsite in a town a few hours away. On the bright side, this prepared me for the copious amount of sofas I'd sleep on while traveling over the years.

During our date night in Zurich, Jack held open every door for me, and when I got cold, he took off his jacket and delicately placed it on my shoulders. Based on my experience with Sam and other guys in New York City, my standards were extremely low, and these gestures felt like he truly cared.

Wow, I've never been treated this well, I thought, feeding into the fantasy about him in my head. After dinner, we went to a bar overlooking the city and stayed until closing.

"Let's watch *Downton Abbey*," I said when we got back to his apartment, trying to set the scene for some lovemaking. As he was rich old money and I had spent my entire life pretending to be rich old money, we both loved this show. Crawling into his bed, we watched it on his laptop. Sitting rigid next to him, sexual tension raged, but he was hard to read. Was he going to make a move? Like school kids, we were both awkward and unsure how the other person felt. I waited patiently, hoping he would lean in.

Throughout the entire show, he didn't even attempt to kiss me. Finally, as the credits rolled, he closed his laptop and nearly robotically turned to me, and we started to kiss. We kissed forever. He had these giant lips, so it was kind of like my lips were on their own little sea of pillows. Also, his kisses had no pucker noise at the end; it was like he pressed them against me, and that was the kiss. We didn't have sex, but this taste was enough after many months of dry spell dreaming.

That night, he slept with his arms around me. With any movement, he'd wake from his slumber to adjust to make me comfortable. Having never been cared for like this, I was grateful for even a crumb of care from a guy. My standards were lower than a raccoon digging through trash.

The next day, we had to wake up early to head on a ski trip. Jack worked in environmental banking and that day, he was leading a group on an environmental tour and ski trip. I didn't really understand what this meant, but we were headed to see the progress on the Gotthard Tunnel. The passage would cut down on gas emissions, as vehicles could travel directly under the Alps instead of on icy, winding roads. These were the kind of things you didn't think about when sucking on a melting paper straw to save the world.

Building this tunnel would take years and was a feat of modern engineering. Hard hats on, we admired the huge construction project. Jack treated me like any other member of the group, to the point that one of them asked me if I was visiting with a boyfriend and another very clearly hit on me in front of him. Jack seemed awkward and conservative, or maybe he felt that, as the leader of the group, it was inappropriate to flirt with me. Regardless, this amplified my yearning for him.

That night, we arrived in Andermatt, the ski village we'd be staying at for the weekend. As we walked through the fairytale Swiss village, admiring the gingerbread house trim on the homes, I pictured my new life as one of those people who ski.

"It's so nice to have a chalet in the Alps when it gets cold in the city," I would casually tell people while sipping my après-ski hot toddy in my white ski suit, rabbit fur earmuffs, and cashmere gloves.

That night, we had dinner together, and I ordered a veal cutlet, the breadcrumb cover baked in a thick layer of butter because it felt like something old money would eat. The kind of recipe passed down, generation after generation, from one's patriarchal German ancestors. That night, Jack and I shared a twin bed in a ski cabin—still not having sex but snuggling to stay warm.

The next day, the entire group headed to the slopes to ski. As a true New Englander, Jack lived for this. It seemed like he was looking forward to skiing more than seeing me.

When my mom started dating my stepfather, we started heading up to Vermont to ski as a family with his kids. Having skied in the same spot since the 70s, my stepdad, a public high school physics teacher, had friends who filled their house with bunkbeds—up to eight beds in a room—and rented the place out to friends. To keep prices down, dinner was served potluck-style with everyone chipping in on groceries, cooking, and cleaning. While grateful to be able to afford to ski because of this shared system, being in their home was absolute chaos, and a nightmare for an introvert like me. A ton of people in a confined space, children flailed as they struggled to walk in snow boots; they slipped from the door through the kitchen—filled with adults waving knives in the air as they went to wipe away the tears blurring their eyes from cutting onions. The whole home had mustard yellow carpet that—with tipsy adults stumbling in thick wool socks—was drenched with years of spilled whiskey; one match and that whole log cabin would have gone up in flames. Even so, I was lucky to have the chance to learn how to ski, so that in the Alps, I could start my new life as a snow bunny.

At the top of the slope, Jack climbed under some caution tape that roped off an area.

"Follow me," he said, waving me over, "I'll take you off-piste." I was excited to go off the trail to be alone with him, but I only went skiing for a few days every other year, making me an intermediate skier at best. Surely, for safety reasons, he wouldn't take me on something too dangerous, would he? I had never skied off-trail before; I usually stuck to green hills and maybe blue if I was feeling feisty. At the top of the hill, I looked out at the rolling mountains covered in fresh, untouched powder before me, feeling at peace. I was grateful to be one of the few who would ever have a chance to stand on this precipice.

"This way," Jack said. He waved for me to follow.

I followed him down the trail, zigging and zagging until I abruptly stopped, looking down in shock. The hill had turned into a 45-degree decline. I looked at him powering down the slope below me. He had taken me to a double black diamond, a level I had never done before. As it was off-trail, the snow was not groomed or checked for safety, which meant you never knew where it was secure to stand. The thick layer of powder made all terrain appear safe, but underneath that top layer, the snow could be thin or thick. Depending on how tightly packed it was, you could potentially fall through and become trapped in what's known as a "tree well."

I am a pretty determined person, and in most aspects of my life, if I wanted something, I would do absolutely anything to get it. I desired this man, which meant that, at that moment, I wanted more than anything to show off, to effortlessly glide down this hill like a sexy slope bunny. I froze. I couldn't move, I was so afraid. The worst part was that I had already followed him too far down. There was no turning back. The only way was down.

"Come on," Jack said, waving at me farther down the hill. "You still haven't fallen enough. I learned to ski by falling; I expect fifty more falls out of you today."

Slowly, I tried to force myself to ski, shaking in fear as I turned a corner, getting a glimpse of an icy cliff with deadly rocks below. Had I gone a few feet farther, I'd be on those rocks.

Finally, I fell face-first into the snow. The graceful thing would have been to try to pull myself up, but I was trying to survive. For at least thirty feet, I barrel rolled headfirst like a sack of potatoes, skis flying up in the air.

"That's not the safest way going skis first, but ... okay," I could hear him say as I somersaulted, snow in my face, down the hill. Once we got to the bottom, I could hardly pull my skis out of the snow. Peering up at him, snow sticking to my bright red cheeks, I had a look of bewilderment in my blue-rimmed hazel eyes.

"Don't you feel great? Don't you feel accomplished?" he asked as we finally slipped back under the caution tape onto the trail.

"No, that was not fun. I am not happy I did that. I just fell down a steep mountain and have lost all my confidence in my ability to ski," I snapped. I didn't want to ski at all anymore. All the fun had been taken out of it. My legs hurt, my face was cold, and I was exhausted from the massive amount of adrenaline now tapering off. At this point, I was pissed. This motherfucker had tried to kill me. I was terrified, hurting, and exhausted. Fuck being a fancy snow bunny, take me back to go-carting and how normal people unwind. Forget putting a down payment on a château.

We headed back to the group, and I sulked quietly over my French onion soup at the ski lodge. Jack told us another story where he took a friend down a crazy hard trail and someone joked, "And after that he still wanted to be your friend?" He laughed, but I shook my head.

After lunch, he tried to get this other woman to go down a hard trail, and she refused and seemed angry at him for trying to pressure her so much. This made sense to me. I was scared for my life. Was he attempting to kill all these people trying to enjoy a day of good powder on the slopes? Jack and I took a T-lift together up another slope.

"I am sorry I was in a bad mood," I said, having collected myself. At the time, once the anger had passed, I was filled with shame. I had lost it.

When I was a child, due to a restraining order, my parents were not legally permitted to speak to each other, and at the age of ten, I became the family negotiator.

Some weekends, my mom would say, "I want to spend time with your stepfather. I've cared for you and your brother all week, so have your father to take you."

My father would say, "I can't afford a hotel. Convince your mom to take you."

Caught in the middle, I resolved their fights. For example, camping is cheaper than a hotel, or, what if we go to the movies with our stepdad?

Now, I was a grown-ass woman, but I still felt responsible for the behavior of the adults around me. I still thought it was my job to fix any conflict. In my head, I was focusing on myself, showing my feelings, and being vulnerable instead of the reality: he had led me into a very dangerous situation. I blamed myself, not him. It takes time to break our unhealthy patterns, and in my early twenties, I was still not ready to break this way of thinking.

"Really? You were in a bad mood? Are you sure?" he said, teasing me about it. *Too soon.* We headed down the last trail of the day. I was so tired that with every stroke, I could hardly pull my skis up out of the fresh powder. Finally, I fell, hitting the ground so hard my ski flew off. Apparently, many ski accidents occur when people are tired and get sloppy.[6] That was me.

With the ski trip over, Jack and I sat next to each other on the train back to Zurich. Attempting to connect with him, I tried to strike up a conversation. "Stay awake and talk to me," I said as his eyes drifted closed.

He smirked. "What do you want to talk about?"

"What's the difference between an aardvark and an anteater?" I asked.

He laughed. Maybe we could get through his attempted murder.

When we finally got back to his place, I lay flat in his bed, completely exhausted, but I wasn't going to leave here still on a dry spell, having dreamed about him for months. We started to kiss.

"What do you want to do?" I said after a lot of heavy petting but still no sex.

"Well, sex is always a risk."

"A risk of what?"

"You getting pregnant."

"You have condoms, right?"

"Yes."

"And I'm on birth control."

"You are?!" he responded. Keep in mind, this man's sister tried to fuck me in a threesome. Was he, dare I say, a prude? Why would he be shocked that a woman in her twenties was on birth control?

"We are double protected," I said, still determined.

"Well, I think we should wait," he responded.

"Okay, I respect that," I replied. Seriously, he didn't want to have sex because I might get pregnant? What? He was twenty-eight. Maybe he was so into me that he wanted to wait? After all, other than trying to kill me, he appeared to be a gentleman. Maybe my obsession with him was making me put on rose-colored glasses. At least I'd checked off "abstinence only" and "murderous ski fiend" on the list of things I didn't want in my future.

On the train back to Luxembourg, I slumped in my seat. All I'd gotten was a sore knee from a bad fall. Having seen so many wild sex-capades in Berlin, on this adventure, I'd failed to get some very vanilla, monogamous lovemaking. I'd take missionary!

I still had a ton of adventure and mischief ahead of me. I had to become my own Prince Eric, whisking myself away to the dream life I wanted. Better yet, maybe I'd become Ursula: a badass bitch who lived alone in a cave with her pets and had the power of her own magic. She could live however the fuck she wanted.

CHAPTER 6: LIVING IN LUXEMBOURG

A City Girl Trapped in Foreign Farmland

Four months later, Luxembourg City, Luxembourg—A few days before, I had presented my Fulbright Research project to the *Service Information et Presse*, the Luxembourgish government body in charge of nation-branding.

"You spoke a little bit fast. I don't think anyone could understand you," the professor who had sponsored me in the program told me. It was not the best to hear that no-one could understand my year's worth of research.

"Why are you in Luxembourg?" People would often ask, as there weren't a lot of Americans in their early twenties there.

"I do research for the government," seemed to be the easiest explanation. Apparently, this is also what actual spies say when asked about their profession. Having gone to an International Affairs school in Washington, D.C., many of my classmates would go on to work for the CIA. I took a tour of their Langley facility, organized by my university for students who might want to work there. Our guide explained that if you work for the CIA, you cannot tell people. Your entire life is a secret because anyone who knows anything could be tortured, blackmailed, or sell those secrets.

"If I'm in a bar and someone asks what I do, I say I do research or accounting. That's boring enough no one ever asks any follow up questions," our guide said.

Later, in Shanghai, I would be approached on LinkedIn by a consulting firm looking for American research assistants. I met the two women who owned the firm in a coffee shop.

"We need someone who can do academic research and write reports," one said.

"I'm a Fulbright Scholar. I have a lot of academic experience," I'd said.

"We also need that person to know what decisions are being made in the White House ... before they're made public."

Speechless, I couldn't tell if these were two very dumb entrepreneurs truly pivoting their consulting business, or two geniuses sent by the Chinese government to recruit spies via ... LinkedIn?

Since I had made my big presentation in Luxembourg that absolutely no one understood, I extended my stay a few extra weeks to celebrate the Duke's Birthday, a national holiday.

During this period, I wasn't sure how to fill my time or, even more terrifyingly, what was next for me. In French, a tax haven is a paradis fiscal, which figuratively translated means "fiscal paradise." Rolling out of bed, I put on some workout clothes to go for a jog, something I'd been doing a lot lately, even though I was never athletic.

For my usual running route in Luxembourg, I headed up from my stageur house—a short-term rental for interns—past the Russian embassy, surrounded by cameras, up a steep hill, and past a local farm. I was so grateful to be surrounded by nature: the feeling of tall grass against my fingers, the sheep who ignored me as I ran by, the light suck on my foot as my shoe sunk into thick mud on a logging trail. Climbing up to the top of the farm's hunting or bird-watching fort, I'd look out at Luxembourg City in the distance before running back.

Next, I'd plan lunch. The worst part of the experience? Opening the fridge at the stageur house. Let me tell you: French people do not believe in Tupperware, so all their stuff was left open in the fridge. Mixed together, all the cheese, milk, and yogurt reeked. Being on a budget, I was reading *An Everlasting Meal: Cooking with Economy* by Tamar Adler. This book is a modern version of *How to Cook a Wolf*, a book popular during the WWII rationing period, focused on using every piece of your produce to make delicious meals with minimal means.

I'd head over to Aldi to buy my ingredients—daily fresh produce is the European way. Walking through the aisles, my toughest decision was to choose how much I wanted to spend on eggs. In the book, she insisted expensive eggs have a brighter yolk and significantly more nutrients. Going through her eggs chapter that focused on every way to cook them, my diet had changed to nearly entirely eggs. At this point, with nothing to do, I had spent hours of my life perfecting mediocre frittata.

After lunch, I'd sit, my eyes glazing over, in front of some terrible crime drama, or even worse, replays of the morning news. Sometimes, I'd read *The Sun Also Rises* or another classic book. This would go into the evening where I'd eat another egg-based dish I'd cook from scratch, have a *Bofferding* local beer, and go to bed early.

In between weekend travel trips, I'd been doing this before my final presentation, but at least I could sit at my computer and do research on my paper for fourteen hours a day until my back hurt too much to continue. As the days progressed, I started to dread waking up. For the first time in my life, I had nothing to do! I was twenty-three and living the life of a retiree. Life was peaceful and that was terrifying.

Having spent so much time focused on my job, I had become distracted from my personal growth and life outside of the nine-to-five. This was my chance to finally stop obsessing over work and really think about what I wanted in my life—a luxury that I was grateful for that most people never get to experience. At first, it felt great having zero responsibilities, but that's when the scary thoughts started popping into my head. *If I have nothing I have to do, what do I want to do?* That led to an even scarier question: What was I going to do when this was over? Having been to 35 cities over my ten-month Fulbright Scholarship, traveling nearly every weekend to another part of Europe from centrally located Luxembourg, I'd had this life-changing experience. I'd learned critical life information, like if you don't make eye contact when you cheers, you'll have bad sex for seven years. After all that learning I was supposed to go back to New York and ... spend most of my waking hours trapped in an office? Or even worse, having bad sex? What kind of career did I want? While I loved doing research, I'd realized that I hated consulting. I was at the whim of whatever the client wanted. I had to work ten-hour days and that earned me ... free delivery sushi dinner on the company dime? What was the point? These companies I was helping market themselves were already rich. I thought back to what I'd heard

Dorothy say in Berlin: that if you write, you at least have some kind of legacy. Were there any writing jobs where I never had to step foot in an office again?

When I finally got back to New York, I didn't want an office job, so I didn't get one. I was also adjusting back into my home culture, which resulted in trouble connecting with my friends from high school. My experiences didn't match office life, but neither did my budget. I was suddenly unable to afford day-drinking at brunch in Greenwich Village on the weekends, let alone rent on top of my student loans.

I moved back in with my mom in my hometown and did pretty much what I did in Luxembourg: I'd head on over to the local park for a quick run and then maybe do a workout class. Without the gym routine, I would have collapsed into a ball of goo. Before I started going, I had no purpose, waking up every day mainly to eat and get back in bed. Filled with a cold sadness, my muscles weakened, and I no longer wanted to move. Getting out of bed felt like stretching the thin, nimble limbs of a fawn, desperately struggling to rouse my weak body—and mind—from a state of nothingness. With zero *raison d'être* and nothing to do, in the quiet moments that grew longer, I heard a little whisper in my own voice that said: "I hate myself."

During this break living at home, a high school classmate died in a freak hiking accident. A nature lover, he had an internship one summer where they flew him out to the middle of nowhere in Alaska and he spent the whole summer with one other person, living in a tent with no internet and no connection to the outside world. He finally requested to be airlifted back early. I don't know how anyone could spend months on end in that level of isolation, or even worse, with a stranger who was annoying. After college, instead of moving to New York City like everyone else, he headed to Colorado, where he found a job. One day, while doing what he loved, there had been a rockslide that resulted in a head injury from which he never recovered. He was twenty-four, and the first to die from my high school year.

Everyone from my grade returned to our little town for the funeral. Stoically, all of us sat in the white colonial church, our youthful skin covered in head-to-toe black. It was rare for me to see such young people grieving. Hearing about how many lives our friend had touched, I looked around the room, at all my high school friends having returned from their fancy jobs in the city. Meanwhile, I didn't have to return from anything. I was jobless, living with my mom and stepdad, and having trouble having basic conversations since my life felt so disconnected from theirs. I could feel my high school classmates' judgement as I told them I was "living at home and figuring things out." They'd all *become things,* and I was floundering.

When I got home from the funeral, I looked at myself in the mirror. Had I peaked? One time when I lived in New York City, a guy hit on me at a bar with the line, "You know I auditioned for *Saturday Night Live* ten years ago." Was I going to be one of those people who was a Fulbright Scholar and then never accomplish anything else for the rest of my life? My friend who had passed had had a short life but had committed his few precious years to doing what he loved.

After the funeral, I took a long, hard look at myself in the mirror: I didn't have to keep living like this. As Newton's First Law of Motion says, "An object at rest remains at rest, and an object in motion remains in motion at constant speed and in a straight line unless acted on by an unbalanced force." Regardless of my consistency and speed, I was stuck.

I didn't know what I was moving toward, but building momentum started with baby steps.

Soon after the funeral, a friend from college posted on Facebook about needing someone who could help do research for a book. It paid $10 an hour—exactly how much I made catering before I even went to college—but at least it was something. After this job, another friend posted that their friend had a sublet available in Williamsburg, Brooklyn for a few months, which I could then afford from the money from the book project. Once in the city, another friend, knowing I wanted to do more writing, introduced me to their writer friend who hooked me up with a gig as a theater critic that I could use to build up my writing portfolio. Slowly piecing each of these things I liked together, the next thing I knew, I was a writer living in New York. My days involved working out of coffee shops followed by a dinner of organic eggs in ramen, with a tinge of garlic for my immune system, and most importantly, a side of a multivitamin so my hair would stop falling out from only living off cheap fifty-cent noodles because all my money went to New York City rent.

Once I had myself set up in New York, I felt ready to make the next step: moving back abroad. Using my new skills as a writer, I could set myself up in Asia, doing freelance work until I found whatever was next. This started with telling all my friends and strangers I met at parties my plans and having them introduce me to people they knew already working in Asia. By the time I selected Shanghai as my destination, I had a whole spreadsheet of referrals with notes like: "That person I met at The Frying

Pan said this person they met at a party once but now lives in Beijing, wait no Shanghai, was cool. Mention Lauren Barnaby when you email them." Now I had a list of strangers to hit up once I landed.

The interim before moving abroad again was miserable, but it was a gift. Why is there stigma around taking a career breather? Sometimes, we need to reset and have a good, home-cooked meal. The respite from being constantly in motion made me cherish my time and realize I own my time. My work doesn't, and my loved ones or social circle don't. Only I get to actively choose how I spend every single minute of my life. I don't have to do things that I don't want to, put someone else's feelings before mine, keep texting toxic guys back—I don't even have to live in America. This wasn't something grandiose—it started with the small choices that slowly added up to the life I wanted.

CHAPTER 7: NAIROBI

New Tech in a Male-Dominated Market

Dear Kristen: I was alarmed to see, on the front page of the Wall Street Journal, 'An explosion in Nairobi, Kenya, injured at least 33 people in what officials described as a terror attack.' The explosion took place in a building that houses retail clothing shops and offices, sending a plume of smoke over downtown Nairobi. [...] Kenya has been hit with a series of bomb blasts since its armed forces invaded southern Somalia in October to create a security buffer against attacks and kidnappings by militant Islamist groups.' The State Department has issued a Travel Warning. I feel you are playing with fire by traveling to Kenya at this time.

One year earlier, Beggen, Luxembourg—My grandmother was on a mission to stop me from going to Kenya. I'd been invited by a friend from college, Preston, to help him launch his manufacturing startup there, and she was livid.

Still in Luxembourg, I was honestly terrified of going back to my old life. I wanted a new challenge, or maybe I was seeking my next high. Regardless, Preston's new venture in Kenya seemed exciting, but my grandmother was terrified of me going, and I'd already had to chat with my mother, my uncle, and now Preston. In my mind, to be safe in a new city, you have to learn how to operate there. Preston would arrive a few weeks before me and get a lay of the land, making it one of the safer ways to live in war-torn Kenya.

When Preston picked me up from the airport in Nairobi, we gave each other deep hugs, having not seen one another since graduation.

"Isn't this the best?" he said.

I nodded and looked out the window of his private black car. I could tell he liked the exclusivity of it. It impressed me as well; I'd never been in a private car with a driver before. Is this what life would be like if I kept working hard? Being driven around, feeling important—it felt cool, especially considering we were both in our mid-twenties.

"It's better for safety," Preston explained. "And it's affordable. Plus, it's baller." He smiled.

Outside, the ground was flat and dusty and the day was overcast. As we pulled into his compound, I admired the tall brick walls, laced with thick barbed wire. A guard out front let us in. This was already completely different from Luxembourg, where I'd spent the last ten months. I'd be here for three weeks, or maybe longer! My life was open-ended with no idea what was next.

"Let's grab some groceries," Preston said, once I put my luggage in my room. The apartment had Acacia floors, three bedrooms, and rolling blackouts. Apparently, occasionally losing power was normal. The living room had a window overlooking the bleak parking lot with our high fence.

We walked to the grocery market, a small plaza near our apartment. Upon entry, a guard in military gear asked us to spread our legs and frisked us for bombs. My grandmother had said Somalian terrorists were bombing everyday places.

Inside, we bought some fruit and Preston eyed a bottle of Johnnie Walker Blue Label. Never had I been traveling and thought, "Yes! Imported luxury whiskey is an essential!" Usually, I cracked open whatever local beer caught my fancy. He turned the bottle in his hand, admiring it. He had always liked nice things, status symbols, but he had grown up wealthy.

"Is it good?" I asked, having no idea what Johnnie Walker of any level tasted like.

"Delicious," he thought for a moment, and then said, "Might as well," bringing it up to pay.

As we walked back from the market, an apparently homeless man under a tree yelled at Preston, "Are you dating?"

"No," Preston said, blushing a bit.

"I will make you my wife," he said, pointing at me. We sped up our pace.

"Never leave the compound alone," Preston said. "If anything happened to you, your grandmother would sue me, and there have been a bunch of kidnappings lately. They'd like nothing better than to hold a rich white woman ransom and force her family to pay."

"Got it," I said.

"Got you some cigarettes," Preston said, handing a pack to the security guard.

"Thank you." He smiled.

"Always good to get on the service's good side," Preston explained. "You never know when you might need them."

"Got it." I nodded. Preston's family was rich, but he'd had a tough life. I didn't know the details, but he had been sent away to one of those boarding schools for "bad kids" and then gotten kicked out.

"They'd never wake him up, so he failed out," his mother would tell my grandmother. "I mean, why didn't they send someone to wake him up?" Maybe there wasn't someone whose job was to go around waking up teenagers? One presumed Preston probably stayed up late playing video games. He'd shown me the custom-built computer he'd made. His first business was having people send him their broken computers, he'd fix them, and mail them back—all done remotely before that was the norm. He'd also told me he'd once run away from home and was sleeping homeless, hugging his backpack. When he woke up, the backpack was gone.

"Could you imagine if I'd woken up while they were taking it? I might have been killed." I'd never had this level of hardship nor this level of privilege. In Nairobi, he was starting his business using the $70,000 left to him when his grandmother passed away.

As I climbed the stairs to our apartment, I noticed Chinese lettering on the door below ours and shoes outside.

"There's a lot of Chinese investment in Kenya," Preston explained.

"Oh really?"

"The Chinese government is getting in early here. Most American corporations don't want bad headlines about bribes and stuff, but the Chinese don't care. That's all necessary to do business here."

"This is Sandra," Preston said as we entered our flat. "She is nicely letting us sublet."

"Great to finally meet you!" I said. Preston had told me that she had an MBA from Penn, a BA from Stamford, and was also the founder of a consulting firm helping global corporations, investors, and development organizations grow in emerging markets. This woman seemed like a badass, living out here in Nairobi after a long career in investment banking. She was someone I emulated, and Preston seemed to look up to her, too. Maybe if I played my cards right, like Preston and I had tentatively discussed, I could become the COO of Preston's company, leveraging my marketing background. He already knew that I was smart, but I needed to show him I was also a hard worker and an asset to his team. My first project was writing an interview guide to use with some farmers for market research.

"Why would we need a guide?" Preston asked. "I was going to wing it."

"That way we can make sure we address all the areas such as marketing, how we describe the product, product features, etcetera."

"I guess that would be helpful." The 'I guess' part felt weird to me. When I worked in marketing consulting, blue chip firms had spent six-figures to pay us to do these sorts of things, and I had already offered to do it for free. This was a great way I could add value.

We were all rather nervous before the meeting. This would be our first chance to meet with potential future customers.

"You might want to cover your shoulders. A good woman is like a piece of candy; she needs to be unwrapped to enjoy her sweetness," Gatimu, a local consultant Preston had hired, said. He beamed at me, proud to share this adage. This was despite my—from American standards—business casual attire: a black skirt and a sleeveless silk blouse. I put on a sweater.

Two farmers, a couple in business casual attire, came to our apartment and explained their problem.

"We'd love to raise chickens, but they need more water, and our land doesn't have access to water."

"Can you grab them some tea?" Preston asked me. I paused. As the head of marketing and the person who wrote the questionnaire, shouldn't I be there? I also had the most experience conducting these types of interviews. You needed to be careful how you worded things to not ask leading questions which might bias your results. Yet, they expected me to be in the kitchen? On top of that, the most junior person there was their intern, Abedi. I'm sure he knew how to make tea. Trying to be a team player, I went to make them tea.

When I returned, Gatimu asked, "Would you like to serve us now?"

I paused for a moment.

"Of course," I said, slowly going to pour the tea.

"In the U.S., we are all into that feminism b.s.," Preston whispered to Gatimu, noticing his cringe at my hesitation.

"In our culture, women serve," Gatimu said.

Shuffling on my feet, I felt uncomfortable. Not only was he stating he felt this way, but he was claiming this was also the cultural norm. How could I argue with that? Through some of the questions I'd added, we discovered some additional features the farmers might want on the product. My guide had been a success! Yet, it felt like I didn't get any credit, as if Preston figured that he could have found that information out without my structured approach.

The next few days were a blur. We headed out to Nakuru, the fourth largest city in Kenya, to visit a member of the Kenyan Parliament and Minister of the East Africa Community, who had offered his farm to pilot this new product, hoping it could improve output in his district. It was Preston, Abedi, and me. Abedi was tall, skinny, and constantly nervous, but excited about everything we were doing. Once he heard about the business, out of enthusiasm, he'd cold emailed Preston requesting to join the team. It reminded me of myself at my first job. My first performance review said I rarely spoke up, but when I did, I had good ideas. My silence was to try to show respect to the senior partners and clients and I could see Abedi trying to do the same for us. When I had gotten that performance review, I had been crushed. Behind the scenes, I had been working so hard, but they had wanted me to be more involved in front of the client. In this new role, I wanted to correct this mistake and be more of a leader.

We took a public bus to Nakuru, which included a pitstop for a security check. They used a mirror to search under our vehicle for bombs and then checked our bags. A few days earlier, Preston had bought a short blade, thinking it looked cool.

The soldier in military gear's face lit up as he pulled it from its sheath. The police officer pulled it from his bag. My heart rate increased. They appeared to be searching for weapons, and they'd caught us red-handed.

"Cool," he said with a big smile, handing it back to Preston. On the ride, we also passed what looked to me like slums. In this area, my lungs felt on fire, like someone with molten lava hands was closing their fists around them. This feeling would be a regular occurrence later in my life on the days when it got very polluted in China. There, it felt like I was having a panic attack. My lungs desperately tried to suck in oxygen, but there were other toxins that they were extracting from the air.

"I'm so happy to have you here," Preston said as we sat on the bus. "I remember when we went to that event in DC at the Tanzanian Embassy. You were so good at networking. I get frustrated with my girlfriend sometimes." He looked down at his hands. He was paying for her to live in his flat back in New York City, unsure how long he'd be in Kenya. Considering that we were in our mid-twenties, it seemed odd that he would pay rent for another human. I could barely afford a round of drinks myself, let alone New York City rental prices. "When I take her to meet with investors, she just stands there, looking bored. I need her to entertain their wives while I talk to them." Unsure how to respond, I didn't say anything. Looking back, this was a huge red flag, but at that young age, I had hoped that it was simply a passing comment, not tied to deeper-rooted beliefs. If I wanted this to be my next chapter, he would be my boss.

"Look!" I said, trying to change the subject, seeing a zebra casually chomping away on the side of the road. As a kid, my parents once took me to Amish country. They gave me a disposable camera and when we processed it, it was all photos of fields with little black and white cows. Having never seen cows before, every time we passed one, I'd snap a pic, and scream in excitement, "There are so many cows!" I felt like a kid again. My adventurous side was being fed with all the delights of travel.

In Nakuru, we were staying in an Airbnb, but in the shower, the water felt like trickling ice down my back. Cowering over, I tried to wash my hair without letting the cold water touch the rest of my body.

"Didn't you turn the water heater on?"

"What?" I said, shivering with goosebumps in my towel.

Preston laughed. "They turn the heater off to conserve energy, but if you click here," he said, showing me the switch in the bathroom, "You can have a hot shower."

"Fuck." These are the kinds of things you have to learn when adjusting to somewhere new.

After my shower, I saw a little boy outside. He had crayons and white paper, and he was drawing in the driveway of our place.

"What is that?" I asked when I headed outside, seeing a large brown box drawn on his sheet.

"My house," he said. I tilted my head. Most American kids draw a box with a triangle roof on top. I never thought about it, but were we all taught to draw a house the same way?

"Where's your mom?"

"Working."

At the nation branding conference in Utrecht, an academic had done research on how nonprofits always label African nations as "poor" for their own gain. It's easier to convince people to donate that way, but in the perspective of Preston and the academic, Africa could be a very profitable investment. They believed that Africa's countries didn't need donations but investors to develop economically and technologically.

We headed to lunch with a very senior member of the Kenyan government. He shook our hands and led us inside to a long, burgundy, coffee table. First was tea with milk so thick, a film layer formed on the top of the tea, coating our top lips like sticky mustaches.

Preston and I both laughed as we struggled to politely napkin off the foamy mustaches, which were dripping scalding tea into our laps.

"That's how you know the milk is good." The senior government official laughed, his skin creasing around a large scar on his face. Never having had tea like this anywhere else, I was told it was a sign of respect to offer tea with milk this thick. He looked over at me and winked before giving me a leer while licking his lips. Never before or since have I been eye fucked so hard. This made me feel violated. I was here to make career moves, not to be looked at. In every moment, I was trying to show respect to those around me, but I didn't particularly feel I was getting that back. Preston looked back and forth in the silent awkwardness. A smirk formed on his face.

"Do you have any big projects coming up?" Preston asked, trying to change the subject.

"Have you been to the waterfront yet?"

"No, I haven't," Preston said.

I shook my head.

"They sold all the land on the edge of Kenya to international hotels."

"There must be nice hotels," I said, assuming this was a project he had worked on.

"Now the people don't have access to their own beaches."

"Oh, that's terrible," I said, completely back-pedaling. *Fuck, I hadn't even thought of that.*

"I am working to find ways to give more of the Kenyan people access to their beaches."

"That's great," Preston said.

"I need to do a quick errand," the official said.

"Be patient. Let him speak first," Preston whispered to me as we hopped into the senior government official's car. "People love to talk, let him tell us what he wants." This was good advice.

"You're right. I was excited and nervous." It was so stressful trying to prove myself while dodging these sexist instances.

As we drove, everyone who saw the government official beamed. Window down, he proudly waved at them, his gold watch glinting in the sun.

Once we parked, he got out to speak at a funeral. As we waited in the car, a group of children peered through the windows. They whispered to each other in Swahili.

"What are they saying?" Preston asked Abedi.

"They say you're Dutch people from South Africa, the ones who speak Afrikaans," he said, smiling at how the kids were completely fascinated by us.

Preston and I looked at each other and burst out laughing. As I waved, they ducked below the window of the car, only to slowly creep back up to look at us. Preston turned to me to discuss the meeting.

"He seems pretty interested, which is exciting! By the way, my CFO, Ram, will show up tomorrow, as well as our chief engineer, Alba. I'm not sure if they'll want to join the company, but they're really cool."

Enthusiastically, I nodded. This seemed like just the right project to throw myself into. The product they were creating would help many countries access more food and making it accessible all over the world could truly change lives.

We stopped to pick up honey from a woman on the side of the street who carried a baby on her hip. The driver and Abedi chatted with her in Swahili and then rolled down the back window where Preston and I sat.

The baby looked at me—a pale blond with light eyes—and hissed.

"He has never seen white people before," Abedi explained. We all laughed.

The next day, Ram and Alba arrived. Ram's family moved from India to East Africa in the 1850s to help build railways. Alba was Columbian and kind of nerdy. When they arrived, I immediately felt the energy shift. Ram was a youthful ball of energy, and Alba was quite the opposite: sheepish and self-conscious. Alba and I shared one room, with Preston and Ram in the other. With us, Gatimu, Abedi, and Sandra and her team, whom she occasionally met with at her place, there were now nine of us working out of a three-bedroom apartment. Plus, you could hear everything in every room, and Alba and I were told not to leave for fear of getting kidnapped. We were in a pressure cooker.

The realization hit me: I was being replaced. If Ram shared an idea, Preston would embrace it fully. If I shared an idea, it was seen as contradicting his authority. I can be a little bit persistent and not know when to stop, but I was doing what I thought was best for the company. It didn't feel like I was in a senior position, an environment of mutual respect, or like I was able to add value. Soon, we returned to Nakuru to continue setting up a pilot on the government official's farm. Arriving on the farm, Preston began setting it up, but hadn't planned well enough ahead. We couldn't achieve much that day. Meanwhile, Ram saw me get eye fucked first-hand and relentlessly teased me for it. To show my value, I was taking notes and trying to keep everything organized, because clearly, no one was good at basic project management.

On the ride back to the bus, all Ram talked about was dicks and sex. Since then, I've done standup and that means going to a lot of open mics, yet I've never met anyone so adamant about dick jokes. A lot of them were very vulgar, about the minister wanting to fuck me, and while the men laughed, Alba looked on, perplexed.

"Kristen, he loves you. If we need anything, you should ask him for a favor."

"Yeah," Preston said, clapping his hands together. "He would never say no to you!"

"We can whore you out," Ram laughed.

"If I ask him for a favor, he will ask me for a favor back, and that's something I cannot fulfill," I said, not laughing at all.

"We'd make sure you were safe," Gatimu said.

"Yeah, like be right outside the door so you can scream out if he tries to touch you or something." Ram was not joking. This had turned into a serious conversation about how they could use my body for their economic gain.

"I really don't think this is a good idea," I said calmly. How fucked up that my colleagues—and *friend*—were discussing whoring my body out for *their* benefit.

I really needed this job. Having spent months in Luxembourg trying to figure out my next steps, this was the only thing moderately enticing, especially compared to my only other option: going home to live with my mom and stepdad. I wanted to make this work. As a feminist, I believe that women should be able to work anywhere in the world, and why let these men stop me? I still believed that I could prove myself and at that point, had low confidence. Any time men were mean to me, I believed it was my fault, blaming myself for how I reacted versus acknowledging that they were being completely unprofessional and disrespectful. We're taught we have control of our environments and to control our emotions.

"Look at the garbage!" Alba said, pointing out the window.

On both sides of the road were huge hills of trash as far as the eye could see. In America, we try to delicately spruce up our destruction of the environment, covering our garbage with a freshly mowed lawn. There, all the trash was out in the open, with heat rays radiating off the piled plastic bags, buckets—it was a lot of plastic. I felt the same: like a pile of trash, disregarded, disrespected, ignored—left to lay out bare.

When we arrived back in Nairobi, we all piled in a truck to head back to our apartment, but some police in blue uniforms pulled us over.

"Passports?"

Only some of us had our passports. We hadn't needed them previously.

"If you don't show us your passports, we will arrest you. Get out of the car."

Alba and I had ours, which the police then took. "We can't give these back until we have everyone's passports."

Preston spoke to them outside the car while Alba started to panic. "What are we going to do?"

"Everything's fine," Preston said, getting back in the car. "I bribed them."

On the rest of the ride back, Alba quietly cried to herself, running into the apartment when we finally got back. For some reason, I didn't feel scared at all, I have no idea why, but I guess I usually find these situations exhilarating.

Back home, the boys started smoking spliffs.

"Want any?" Ram asked.

"Does it have nicotine?" I asked.

"Yes."

"Then I'm good."

"You won't smoke it because it has nicotine?!" Ram repeated, laughing at me, as if this was absurd. It felt like it was a high school movie where the bully is teasing the nerd kid for not wanting to drink, except it was a bunch of full-grown adults who had graduated college trying to start a business together. Any tiny thing I did, Ram scrutinized and Preston was starting to jump on board too, sucking up to him like a fanboy.

I excused myself. Back in the girls' room, I could hear the mumble of Preston and Ram speaking through the wall. Going forward, business conversations happened in the men's room.

"What are your thoughts on my role in the company?" I asked Preston in the morning. I could feel myself losing control. I was miserable, but I still didn't want to give up. Looking back, there were so many red flags, but based on my lack of life experience, I naïvely thought their remarks were immature, poor choices of words, not hints at deeper sexist beliefs. I thought I could control my situation and that it was my responsibility to resolve any conflict. In reality, I had no power over what others thought of me. Choosing to work together meant a partnership. They had to want to hire me, and I had to want to be there. While the opportunity looked amazing on paper, in reality the job involved enduring sexism daily.

"I've asked Ram to let me know if he wants to stay on by Wednesday. If you did stay on, Ram would be your boss and have more equity than you."

I blinked in shock, not sure what to say. He was going to let one of the most childish human beings I'd ever met be his second-in-command? I couldn't speak to his skills in business, but I could speak to his character.

Nothing about Ram impressed me, and I would never want to ever spend even two minutes at a bar with this person.

"Good character is the key to business," my step-grandfather had always taught me. Working at one of the Big Four accounting firms his entire life, he'd seen how character flaws had led successful men to ruin. When he was a young boy, he saw a couple drowning in Lake Michigan and, without concern for his own safety, he rushed in and saved their lives. For this he was awarded the Carnegie medal for bravery. In spite of family financial problems and alcoholism, he earned an academic scholarship to Cornell, and later an MBA from NYU. I'd always believed in this: be a good person and you will succeed.

"I'm also a little worried about your attitude," Preston said, "Sometimes you challenge me, and at the end of the day, it's my company." *My* attitude? I wasn't making fun of people or making dick jokes.

"If I think something is a good idea, shouldn't I share my opinion?" Coming from consulting, blue chip firms had spent hundreds of thousands of dollars for our thoughts on their businesses.

"You just get stuck on something and repeat it over and over again."

Thinking for a moment, I guess I course-corrected a little too much from my last job, where they said I didn't share my opinion enough.

"You're too emotional," he said, repeating the age-old criticism—a stereotype used against anyone who is not a cis-gender white man. If everyone around you refuses to listen or respect you for reasons out of your control, isn't it human to become emotional? That's how we show that something is important. When cis-gender white men are in this exact same situation, why are they never labeled this way? In my situation, everyone around me was dealing with this intense experience differently, but it's not like the men weren't emotional.

Over the next few days, I continued to clash with Ram and Preston. Preston suggested the team head to Watamu on the coast for a few days to reduce tensions.

The Indian Sea had clear blue water as far as the eye could see. We rode through the mangroves on a boat made out of a hollowed-out tree, far away from the Somali–Kenyan conflict going on in the city. The sexist jokes and bullying continued.

I wish I could say that I was handling things well, but I was not. I had no friends there and no alone time, I was dealing with misogyny, being eye fucked and asked to whore myself out, and I was told that I couldn't go out of our place for fear for my life, which prevented me from doing my normal de-stress activities of going on a walk or jogging. I felt like an animal trapped in a cage. It was making me short-tempered, frustrated, and irritable. How could I handle this better? Trying to be professional was not a successful way of dealing with unprofessional people. My points of disagreement were only around the business, and I was trying to not play into the stereotypes—women are too emotional, they can't think straight under pressure, etcetera. For women to overcome sexism, don't they have to prove those assumptions aren't true?

Back in Nairobi, we went to Westgate Shopping Mall, which had the generic white tile floors and walls you see at a mall pretty much anywhere in the world. There were newly-adopted local children there with their white families, something Preston referred to as "adoption tourism," where the family comes to Kenya to adopt a child. This was bizarre to watch. The children looked shell-shocked, wandering around, wide-eyed, presumably experiencing a mall for the first time. Seeing the looks on their faces, I thought that it must have been so different from wherever they grew up. They were still in their home country, but the mall likely felt foreign.

"You want a dress, sweet thang?" one of the smiling white women asked a five-year-old Black girl. "You can have whatever you want."

We walked to a shoe store.

"What do you think of these shoes?" Preston asked.

"I like these ones," I said, pointing to a pair.

"How about these?"

"They're okay," I said, giggling. They looked pretty awful.

"I don't care how you feel about my style. I'm a grown man," he snapped.

I bristled. After all, he had asked my opinion. Should I have lied? He wasn't snappy like this in New York. Also, *he* had called *me* emotional only a day earlier.

In the mall restaurant, I watched a teenaged, Black girl, sitting on the lap of her boyfriend, a white man in his forties. This made me realize that not everyone saw visiting a country the same way. Some people went to a country with the sole purpose of taking from it, while others saw being in a host country as a gift and wanted to give back and be grateful for their experience there. Sometimes, intelligent people intentionally go to areas without the safeguards of human rights because it is significantly easier to get away with doing bad things. They could live with their character flaws unchecked and unquestioned. In 2020, at this very mall, sixty-seven people would be machine-gunned down as part of a militant attack.[8] Shocked when I saw the headlines, I reflected on my time spent wandering there. Sadly, similar violent attacks also happen in malls across America.

That night we went to Ram's uncle's home. To get there, we passed a checkpoint to their private community. The guard had a glazed look that made it seem like he didn't see you as a human, but as an object that at any moment could potentially cause harm.

Ram's uncle's house was huge. Since he was an electrical engineer, he bragged about the—in my opinion, tacky—rainbow lights he'd added above his pool. We headed to the backyard. A man with a machete walked around the back of his lawn, patrolling the property for safety reasons.

"Whatever you guys need, you are family. I'll, of course, help introduce you to the right people," he said as he cut up a glistening steak. "Government officials, big corporations, you name it—I know everyone."

"Take this," Ram's uncle said, calling over their maid, who wore a blue prairie dress with an apron. He handed her a bone with meat scraps left on it, having cut off the rest for us. She grabbed the bone and ran into the shadows, eating it out of view. Seeing this, my hair stood up on the back of my neck. It felt like when someone gives their dog table scraps.

"That was so fucking baller!" Preston said on the ride home.

"Seriously, he has good hookups. He'll introduce us to everyone we need."

I looked out the window at the darkness. Ram had something else I didn't have: a local network. I thought back to my grandfather's teachings on good character and hard work.

Once we got back to the apartment, I was barely on speaking terms with the guys. I had started to try to speak up when they said sexist things to me.

"We're just kidding, stop being so emotional," they'd snap back, as if I was in the wrong.

The three of them left to run an errand while I headed back to the apartment to pack. They'd texted that we were going to a networking event later that night.

Ram says wear something tight, Preston had added to the end of his text.

Hey Preston, that last comment isn't something a friend who respects me would say. I am pretty surprised by it, as I thought we were friends, and I thought you had my back. I was over this shit.

"He showed everyone in our car your text," Alba said when she got back. "He said, 'Doesn't she know it's a joke?' They're awful." She shook her head. "I hate it here."

"I've been friends with him since I was ten," I said, in shock. This wasn't the person I'd known. All for what, to win favor with Ram, another jackass? For what, his business? Had he always been like this, he would entirely change his personality to please whoever he was with? Maybe the world was one big transaction to him, calculating the return on investment of each relationship.

Alba and I quickly got dressed and headed to the bar to meet Preston and Ram.

"IDs?" the guard said at the bar.

Alba and I looked at each other. "We didn't bring ID." We hadn't needed our IDs before and after they took our passports that one time, we'd decided to travel without them.

"Bye, suckers," Ram said, heading in.

"What's the drinking age?" Preston asked.

"Sixteen."

"We're clearly not sixteen." I laughed.

"It's the rules here."

Preston snickered. "Guess you can't come in." He loved this power trip, that we were at the whim of his choices.

"What do we do?" Alba asked, eyes wide.

"Let me see," Preston spoke to the guard and returned to us. "I bribed him. You're fine."

We went and joined the group at a long table. It was a networking event for startups filled with other foreigners from all over the world.

"How'd you hear about this event?" one of the other expats asked.

"Our roommate, Sandra," Preston said.

"She's kind of sexy, right?" Ram asked.

Preston laughed.

"Yeah, I could fuck Sandra," Ram said, nodding his head, "I'd consider her hot enough to fuck. Yeah, I'd do it." Some of the guys around us burst out laughing while others shifted their weight in silence. That's when it hit me: it wasn't ever about how hard we worked. We were still women. If they were making these comments about someone far more experienced, successful, and hard-working than themselves, it would be impossible for me to ever rise above these comments. Alba and I looked at each other.

"I have to go to the bathroom," Alba said.

"I'll come," I said.

"What is wrong with them?" Alba asked me in the bathroom.

"Seriously. What the fuck? She's our roommate!"

"I'm ready to leave," Alba said, on the brink of tears. "I can't take this anymore."

"I know; we'll go."

"We're heading out," I said, waving to Preston and Ram.

"What, you can't keep up? Not ready to party," Ram yelled across the table in front of everyone. He had to put me down at every chance he could.

"Good riddance," Preston mumbled under his breath.

"Excuse me?" I said.

"Nothing," Preston said with a sly grin.

It was better to leave than stay to save face, even knowing they'd gossip about us behind our backs. It's not like I was going to see any of these people again. We headed downstairs and out to the street to find a car. Putting my hand up in the air, I hailed a taxi while Alba tried to collect herself.

"What are you doing?" a local woman asked.

"Getting a car."

"You don't have a car?"

"Our friends do, but we don't."

"They didn't call it for you?"

"No."

She shook her head and looked at me, angry. "You can't just call a car here! They'll take you somewhere and, best case scenario, rob you. Worst case scenario, they'll rape and kill you." She pulled out her phone, "Let me see if I can find you one." She started calling numbers and speaking to drivers until she found one who agreed to take us.

"Thank you so much," I said. "We had no idea. You're a saint; you literally saved us."

"It's fine," she said. "Just know your friends are dicks."

"We know," I said as Alba started to sob loudly behind me. This was too much for both of us. She handled it by crying, and I handled it by shutting down. I was in survival mode.

Sandra was there when we got home.

"Ram was saying how he'd fuck you," we told her, sitting at the table.

"How old are they?" she asked, herself in her early thirties.

"They're twenty-three," I said.

"Babies, you're all babies," she said. "If I had known they were that young, I wouldn't have let them stay here. Preston has that deep voice, so when I spoke to him via video call, I assumed he was older."

She didn't seem to care at all that they had said such things to potential clients and colleagues within her industry. This made her seem even more impressive. I wish their comments rolled off my back. Now that I'm her age, I realize why she wasn't bothered: someone who says that kind of shit is only destroying their own reputation, not yours. If someone I respect criticizes me, I am upset. If someone shows up at a networking event and talks about how fuckable a peer is—they have shown a whole room their true colors. It's like throwing out a fishing rod that will only attract other jerks. You're a professional liability.

In the morning, Ram and Preston told Alba they'd be skipping the safari we had planned for that day. At that point, I was not on speaking terms with them. Alba and I headed off together to spend a day seeing giraffes, rhinos, and elephants, trying to not think about the stress of the past few weeks. We took pictures and felt the sun on our faces, a brief moment of relief from a stressful situation.

When we got back to the apartment, Ram had set up a schedule for Alba, Preston, and him to share and discuss. I headed back to my room to finish packing. My flight would leave the next day.

I got in the car alone.

There was nothing waiting for me at home, but there was nothing for me in Kenya. During the fifteen-hour flight, I processed my experiences, feeling dead inside, replaying our conversations in my head, wondering how I could have handled them differently.

Freshman year of high school, my whole earth sciences class got invited to a party—or so I thought. It was the first one that I—the awkward, scrawny nerd girl who only ever spoke about cats—had ever been invited to. I thought it was my chance to finally be cool and go to an actual high school party where alcohol was served, like I'd seen in all the movies. That weekend, I had to beg my dad to drive me to the party since our housing that weekend was with a relative, thirty minutes away. It had been hard for me to maintain friendships because we were always staying in whatever free housing, campground, or cheap motel my dad could find in other parts of New England, and he didn't want the long trip to drive me to my home town and back for playdates. When I showed up at the huge mansion—five times the size of my mom's apartment—I knocked on the door, and the owners said that the host didn't live there and closed the door. I was so confused, so I knocked again.

"Are you sure?" I asked.

"Of course, I'm sure," they said, annoyed.

When I got back to the car, my dad said that he heard some boys across the street laughing. It turned out that they'd told me their neighbor's address intentionally and, through the bedroom window with a couple of other guys from my class, had videotaped me going to the other house. When we got back home, Dad explained to my extended family my invitation was a mean prank. I thought that I was finally a cool kid, but really, it was a reminder of what a loser I was. On Monday, the boys brought the video to school and, pretending it had to do with history, almost got my teacher to play it in front of the class.

"Please, don't play it!" I begged my history teacher, desperation in my eyes as the bullies laughed with joy.

Luckily, later in the day, there was a distraction, and I had my chance. While the boy was distracted bullying someone else, I opened his backpack, took the video, and threw it in the trash. If I hadn't, they would have brought it up every time they saw me. This trip to Kenya had taken me back to that experience: having guys who had everything I wanted tease me for everything I didn't have.

For months afterward, I blamed myself for everything that went down. *I shouldn't have been so emotional. I was so immature. What should I have done?* There was nothing I could have done. Some people cannot be reasoned with.

A few years later, Preston reached out when he was in Shanghai, checking on a Chinese supplier of his product. I still hated him, but the wound had dried, and I was curious what had happened with the business.

At the first bar we went to, a speakeasy, the bouncer said that he couldn't let us up right away.

"Here," he said, handing him cash.

He laughed, waving it away. "That's not how things work here."

Three years later, Preston's and Ram's company was worth a couple of million, no small feat for an entrepreneur in his mid-twenties. However, I wondered, did being sexist help or hurt their business? They had had innovative technology with hardly any competitors when they'd started off. Their sexist frat bro behavior had clearly resonated with some, but mainly only other misogynists. Preston explained that they parted ways with Gatimu because he hadn't added much value, Abedi was caught trying to steal money (which I could hardly believe), and the senior government official ended up wanting too many bribes to be worth working with. If they didn't go to networking events and open their conversations talking about whether women in their industry were fuckable, could their business have grown by more? Studies show a healthy work environment can increase productivity, improve retention rates, and attract top talent, so overall, avoiding assholes helps a company succeed and on an individual level, it's better for your wellbeing.

"I'm thinking of leaving Nairobi," Preston said.

"Why? Your business is doing so well."

"I'm concerned about safety." He looked away as he said it, and then back at me, "Another founder was sleeping peacefully in his nice home when someone broke into his house in the middle of the night to rob him. They shot him, his wife, and kids in their heads." My head jerked back, gawking at the horrific story.

"Can you run your business remotely?"

"Ram has family there, so he'll stay on."

I thought this was the most shocking thing he could tell me.

"One last thing," Preston said. "I have some news. I'm going to be a dad!"

"Oh my God!" I said, feigning delight. Leaning in, I gave him a big hug, mainly to hide my look of disgust that this man might be responsible for raising another human being and teaching them values.

"I was seeing this chick. The condom broke, or so she says, and she decided to keep the baby."

"How do you feel about that?"

"Terrified. I'm scared I'm not ready to be a father, and she's thinking of returning with the baby to her home in Sweden. I might have to get the courts involved."

"As a child of divorce, try to avoid the courts if you can. Better to try to stay civil, for the kid."

He nodded. On the bright side, maybe the next generation will be nothing like him.

After Nairobi, I would go on to work on a non-fiction book for which I'd interview over 300 women about the lack of female startup founders across the globe. The main culprit was the lack of women in STEM (science, tech, engineering, and math) fields and how people in the startup world are very sexist. From little girls being told they were "uncool" for liking math to experienced professional women being refused capital by investors who were worried that they'd be "too focused on being moms," every step of the process, women were being held back from starting their own businesses. On the bright side, female-driven and diverse angel investors were starting to pop up, solely to invest in women and people of color. Why? Not for "charity," but because they'd done the math, and investing in these groups had a higher return on investment. One study found that women-led companies perform three times better than the S&P 500 (a stock market index tracking the stock performance of 500 of the largest companies listed on stock exchanges in the United States),[9] yet only around one in ten Fortune 500 companies are led by women.[10] Imagine what the world would be like if more opportunities were given based on merit.

I run my own business and always try to avoid working with difficult people. They are like emotional bombs that could go off at any moment and always underestimate and undervalue those around them. Having said no to well-paying projects, it's not worth the emotional stress and communication gymnastics it takes to effectively work with douchebags (sadly, that's a privilege not everyone has). They take so much more energy than working with nice people, so I can take on a bigger workload—and thus make more money, be more successful, and be happier. On top of that, when people like working with you, they give you more referrals. It pays to be nice.

Chapter 8: Hangzhou & Austerity Measures

Thanksgiving Dinner in a Cold War Era Bunker

One year later, Shanghai, China—My first couple of months in Shanghai were a rush to adjust to a completely new home. Luckily, I had a few freelance writing projects to hold me over while I adapted to the city, which mainly involved multiple bouts of food poisoning, losing my bank card to an ATM, and adjusting to headaches caused by severe pollution levels. Unsure how I was going to support myself, I would frequently wake up in a panic. If I didn't find a job quickly, I was going to run out of money. Would I be able to? Part of the excitement was the challenge, but I had zero idea what executing that plan would be like. I needed this change. I needed to run away from the familiar and continue my discovery of what made me happy, this time on the other side of the world.

Shortly after arriving, I moved into a *Harry Potter*-esque closet of a room in an apartment with two European rugby players, who had nicely taken me under their wings and invited me to all their rugby events. These events featured very jacked, stunning people from all over the world getting drunk on beer and talking about a sport I knew nothing about.

"I love it when the one guy rams into the other guy and then everyone piles on top," I'd say, desperately trying to connect with those around me.

"You should play rugby! It's a great way to meet people," my roommates would tell me.

"I'll think about it," I'd said, looking down at my frail body, T-rex arms, and petite stature. I'd crunch like a potato chip if anyone piled on top of me.

With both the women's and men's Shanghai rugby teams, I spent my weekends in clubs, predominantly in a marble bathtub elevated in the center of the dance floor, until a bouncer would scream, "No!", spank my bottom, hoist me over his shoulder, and put me back on the ground. "You can't dance in the tub!"

After that, the other female rugby players and I would wait a beat, and then struggle in our heels to climb back into the tub to keep the party going. I still have no idea why there was a bathtub installed in this club … or why the bouncers would spank us. While this was fun, partying wasn't leading to close friendships and, at the end of the day, I wasn't a part of the team and athletes were not *my people*. I preferred to be hunched over in a corner, typing away at a computer, rather than do anything athletic, like, say, stretching. I needed to find a way to make close friends, the kind you can turn to when you ugly cry. At the time, this was a frequent occurrence. With the stress of not knowing how I would pay my bills, get passport photos, or even where to find comfort food, I was completely starting over on the other side of the world from my home.

Luckily, in my search to make friends, I used some online networking groups and met Carolina, who had also recently moved to the city. Italian, single, and in her late forties, she wore only Gucci and had celery-straight hair dyed chocolate lab brown.

"I am the Marketing Director for a wine importer," she said as she sipped on her espresso.

"My senior thesis was on wine," I said. "And I used to work in marketing."

"Really? We're hiring. Send me your resume."

At this point, I was running out of money. In the past two years, I'd worked as a freelancer making hardly anything, which is why I needed this job.

Prior to the interview, I spent the whole night reading everything I could about the wine market in China. However, none of this information proved accurate.

"This is China. Wine is sold through the gray market and the Chinese government doesn't share that kind of data. If they do, it's all fabricated," my interviewer, Wallace, a Briton with dark yellow stains on his teeth and nails from chain-smoking cigarettes, explained.

I nodded enthusiastically, although I had no idea what this meant. Luckily, he was impressed that I did any research at all and that I took illustrious notes on anything he said. He could have said, "Wine is sometimes red," and I would have written it down with the fervor of someone telling me the nuclear codes.

By the end of my first month, I was on a trade trip. This involved acting as a "handler" to a winemaker or export manager who would be in the market to promote their wine brand. In this case, I was traveling with Oliver, an Australian Export Manager, repping one of the largest wineries in Australia. He was pencil thin with a big smile and charming Australian accent.

The goal of these trips was to build brand awareness, educate the market on Australian wines, and build brand credibility. There was a lot of fake wine in China, and at face value, having a foreign face promoting a brand made it feel way more genuine and likely to be the real brand's wine. In this case, it was Oliver and I selling Australian wine.

We were headed to Hangzhou, which is the equivalent of Orange County to Los Angeles or Greenwich to New York City, in that it's a wealthy suburb outside a major city, in this case, Shanghai. To get there, we headed to Hongqiao Railway Station. We went through basic security when we entered; a metal detector, and our bags were scanned, then we walked onto a platform overlooking the main terminal. The station had lines of doorways to different tracks and rows of seats outside each, and a hallway and store kiosks in the center. I gasped at the sheer number of people below. Commuting from Connecticut, I was used to the hustle and bustle of Grand Central, but this was eight times that crowded. I'd never seen this many people in one place before. It made New York City seem like a small village.

"Let's go," Oliver said, reading his ticket. He traveled all over the world doing trips like this. While I'd traveled to over 35 cities in Europe on my Fulbright, I was new to Asia, and still had a long way to go to become an international woman of mystery.

"Hello," a man next to me said as we waited at the train entrance. Since Chinese is a tonal language, he said it with an abrupt sharpness. The fact that he said "hello" instead of "hi" felt more professional and respectful. He pointed at his phone, lifting the camera toward me, asking if he could take a picture.

"Okay," I said with some hesitation.

"Xie xie." I knew a few words in Chinese at this point. This meant "Thank you." He bowed and took a photo of me.

Seeing this, Oliver laughed.

"Your hair." He pointed. "There are not a lot of people here with blond hair."

"Oh." I laughed, too. It was funny to be treated like a celebrity for something so silly, but I suppose if you had never seen someone with blond hair before, it might be kind of odd. I must look like a ghost, a short glass of milk, a piece of toast?

The red Chinese lettering outside the gate turned to green and everyone around me jumped up in unison, pushing each other to get to the train. It's like when a plane lands and people stand up to get off first but turn that up to an eleven.

"Watch out for the old grannies," my high school friend had warned me when I moved here. "They . . ." He thrashed around with his elbows, suggesting they'd hit you right in the rib as hard as they could. "They had to fight for food growing up. People were starving to death, and you wouldn't eat unless you were at the front of the line."

Wary of this information, I held the strap of my bag tighter. My great grandma had been feisty, but the only thing she'd fight you for is another shot of vodka if you tried to cut her off.

Out on the platform, the train approached. It didn't look like a clunky metal box a la Amtrak, but a sleek, futuristic white plane. After it glided seamlessly into the station, I followed Oliver as he walked along looking for our car. Technically, I was supposed to be his handler and if I were earlier in my career, I'd probably be self-conscious, but more confident. Since it was my first trip and he'd done a million of these, we both knew that he should lead. There's an understanding between expats and the well-traveled that it's really about learning how to operate in a new place. There's a camaraderie where the experienced loved to share their learnings as well as laugh at those earlier on in their travel journey. It's a weird cult.

My company had gotten us first-class seats, which, surprisingly, cost only about twenty-five American dollars. The brown seats were thick, padded leather and looked like La-Z-Boys. Oliver caught up on email, while I studied the train. This was the bougie corporate life. I could get used to this! I'd only been in first class once before, and it was because my ticket was bought on the CEO's credit card and they did a complimentary upgrade of me but not him. Not realizing until I was on the actual plane, I hid my face when he entered the plane and never admitted to the mishap. This time, my company had paid for me to be here. Having found a job in a foreign land, I had earned this seat.

I opened the chair pocket in front of me and pulled out white disposable slippers and whatever the train version of an inflight magazine was. Looking around, I checked to see what other people were doing with the free slippers. Was it a gift to fondly remember your time on the train, or was I supposed to wear them now? Were they there to protect the rough carpet from my shoes? Opening the plastic wrap, I put them on. Was it unprofessional to wear these instead of my kitten heels? I was in a full Elie Tahari suit that my grandmother had bought me on clearance at Bloomingdales for job interviews when I graduated college and slippers. She'd always told me to dress for the job you want, and I was finally doing it!

As the train doors closed, I settled back, still excited. This was my first time on a bullet train. Would it feel like flying through space? I was half-expecting everything to zip by in a blur, but I could still see things if I looked straight ahead. It felt like a less bumpy Amtrak ride.

Playing with the side of my chair, I made it recline. My legs were too short to reach the ground, so I fluttered my feet in the slippers until one fell off.

"Oops," I said, looking around. Reaching my leg out to slip it back on, I then opened the magazine. Everything in the magazine was in Chinese and thus illegible to me, but I looked at pictures of a sales guy in a brown suit, a beautiful woman on a tropical island, and a red box surrounded by what looked like little pinecones. Squinting, I read the small English lettering that read, "sea slugs." Why did they put sea slugs in such a beautiful box? Were they meant to be pets? My hamster growing up had lived in a lovely cage with big red tubes. Maybe the slugs were the Chinese equivalent? I would learn that they were a common expensive luxury gift and great in soup. A British friend in Shanghai had a Chinese colleague give him a box of them. They are purchased dehydrated so that when you pop them in soup, they grow like those sponge dinosaurs that come in pellets. He promptly gave them to his Chinese cab driver on the way home, who was absolutely delighted, and also confused why a foreigner would give up such a great gift. I settled into my seat for the train ride ahead.

Had I made the right choice moving to China? I had slowly started to make friends, and I was excited to work in an office again, something that I had refused when I was back home. Did I like my job? I was starting to. Like most jobs, it was a lot of answering emails and making Excel sheets, but it had perks: going to tasting events and trying wines worth hundreds of dollars nearly every week, all for free. I'd even convinced my company that I needed "wine training", so once a week they'd have their trainer walk us through extremely expensive bottles to train our palates. If they made a movie about my life, it would be a bunch of scenes where I was dehydrated, yet constantly choosing to drink anything but water. This would be my first big travel trip. For my employer, it would be a test to see if I could handle it. For me, it would be a chance to convince them that they needed to send me on as many trips as possible across Greater China.

Once we arrived in Hangzhou, our local sales rep, Zhang, met us at the train and called us a cab. He had a big belly and a gold chain, signs of affluence. Zhang pulled out a red cigarette box from his coat. He lit a cigarette, cranked down the old taxi's window, and breathed the smoke out until we got to the dinner venue.

"It's owned by the military," Zhang said, waving his cigarette at the building atop a hill, "Austerity measures were bad for business. We had to go underground."

To cut down on corruption, Xi Jinping, the President of the People's Republic of China, passed new laws preventing too much military and government spending on fancy gifts, frivolous banquets, and so on. After all, under communism, government leaders shouldn't have expensive, luxurious lives. The wine and hospitality industries had been particularly hard hit by these new laws. One of the other wineries I repped had had their wine at a banquet with Obama and Xi Jinping, a great honor and excellent for promoting their brand. They had tried to post about it on social media, and it had turned into a code red at work.

"I am not going to jail for you!" the founder told them over the phone. "Take the photos of Xi drinking your wine down immediately." Another wine importer had recently been caught lying about the value of wine to reduce their import tax. Local officials threw the Spanish CEO in a Chinese jail cell and our founder had been sweating bullets ever since. He was very good about following the local laws, but it was a reminder that the government could always make an example of you.

We walked by reception, then went down in an elevator to an actual underground bunker. *Oh ... the 'underground' thing was literal.* A Chinese couple and their daughter met us at the bottom of the stairs. They apparently owned this venue in the basement of a government hotel.

"It was built during the Cold War," Zhang explained. "When there were air raids, everyone came down here." He waved to Oliver and me to follow.

After walking down a narrow, high-ceilinged, brick hallway, we arrived at a rounded metal gate. The wife had a sweet face and a strong neckline. You could tell she was the brains behind this venue. The husband was like if Silvester Stallone and Marlon Brando had a love child. His skin was a bit patchy with scars and his jaw was a little off skew, as if he'd been punched in the face one too many times. Their daughter wore pink florals, spoke the best English, and had contacts that made her pupils look larger, a common beauty trend in China.

Returning to the main hallway, we turned a corner. This hallway was refurbished with plastered white walls and thick, purple, velvet curtains. Along the walls were shelves stocked with with Canadian ice wine. Ice wine was hard and expensive to make because the grapes have to freeze while still on the vine, meaning that a flash freeze has to set in naturally. While the water freezes, the sugar and other dissolved solids don't, enabling a more concentrated dessert wine to be made.

"I love the curtains," I said politely. They were hideous. It was as if a magician had tried to design a retirement home.

The daughter translated and her mother's face lit up at the compliment. "My mother designed the place to look like Canada!"

What?

"We have another house there. My brother lives there!"

"I thought you could only have one child?" I blurted, then realized maybe this was too personal.

Luckily, the daughter only giggled. "We have Canadian passports. I live here, and he lives there."

Having your family grow up on two continents sounded fascinating. Could he return to China? Was he cool with this, or had it caused childhood trauma he'd live with for the rest of his life? I will never know the answers to these questions because it felt rude to ask how, specifically, they were breaking the local laws.

Next, we arrived in the main room, which made me gasp. It resembled a hole blasted out of a pit of rock, yet it felt like an architectural feat creating a chapel-like, curved space. Layers of glass in between steel beams covered the ceiling.

"It's so beautiful!" I said, in shock. "Why is there glass on the ceiling?"

"To stop the rocks from falling," the daughter explained.

How had they discovered that murderous rocks could fall from the sky at any time? Regardless, I was grateful they'd prioritized keeping us safe. The sides of the cave had purple curtains between rounded columns and the kind of faux-brick rocks you'd see on a 90s home fireplace in the US Midwest. It was hideous and awe-inspiring at once.

My heart beat with excitement. While some people buy travel mementos, I collect unique experiences. My whole life I've never really owned much.

As a kid, shortly after my parents' divorce, I remember curling up next to my mom on the sofa while she studied some white pages.

"What are you doing?" I asked.

"Looking over our items documents," she said. "Your father says he owns this silk." She pointed to the silk behind her on the wall. It was a jungle scenery with tigers, giraffes, and more painted on a framed piece of fabric. "We were in India, in a small market on the side of the road. I went through the shelves of rolled up fabric, and when I pulled this one out, I knew I had to have it."

"That's a lie, I found it and I paid for it!" My dad would later tell me. To this day, I have no idea who was telling the truth, all I know is that it's now in storage. The white pages were a long list of items they had the lawyers negotiating over. One time my mom dropped me off at a soccer game with a water bottle. It was one of the free ones you get as a promotion when you sign up for a new bank account with a maximum retail value of $25. When my dad picked me up from the game, he claimed it was his and sent me home without it.

"Are you kidding me?" my mom said when I got home. Even at that age, it seemed so silly to fight. Since then, I have never really put much stock in nice things, and living out of suitcases wasn't much of an issue for me. Why spend enough money on something that it stresses you out? I would rather eat cake or something more within my means. Maybe part of me was running away from all that.

Being in a bunker in a government-run hotel felt pretty unique. Perhaps this job was worth spending the majority of my days trapped using Microsoft Outlook. I needed the money, and it was far more interesting than meeting with healthcare executives in the middle of nowhere America to tell them no one wanted to repeat-purchase healthcare plans from them because their customer service sucked. Plus, I got to drink fancy wine, becoming *that* person who could swirl their glass, take a sip, tsk, and say, "Ugh, this Malbec has *far* too many tannins."

Guests started piling in and taking their seats at a long table in the center of the bunker. To pair with the Australian wine, we'd be having Australian beef cooked by an experienced onsite chef. With each course, Oliver would stand and walk through the flavor profile of each wine, ending with the most expensive of bottles. This would eventually be my job. Everyone seemed very engaged.

At the end of the night, the daughter of our host asked if she could take a picture with me.

"Of course!"

We smiled together.

"Can I take one too?" a stylish man with a billowy, open in the front shirt and multiple silver rings asked.

"Sure."

"Me too!" A line started to form.

Oliver burst out laughing. "I thought that I was supposed to be the main attraction," he said in his melodic accent. "You know the Barossa Valley has a lot of blondes like her. The Germans came over and settled the region. A lot of them knew how to make wine from their mother-land."

Because of my marketing background, I had been assigned the New World wine portfolio, which was basically anything non-European, including wines from Australia, New Zealand, South Africa, and the United States. Since French wines were the most well-known in China, wines from outside of Europe needed additional marketing to educate Chinese wine drinkers on these less famous regions. This was a fun challenge because I could take the ideas and visual assets sent over from the vineyards and brainstorm entire campaigns. For example, white wine isn't as popular in China, so I made a campaign with a New Zealand winery about drinking refreshing sauvignon blanc on a hot summer day. On the table cards they'd put at restaurants, if you bought their wine, you could get a scratch card with a chance to win a trip to their vineyard in New Zealand. This campaign was so successful that, across the country, we ran out of wine to sell.

As we headed back in the taxi, I was on a high from such a successful night. Having arrived in China with nothing, within three months, I had been able to create something I was proud of. Although I hated office life, there were fun full-time jobs out there. This one fit my desire for adventure, travel, and memorable experiences, and I was finally an international business lady—the dream I'd had since high school.

CHAPTER 9: BANGKOK

Creating Drama During a Coup D'Etat

Three months later, Bangkok, Thailand—Having only recently settled into my new job, I wasn't planning on leaving for Chinese New Year, however, a couple factors made me decide to take a trip to Thailand.

First, there was a political crisis in Thailand. A little over a month earlier, 160,000 protesters marched to the Government House, pushing for the removal of incumbent Prime Minister Yingluck Shinawatra. This meant that most tourists heading to Thailand for the break canceled their flights, so visiting was unusually cheap.

Also, my best friend had recently moved to Thailand, and had an apartment in Bangkok. Originally from Vermont, Sarah and I first met when we moved to Brooklyn and knew no-one.

Sarah and I were inseparable. Based on my commitment to having unique experiences, I will say yes to nearly everything, and she is charismatic and could get anyone to open any door for her. Sarah's sister was a matchmaker at the time who taught us everything you needed to know to commandeer a social life in any city. The trick to getting into an exclusive club? Only bring women. To get wealthy men to buy bottles, a club didn't need to offer competitive pricing or a sommelier; they needed to surround them with attractive women. Sarah would roll up to the front of a long line in front of the hottest clubs in New York and say, "I'm with eight women, can we skip the line," then Vanna White motion to all of us in our tight bandage dresses. Nine times out of ten, they'd say yes. She got us into every exclusive club, found ways for us to get free tickets to big events, and we never paid for drinks. She was at the center of every party and the keystone of my social life. I loved her. She was my best friend.

Sarah saw her love for travel as her identity, and after her first job, she'd found a place working at a travel agency. One day while I was on a trip into the city, shortly before my planned move to China, I saw her slumped over on the sofa of our friend's apartment. She smiled at me, but I could immediately tell something was wrong. Sarah was the most fun, go-getter person I knew. As I saw her on the sofa, a weak smile attempted upon my arrival, I immediately gasped.

"What's wrong?" I asked.

"I got fired." Like a balloon deflating, her body slumped. She'd worked so hard to get her dream job in the travel industry, but the place had been extremely toxic.

Usually when I say, "You should move abroad, you know, live on the beach, drink cocktails with gorgeous men from all over the world, work off a laptop by a pool," people reply, "Oh my God, I know, right?" They never do. Sarah was completely lost and sick of paying New York City rental prices, so moving to a beach in Thailand sounded like a dream.

Sarah begged me to come visit, and I was excited to go. We were family. She came to Fire Island on trips with my family and I did the same with hers on Martha's Vineyard. Whenever we had family or boy drama, we'd call each other. The entire time I was in Luxembourg, we had a Facebook group that was only the two of us called, "A Tale of Two Biddies," in which we'd write to each other every day. She was the closest to a true, loving partner I'd ever had.

Growing up with two parents who hated each other, relationships weren't something I saw as permanent. People change, and it's hard to trust others when you never know what they might do if a relationship soured. The two sides of my family absolutely hated each other and often used me to seek retaliation for the lawsuits that my parents lost all their money on. For example, a paternal family member had my brother and me, ages three and seven, pose smiling in front of my mom's father's grave. Having come from a pool party, both in tie-dye bathing suits, our bright blonde hair tinted green from the chlorine, we smiled awkwardly as the family member took pictures, insisting that they would be a great gift to show my mom that we had visited her dad's grave to remember him.

I didn't understand the emotional implications of this, trusting the adult who insisted that it was a good idea. On her birthday, when I handed them to my mom, she went silent. Her face turned white as she flipped through the photos. Having lost her dad when she was eleven, it was a reminder of one of the most difficult times in her life.

"Who gave you these?" she asked, almost in a whisper. I couldn't logically understand what was wrong. I thought that I was doing something nice for my mom who I loved deeply, when I was emotionally stabbing her in the gut and sharply turning the blade. The family member knew how to cut her deep and maximize her pain. I learned that the people who know you the best can hurt you the most. Growing up in that environment, it was hard as an adult to trust anyone deeply. Sarah was the closest I'd ever been to someone outside of my family and Sam.

While I loved Sarah, the part of me that felt separate was always there—a barrier to growing a deeper connection. I saw this trip as a fun chance to see Thailand, like any other trip, and I had already started to build a new life for myself in Shanghai. For Sarah, this was like a class reunion. It was a chance to take photos and reconnect with her best friend. She loved the story part of relationships. For example, on New Year's in New York, when the ball was dropping and everyone was counting down, one too many champagnes in, she fell down a flight of stairs into a man's arms. For her, this meant that they were meant to be. For the rest of us, we immediately identified this gentleman as a closeted gay man who was abnormally close with his mother. With this romcom intro, Sarah tried to date him for two months, until, finally, she could no longer take his constant avoidance of sex and talking about his mother all the time.

While I tried to avoid telling people about my birthday since I didn't enjoy the attention, Sarah would have an entire birthday month where every weekend she'd dress up in a fur boa, a new $15 sparkly dress from Forever21, and convince a promoter to take us out. One time—all for free—she got us all a limo to eat dinner at the Ace Hotel while a woman was suspended from the ceiling doing acrobatics in a cube.

When I arrived in Bangkok, I was on the upswing from some of the most difficult years of my life. During the Fulbright, I had spent every penny I had on travel and when I returned, I was earning nothing. Once I moved back to New York City and then on to my closet-sized bedroom in Shanghai, I was making enough to cover my rent, but that's it. Every day, I felt anxious about money. I had always wanted to be an international businesswoman, and against all odds, I had secured a job working abroad as a fancy wine lady. It felt good to be able to buy a beer without thinking about whether or not I could afford it. I graduated from being a *backpacker* to an *expat*. There is a clear distinction. While backpackers discover themselves abroad, they bring that experience back home. Meanwhile, expats are often creating a new self in a new home. The former is a tourist, the latter is a resident. Having gone to school for International Affairs and Economics, then studying abroad on my Fulbright, failing to secure a job in Nairobi, moving home with my mom while all my friends had fancy jobs in New York, I dreamed of *working* abroad. It felt like something only my idols could pull off.

"So let me get this straight: you're moving to China without a job, you don't speak Chinese, you hardly know anyone, and you don't have a place to live?" My roommate in Brooklyn asked me about a month before I left.

"Yeah, exactly," I said.

"Yeah, that's absurd," he shook his head, taking a sip of his gin and tonic. The first thing I heard every night when he got home was ice falling out of the fridge and then, "Fuck, shit!" as he prepared his emotional support G&T. He hated his ad agency job. Our other roommate was in agreement. Neither had ever left the country, and, like most people I talked to about my plan, they thought I was an idiot. I wanted a different life, which meant taking a huge risk, and it finally paid off. I had been broke for most of my life. For the first time, I felt financially secure (despite my student loans, but that was for me to worry about another day). I wanted everyone to know about my success as an international business lady.

Before I had left, my father had bought me a big, over-the-top, gold Michael Kors watch using my aunt's employee discount. It was about three years out of style, but three years ago, neither my father nor I could have afforded it. Despite it being out of its prime, I was so proud to be wearing a gold watch. In hindsight, Michael Kors is a mid-tier brand at best, but it felt like I was wearing Chanel. I'd never owned anything I'd paid over $150 for. While I had grown up surrounded by wealth, for the first time I *felt* wealthy. I finally had disposable income; I didn't have to worry about how much I spent on drinks after a night out, and I could buy myself nice things—granted, a value shopper, these were mainly fakes I'd found on the Chinese equivalent of eBay. Previously, my only big purchases were plane tickets. Feeling wealthy was a new experience for me. The best part was that it was my money that I fucking made for myself doing my own career completely differently from everyone I knew. Forget finding myself, I was a badass boss bitch, a captain of industry, an executive in the making.

I grabbed a taxi from the airport and headed to Sarah's apartment. It had light wood floors, two decently sized bedrooms, and a balcony. Honestly, it looked like an apartment you'd find most places, except for something strange in the bathroom.

"Excuse me, repeat that, there's a butt hoe in your bathroom?" My head jerked back.

"No." Sarah laughed. "A butt *hose*. It's to clean off your butt." And sure enough, right next to the toilet was a free-standing little hose with a tiny shower head fixture on the end. For the rest of my time in Thailand, I would try here and there to use this butt hose, and then give up, because I sprayed water everywhere. Later, I talked about this experience on a first date, and the man laughed until he was hunched over crying, and his stomach hurt from laughing so hard. I learned that these hoses are not at all for a delicate rinse of the ass hole, but instead for cleaning your bathroom. In fact, there is a drain—like you'd see in the center of an American shower—in the center of many Thai bathrooms so you can take the *not*-for-your-butt hose, rinse down the floor, and have it conveniently drained.

Once my butt hole was fresh, I plopped down on Sarah's bed, where she'd offered to have me sleep next to her while I was there.

"It's so good to have you here," she said. "It's been hard being away for so long."

"The first couple months are tough." I'd been through this many times and was coming out of the most recent rendition. On the bright side, I had cash money! Any time that I cried, I could wipe those tears away with cold, hard cash. It's fun to pretend to be an evil villain.

"Yeah, and," Sarah said, playing with the trim of her elephant-print bedspread, "it doesn't seem like anyone back home cares anymore?"

"What do you mean?"

"Like, I'll tell them about my life, and they won't respond for a day or two, and then it'll be a quick response. They don't seem to care about me since I'm not there."

Having never really thought about this, I cocked my head. Whenever I left, I assumed they'd go on with their lives without me, and I'd simply reconnect when I got back. Why should my friends care? They're doing their own thing. When I was in Luxembourg, Sarah was the only person I messaged back and forth with, I assumed because she loved travel and wanted to hear my stories. No one else messaged me.

I put my hand on her comforter. "I don't think it's personal, I think they're busy."

"I talked to them every day before I left."

"It's hard for people to relate. You are having all these wild adventures, and they're going to the office every day."

"Aren't they interested?"

"Maybe, but it doesn't impact their daily life, and they don't know how to give you advice or carry the conversation." Despite traveling more than anyone else I knew, travel was never part of my identity. It was a thing I did for *myself*. I feel that travel made me a better person. Whenever I had returned to the US, I wouldn't talk about travel when I met people. Not everyone travels, and that's okay. I had learned to bring up my travel stories sometimes, and other times to keep my mouth shut and listen.

"I just ... I thought we were close, you know?" She looked down at her duvet.

"You are still close. They'll be so happy to see you when you're back, but in the meantime, I'd focus on making your new life here." That's the best advice I could think of for dealing with loneliness. She would soon be an *expat* here. Better to look forward than to look back. "Have you found your go-to spots in Bangkok yet?"

"Not really. I got here two weeks ago and have focused on interviewing at English teaching schools. Luckily, I found a job."

"That's great! Now you have income, so that's a stress reliever."

"But this weekend, I'm taking you to Koh Samet. It's an island nearby I've been dying to visit."

Since she was working, and I'd be there for a little less than a week, we decided that the island near Bangkok would be a convenient weekend trip. After six hours on a bus, an hour on a boat, and wading through the ocean in pitch black with our luggage over our heads, Sarah and I arrived on the picturesque island. Our "hostel" was nicer than most hotels I've seen, and we shared a private room. The queen sized, four-poster beds had maroon comforters and mosquito nets. That night, we ate octopus while overlooking the ocean and watched a fire dancing performance before heading to bed. It felt so luxurious. Before this, the majority of my travel involved sleeping on a friend's sofa and waking up to the sound of potato chips crunching in between their couch pillows.

We spent the next day on the beach, drinking straight out of coconuts that we bought for forty cents. This was the life that I had worked hard for.

"They love the king here," Sarah explained as we handed the salesman our change. "It's disrespectful to drop their currency on the ground because his face is on it. You could even get sent to jail for disrespecting the king.

As we sipped on our coconuts, a stray dog slowly wandered down the beach. They ran free here and seemed to be pretty healthy, since all the tourists would give them free food. Oh, to have the life of a beach dog.

That night, we decided to go clubbing. We put on flowy dresses and walked down the beach to a tiered beachfront open bar with a raging dance floor.

"I love your necklace," the bartender said, a shirtless local with chiseled abs. It was a thick gold statement necklace I'd bought for cheap at Forever21. Growing up, my grandmother always wore statement necklaces. Sometimes she'd let me try them on, delicately removing them from a silk box and fastening the thick beads around my neck.

"You can wear it," I said, undoing the clasp in the back and handing it to him. He took it carefully, as if I'd handed him a $40k Cartier version. He softly put it around his neck and he looked so confident as it glistened against his bare skin.

"It's not worth anything," I said.

"What?"

"It's a cheapie."

He looked shocked. Later, I'd learn this is what all the influencers do in LA. They'll pair a Gucci belt with a pantsuit they bought from Shein. People see one designer logo and assume the whole shebang is expensive.

He continued to wear my necklace as I followed Sarah to the dance floor. She'd made friends with a local guy with two tattoos on his chiseled pecs. We danced with him on a table until he lost his balance and fell into the crowd.

Sarah hopped off the table. "Are you okay?"

"I'm fine!" he said as he hobbled over to sit on the bench next to the table. "I need to keep dancing." He tried to climb back on the table, but immediately fell.

"Let me see your ankle," I said. It was twice the size of the other one and was sprained, at a minimum, if not broken. Sarah and I looked at each other. "This is not okay."

"I'm fine!" he said, pushing us off. He stood up, trying to sway to the music, but whenever he put his weight on the bad foot, he'd fall a bit.

"No, you need to go home," Sarah said, firmly.

"You sure?" he said, completely devastated.

"Yes."

We helped him hobble off the dance floor and then a friend agreed to take him home. While I've never seen him since, we added each other on Instagram and for years I've watched his life unfold. He regularly dances on boats in short shorts, luckily having recovered from his ankle injury.

"Let's grab more drinks, I want to find someone cute!" Sarah said. At the bar, the bartender handed me back my necklace and handed us local Chang beers.

"Is this your first time in Thailand?" a guy asked me as Sarah paid.

"Yes! How about you?"

"Fifteen years, I come back every year."

"Fifteen! Wow!" I had only returned to places to see friends, never because I loved a place that much.

"This is my first government coup."

"A bit wild, isn't it?"

"Oh, this is their twelfth government coup; it's a thing here."

"Really?"

"I wouldn't get too worried about it. It's not anything serious like how the Illuminati killed Michael Jackson."

"Um ... what?"

"Oh yeah, they definitely killed him. He wouldn't play ball."

"Really?"

"Back," Sarah said.

Oh, thank God.

"He was just telling me how the Illuminati killed Michael Jackson."

"Really?" Sarah said, recognizing it was our cue to move on. "I think I need another drink." She tugged me after her, despite clearly having a fresh one in her hand.

She had spotted a stunning man at the bar. He had a shaved head and emerald eyes that stood out against his perfectly tan skin, his muscles glistening in the moonlight. She started flirting with him while I chatted with his friend. His friend seemed into me, but he wasn't really my type. He had floppy, long curls. It turned out that both men were soccer players from Spain who had come to Thailand to train and play on the professional team. They barely spoke English, but that didn't matter.

"Do you like the beach?" I asked my guy. Such a stupid question, but I didn't know what to say that was in basic enough English.

"Uh ... yes." He smiled intently. His eyes lit up no matter what I said. Being horny makes everything sound sexy. Oh, to ponder all the red flags that have been ignored.

We went to a couple more bars with them. Sarah looked lovingly into her guy's eyes while they shared a hookah, while mine looked intently into mine. She soon disappeared with hers and returned without him.

"What happened?"

"Oh, you know."

"Where's my friend?" my guy asked.

"On the beach!" the friend called out.

Once he was out of earshot, I asked, "So?"

"We were chatting on the beach, and then started kissing, and then hooked up on a beach chair." We both laughed. "He's so hot, but I don't want a relationship, and will probably never see him again. I just wanted something fun."

"Nice." We all need to treat ourselves.

The next day, we were hungover and spent most of the day, heads throbbing, on the beach. At one point, we saw the soccer players from the night before. Seeing her guy, Sarah's entire face lit up, and she waved at him excitedly. Seeing her, his face dropped, and he looked away.

Sarah bounded over to say, "Hi!" I waved at his friend who I had spoken to the night prior and watched Sarah and her guy awkwardly interact before she returned to my side.

"Let's go." She grimaced.

"What's wrong?" I asked once we were farther down the beach.

"He didn't have to be like that."

"Like what?"

"Such a dick. It's not like I wanted a relationship, we only hooked up, doesn't mean I can't come and say hi."

"I'm sorry," I said. I wanted to say, "You knew this could happen," but I didn't. Guys are assholes sometimes. I envied women who could have sex and walk away without a care. I couldn't do it; I still felt a longing for something more, unable to disconnect physical intimacy from the emotional one. I hadn't had sex in months because of my self-imposed dry spell until a guy met the standards in the dating book I'd read on the flight when I moved to Shanghai (none did) or I could figure out how to better handle my own emotions around sex.

On the ferry and bus ride back, Sarah was distant, her personality less bubbly than usual.

Back in Bangkok, she had work in the morning and I had my own plans to see one of the local markets. Taking the metro, I arrived early before most of the shops had been set up and as it was a Monday during a coup, hardly anyone was there. Ordering a Thai iced tea from one of the vendors, I wandered around looking at elephant harem pants, hippie fabric-patched pants and bags, little paper mâché elephants, golden trinket dishes, and more. Every shop had the same selection and a shopkeeper ready to insist I pay an extraordinary amount until I mentioned the shop next door had it for fifty percent less.

Next, I headed over to some other markets across the square. Inside, I found a nail salon. I sat down in front of a free nail stylist, "Are you free to paint my nails?"

She couldn't speak English, but her eyes lit up, likely because she'd had few foreign customers.

As she brushed on bright orange laquear, a cockroach scurried behind her up a shelf. We tried to speak in broken English.

"You are," she whispered to their friend, who whispered back, "Pretty."

"Thank you, you are very pretty, too."

A few moments later, a mouse walked onto the edge of a shelf and sniffed a bit, as if unsure where to go next. They all looked at my face to see if I was shocked, but I was unfazed. This was nothing compared to what I was prepared for. One time in New Orleans, I was lying in bed, peacefully reading Benjamin Franklin's autobiography, when a huge cockroach the size of a thumb climbed up my bare arm. Nothing would ever be more traumatizing than that experience, especially a small mouse. We all laughed together.

That night, Sarah, and I headed to Khao San Road, the main tourist bar street. Everyone on this street wore elephant harem pants, carried hippie fabric-patched bags, and looked like they hadn't showered since birth. I edged through the crowd, trying not to get a layer of body sweat and patchouli essential oils on the new, wispy chemise maxi dress I'd bought at the mall earlier to vainly show off my new business lady self. Sarah was also there to find herself. Her eyes lit up when we chatted with backpackers about seeing a local woman shoot ping-pong balls out of her hoo-ha.

"Can we go somewhere else?" I asked. "I hate it here. Is there somewhere more local?" Hoping to find people who lived abroad, not casually passed through, I wanted to hear about the work that brought them abroad or speak with locals to learn about everyday life and cultural differences. Most importantly, I wanted to sit beside people who didn't smell like armpits.

"Kristen, I just moved to Bangkok; I don't know any other places, and this place seems cool."

I shrugged. Knowing who I wanted to be, I didn't want to spend time with backpackers finding themselves. This whole street felt so artificial. We went and got hookah.

"And there's nowhere else we can go?"

"You're being difficult," Sarah said. She was right. Part of being a good travel partner was being low maintenance and going with the flow, but I had finally become an expat with a real job abroad, the international business lady I had dreamt of becoming since high school. Yet, I was surrounded by many people you might find in my hometown. My choice to move abroad was intentionally to take time away from the familiar and experience the new.

"Is there anywhere we can go for a nice cocktail, maybe a rooftop with a view?"

"Not that I know of. I just moved here."

This trip felt like a total bust; it was impossible to escape all the tourist traps. Maybe I needed to head outside the city.

The next day, I headed to Ayutthaya. Founded by King Ramathibodi I in 1351 and the former capital of Siam, Ayutthaya was filled with clay-colored, triangular Buddhists temples that rose up into the sky. As I got off the bus, I was swamped by men driving tuk-tuks offering me a ride.

"No, thank you!" I said to all of them, determined not to do the touristy thing. Grabbing a map, I walked for half an hour to the first temple. All the while, tourists in tuk-tuks rushed past me. The same thing happened at the next temple, and the next. Finally, I found a random building that had bottled water for sale. Inside, I looked at paintings of the city when it had been a prosperous port. Skinny boats with dragon heads at their bows snaked through the old city, full of little houses with bright red roofs.

This journey reminded me of my last trip into New York City with Sarah before I'd moved. We went to the Museum of Modern Art together. Having gone to what felt like a million museums all over the world by myself, I always explore them like a cat with the zoomies. I walk quickly from room to room and only stop if something catches my eye. By the time I'd returned after reviewing the entire floor, Sarah was still standing in front of the one painting where I'd left her, Vincent van Gogh's *The Starry Night*. She just stood there, completely enraptured. This was so foreign to me, but the same way I zoomed around, this was her way of enjoying the museum. I loved Sarah. She was different from me, and there was this magic to her. Her enigmatic energy was like a magnet, drawing you in. It was beautiful, but at this point in my life, I didn't want to be surrounded by calm, I wanted to be swept up in climbing the corporate ladder. There was no time to dilly-dally.

After about two hours of walking, I was dripping sweat from the heat and humidity. I should have taken a tuk-tuk. Giving up, I took a bus back to Bangkok. The entire economy felt like it was designed around making sure tourists all had the same experience. I hated it.

That night, Sarah and I went out for my last night. Once we arrived, I realized this new road looked exactly like Khao San Road, and Sarah started chatting with the same type of people.

"I hate it here," I said quietly to Sarah.

"Would you relax?" Sarah snapped. "Just try to have fun."

"Everyone feels like they've changed from back home and are different, but they are all wearing the same pants." I had probably seen hundreds of pairs of harem pants on this trip—all the exact same style I'd seen at every market I'd been to.

"Let them enjoy themselves!" Sarah said.

"Any idea where we could go that's a little less touristy?"

"Kristen, I just moved here. I don't know! Can I talk to you for a minute?" She pulled me aside. "What is up with you?"

"I feel so trapped here. It feels so hypocritical and everywhere I go people are trying to rip me off and selling all the exact same things. It's such a tourist trap."

"You've changed," Sarah said.

"I have?"

"Yeah, you're materialistic and judgy."

I went silent, processing what she had said. "I'm going to go," I said. I called a taxi and left.

By the time Sarah got home, I had packed and moved a blanket from her bed to the sofa. We would not be sharing a bed tonight.

"What is your problem?" Sarah said.

"I finally got a job and am becoming successful and here I'm surrounded by backpackers who don't have any purpose."

"Who gives a shit?"

"And you're finding yourself, too. You're so upset no one from home is cheering you on, but who cares?"

"Who cares? I moved my whole life over here, and I feel like they abandoned me."

"They didn't abandon you. They are just focused on their own lives."

Despite the government coup, I had created my own drama. Maybe it was the alcohol or the sadness making me block it out of my mind, I don't fully remember our conversation. Regardless, it doesn't matter. I'm sure I said some mean things about how I had been feeling about my trip. I was in the wrong, but neither of us was actually wrong. We were growing apart. It was a friendship breakup.

The next day on the flight, I felt numb inside. Sarah had been my best friend and she felt like a stranger. She was grasping to become something else, but it felt so different from whatever the hell I was becoming. I had been the dick; difficult to travel with, high expectations, judging everyone else for trying to have a good time, and expecting my friends to show me around. I was being needy. Sarah was being emotionally needy and that's not my strong suit. People came to me for life advice: how to invest or to suggest ways to get over a guy. I wasn't the person they came to when they were going through emotional stuff. She needed me and I did not feel empathy for what she was going through. I didn't understand the things that were hurting her.

On my flight home, I thought about my trip. Losing my best friend felt like my fault. In reality, we were going in completely different directions. I wanted to lean into business and become a professional, and she was discovering she wanted to be something else. It wasn't that either of us was wrong, it was that we didn't connect the way we used to. Our values had changed.

After Thailand, Sarah became a vegan yoga instructor, traveling as a backpacker to over eighty countries, living in a new city every few weeks. Today, she lives in the Maldives, where she runs a six-figure business as a life coach teaching others how to practice yoga and meditation and spends every day in chaturanga dandasana, overlooking the sea. I message her "Congratulations!" or "Happy Birthday" here and there on social media and she thanks me, but she never initiates a conversation. Still, I am so proud of her. She's such a beautiful person, and she deserves the world. Should I apologize? Someday. Shouldn't that happen in person? It doesn't feel genuine over DM and considering we're both travelers, we haven't been in the same place ever since my visit.

Losing her friendship is one of the biggest regrets in my life. We grieve the loss when people die, but what about when we drift apart from a friend? It hurts. Maybe someday I'll find myself in Maldives and over some drinks, her glowing smile looking back at me, we'll resolve things, or maybe the closure I needed was accepting that we'll never again be two starry-eyed girls, living in shitty Brooklyn apartments, seeing the world as ours to tame.

Chapter 10: Changzhou

A Ghost Visits a Ghost City

One year later, Changzhou, China—According to Google Maps, there were seven Starbucks in Changzhou. Unfortunately, there was no "Changzhou" Starbucks mug to remember the city. If you visit a city without getting a Starbucks mug with its name on it, did you ever really visit that city? This would have made a great gift. When visiting my father's side of the family while home two months prior, I'd brought them some of the most expensive coffee in the world.

"Wow, this is the best coffee I've ever had," my brother said as he took a sip.

"Isn't it good? I bought it in Vietnam," I said, sipping my coffee. My Dad grabbed the coffee bag to read the back, trying to figure out how it could possibly taste so delicious.

"Wait. Is this the coffee that's pooped out by cats?" Dad asked.

"They're technically civets, which I think looks more like a ferret—"

I was abruptly interrupted by my young cousins, aunt and uncle, brother, father—all spitting out their coffees. Brown liquid spewed across the room, covering the table and carpet. They all looked at me in shock.

Apparently, you're supposed to tell people that kind of information in advance. Having spent so much time abroad, what was socially normal to eat, drink, or do was starting to become different for me compared to most people back home. Riding my baby blue racer bike to get around the city, eating three-dollar dumplings for lunch, going to the wet market and watching the big fish swish around in their tanks, or crawling through old hutongs to chase stray cats, I had adopted new norms in my new home. The city had constant delights: poor translations that made you laugh, adorable kids excitedly taking their first bite into a bao bun, or a hole in the wall where you could try a new delicious type of Chinese food—cumin ribs Uyghur style, Sichuan peppercorns that made your mouth go numb, chicken hearts boiled in hot pot, or delicately made street corner soup dumplings made by a pinch from an ayi's fingers quick from years of experience. If you lined all her grandkids up and she consecutively pinched all their cheeks, I bet the first kid still wouldn't have noticed by the time she finished. On second thought, the one-child policy makes this less impressive.

Shanghai had constant surprises. Sometimes I'd go over an unpaved road and pop a tire, sending me to my local bike repair shop where the guy knew me now and would fix it for under eight dollars. A motorist and I would bump into each other and, unable to speak the same language, there would be no anger or animosity, we'd shrug, smile at each other, and head on our way. I'd be on the subway and see a woman holding her son over the garbage, pants down, ass out, pee trickling directly into the can. Or heading to a club, I'd see a wall-size tank filled with slowly circling sharks.

The constant change made the city exciting. You never knew what would happen next. It made me feel like I was part of something. When my best friend, Jade, invited me to spend Chinese New Year with her family in a suburb of Shanghai, I was excited to learn more about the country I now called home.

We pulled into an apartment complex, a thick white fog hanging between the buildings. The car bounced over uneven tiles as we headed down a row of homes. Chinese New Year represented a unique opportunity for the new, urbanized China to meet around a circular table with the old, agrarian China. As I would learn, old and new China were very different. So were my old American and my new Shanghai lives.

Jade had four Chihuahuas—Lucky, Helen, Kana, and Lisa—all English names because Jade's mother, who did not speak English, considered this 'fashionable.' Changzhou in Jiangsu Province was about a three-hour drive outside Shanghai. Having been back to my American hometown two months prior and having lived in China for over a year and half by now, the trip was a time to reflect on how I felt in my new home as well as how it was shaping me.

"We're here!" Jade chimed. As we parked at the end of the apartment row, an elderly woman ran out of the building to greet us, wearing a Chinese cooking apron. Unlike an American apron, this looks more like a hospital gown made of a faded plaid tablecloth, tied in the back with strings. She had rosacea-stained cheeks and skin the color of light cowboy boots, and her face creased into a million lines when she smiled, like a mille-feuille. She had spent many days under an unforgiving sun. Jade explained this was the sister of her grandmother, who had passed away, and who we were visiting for Chinese New Year's Eve dinner.

Two months earlier, I'd flown home to surprise my family. My grandmother reacted as if she'd seen a ghost—as if I wasn't there in the flesh before her. She ran to hug me, in her bright sweater, pearls, and white pants, her bright blond bob immaculately sprayed into place. She always looked like she'd just stepped off a yacht in Monaco. With my parents on a budget growing up, my grandmother used to take me shopping for school clothes. It's how we bonded. However, as one might expect if you're dressed by your grandmother, my Sunday church dresses—with their tulip designs and A-line toile hems—didn't make me very cool in a room full of middle schoolers wearing tight Abercrombie and Fitch layered popped collared shirts and velour pants that proudly said "Juicy" on the ass. Whoever created Juicy pants belongs in jail. They got a bunch of underage kids to walk around with Juicy in terrycloth on their bums.

In China, Jade had taught me to use Taobao, the Chinese version of eBay, where could buy immaculate quality fakes—a fur Marni bag (I pray it wasn't dog fur, although a local friend told me this wasn't unheard of), what I called "Franken-Lilly" (Lilly Pulitzer print cut into a non-brand approved style T-shirt), or a gold Goyard clutch (gold represents "good fortune" in Chinese culture, but this fake's gaudy color was likely not approved by the Parisian headquarters). The new me was embracing "Tuhao," which translated is basically "new money." This was both Jade's and my vibe. Having both worked back-to-back at desks at the wine importer together, we were up and coming in this world and ready to flaunt it.

Having someone react to me as if I was a ghost wasn't new to me. It was common when I visited rural parts of China, where many had never seen a blond with light eyes before.

"Yáng guǐzi," a local might say, using a slang term meaning "foreign devil," what I was later told was a racial slur.

"Shuō Cáo Cāo, Cáo Cāo dào!" I'd respond, which means, "Speak of the devil, and the devil will come." To this, they'd sit up straight, tilt their head in shock, and we'd laugh together. Having spent more time in China, I was picking up the basics of the language. This made everyday life a lot less stressful.

Changzhou itself was a "ghost city." During the 1990s, due to social market reforms in the region led by Deng Xiaoping, the leader of China after Mao Zedong, Jiangsu Province and other areas near the wealthy port city of Shanghai, were flooded with foreign investment and rapidly grew. This created a real estate bubble in China, creating "ghost cities"—cities with high levels of construction but low occupancy rates.[11] This inflated property values, causing a push for people to move into urban housing. Families like Jade's moved from farmland to apartments.[12]

Within parts of China, there had been a dramatic shift in living standards and daily life over the past three generations. For example, as a child, Jade's entire family lived in a single room with a bathroom down the hall shared by her entire apartment building's floor. Today in Shanghai, she and her mother shared a queen-sized bed in a one-bedroom apartment with their own bathroom, a huge upgrade.

Jade's grandmother used to make a living on a farm, and not the type we have in the U.S. with industrialized tractors or Monsanto seeds. This was an old-school, bare-bones farm. The kind I used to learn about at the

Historical Society in my hometown, where I was taught to churn butter, make cranberry sauce, and that colonial American life sucked—like
wake-up-with   your-breath-frozen-into-tiny-icicles-on-your-blan-
ket-and-maybe-your-little-sister-frozen-to-death-next-to-you kind of
sucked. That was 200 years ago, but for Jade's family, that was the level
of poverty during her grandmother's generation.

"The countryside is a bit 'peasant,'" Jade explained to me as we ate
zongzi, rice, and meat stuffed in a bamboo leaf at a truck stop on the way
to Changzhou. Growing up in Shanghai, Jade had the sass of a teenager
from *Gossip Girl* and her mother was like a wife on *The Sopranos*—very
kind and generous, but she wore a red, fur-trimmed biker jacket and
was powerful enough that all her male cousins were terrified of her.
They were not going to lower their *Sex and The City* level standards
simply because they were in the country. We visited every one of the seven
Starbucks on our trip.

The first night, dinner was in Jade's great-aunt's apartment. Upon
entering the apartment, we put blue plastic boot covers that looked like
shower caps over our shoes to keep the floor clean. Most of the family
was seated on the sofa watching television together. This reminded me
of Thanksgiving at home. The young girls giggled at the sight of me, the
weird "laowai", or foreigner, in the room. In the area adjacent to the living room, a few traditional cold plates were already laid out on the table:
barbecue ribs, shrimp, huge black-striped lima beans, water chestnuts
and black fungus, chives, and a jelly-ish fungus that's chewier than you'd
expect, along with a plate of pig intestines cut into thin porous slices
(looks kind of like yellow Velcro with a tofu texture). Served as a first
course for more practical than cultural reasons, these cold dishes were
for eating while the main dishes were still being prepared. This was later

accompanied by warm dishes, including my favorite: duck lungs, which look like miniature human lungs, but are maroon in color and taste like a thicker, less buttery, foie gras. As I settled into my new home, I had become more adventurous in my eating and realized why other cultures loved some of the foods Americans considered "disgusting" (spoiler alert: it's because they're delicious). Perhaps other countries would say the same thing about Jell-O (cow hooves), gravy (turkey giblets), or Cheese Whiz (pure chemicals).

"This is my mother's favorite," Jade said, pointing at the Asian swamp eel, which lives in the water of the rice fields and tasted like its muddy origin, often served with a thick, brown, sweet white pepper and soy sauce. "She used to eat it on special occasions, growing up in Changzhou," Jade said. We didn't serve eel in my family, although this was in fact a dish the pilgrims ate at the original Thanksgiving, offered by their Native American counterparts.[13]

Jade and her mother were very close. When her mother was pregnant, her father's family offered her a beautiful jade necklace as a congratulatory gift. When the baby was born, it was a female. Under the one-child policy, this meant that their family would never have a son. Shortly after Jade's birth, the family asked for the necklace back, scorned her mother, and pushed her father to divorce Jade's mom. Jade's mother put everything she had into raising her daughter.

My grandmother did the same: loving and caring for her family was her number one priority. Her mother was a talented pianist who lived in Paris in her youth, studying under a famous teacher. When she returned stateside from this life-changing experience, it was to a disastrous marriage, and she had to flee with an infant child, my grandmother, back to her parents in Connecticut.

From this experience, my grandmother put everything she had into helping her family. She would never abandon her blood. When my parents were financially struggling, she took her savings to support us however she could. Whenever my mom had to work late, my grandmother was there to care for me after school. Thanksgiving was one of those opportunities to invite all her children and grandchildren together at a table to eat a wonderful meal and give thanks for family.

It was an immaculate theatrical experience, orchestrated by my grandmother. To kick off the day, my grandmother set up little "stations" around the kitchen with ingredients for each dish—sweet potatoes, green beans, corn bread, creamed onions, stuffing, cranberry sauce, gravy, pecan pie, pumpkin pie—the same dishes every year. Then, we picked little pieces of yellow notepad paper out of a hat to determine who cooked what. Everyone wanted to cook the cornbread, the easiest dish, while sweet potatoes with toasted marshmallows took the most labor.

As dinner wrapped up at Jade's family's place, fireworks were visible outside the windows of the apartment. Jade and I watched them from the porch, sipping rice wine. Afterwards, we gathered around the TV to watch a Chinese awards show. I explained to Jade that on New Year's, in America, people watch "the ball drop."

"That's strange," she said.

"Indeed."

Pulling out of the driveway, the same woman we saw when we arrived stood over a new pile of fireworks, her face close to the newly lit stack. Clearly, her concern was singular: ignition at all costs. As we drove away, I thought about Jade's great-aunt's worn face and wondered what her life on a farm was like. Her living standards had risen, but had her sense of community been demolished? I thought it was tough teaching my grandparents how to use the internet; I couldn't imagine teaching this woman. Did she prefer this life over her farming roots? It might be nice to have a modern apartment over having to till a field for onions, but I've never lived on a farm. A Mormon momfluencer I followed on Instagram seemed very happy on her pig farm in Utah with her six kids, churning butter in a prairie dress for her followers' delight. Not emotionally mature enough to care for children, following her big family was my daily reminder to take my birth control.

The following night, we arrived at another dinner, and in the distance stood an eleven-story building with a parapet along the edge and a round top, designed as a replica of something I recognized. I squinted.

"Is that the U.S. Capitol building?" I asked.

"It's a factory," Jade explained with a wink. "The owner had big dreams." Replicating famous architecture was common in China. Known as 'duplitecture,' it was seen as a way of showing the technical skills of China's architects. A kind of "They can build a tower so poorly constructed in Pisa that it leans, well guess what, we can make these kinds of things too!" On another trip, I'd seen an entire street designed to look like the Champs-Elysées with a third the size Eiffel Tower at the end. The fact that this Capitol Building replica was ordered and constructed atop a large factory reminded me how far away I was from home. It was also why I loved China.

A developing country with such rapid growth, if you wanted to build a factory in the middle of nowhere with another country's Capitol Building on top, who was there to tell you no? The same rules applied to me and my life: living in China meant stripping away all things familiar—social norms, everyday routines, and cultural expectations. By forcing myself to adapt to a place where nothing was expected of me, I went through the cathartic process of rebuilding my identity from the ground up. There were zero expectations of me, this weird pale girl who likes pooped-out coffee—a new and improved replica of myself.

"Let me show you the big rooster," Jade said, peeking in a shed. All we could see were chickens. "Over here. He's not here," she said. "He is so big, the biggest rooster I have ever seen. Maybe ten kilos!" I did the math in my head. Ten kilos was twenty-two pounds, so like two or three cats.

As we stood on the street, other family members rolled a big circular block of wood into the house; this would be our table for the evening. Dried herbs hung from the walls under a vaulted wood ceiling which opened directly onto the street.

The wheel of wood was covered with a clear polyethylene material that was used instead of plates. The family's kitchen had a traditional stove, including a brush-burning "stovetop"—a large wok-like metal bowl, currently filled with steaming rice. An oven underneath the bowl was stuffed with kindling. Brush was stacked against a white brick wall for easy access. It felt so cozy.

In another room, the husband of our host showed me his pride and joy: his homemade mijiu distillery. A large clay vat was filled with rice disintegrating in water. A vertical, wicker basket tunnel in the center allowed the mijiu to be separated and ladled out. The fermented rice of the exterior, if eaten directly, tasted like cheese rinds (it's not supposed to be eaten, but this foreign devil was feeling adventurous).

Soon after, we were served chicken soup with black fungus, ginger, and bamboo shoots.

"I think I know what happened to the rooster," Jade said as the chicken soup was ladled into each of our bowls. The broth was fresh and vibrant, a rich sunflower yellow—the freshest, most delicious soup of my life. I had so many servings, I peed for days. I even took some home in a plastic bag, which I ate immediately.

Suddenly, Jade's drunk uncle (from now on 'Drunkle') decided he had something he needed to get off his chest. "I like Americans," he said. "But do you know who I hate? *The Japanese.*" He repeated this about fifty million times, all in Chinese. Jade politely apologized and the rest of the family lightly prodded him to change the subject. There was some kind of fucked up comfort this gave me, knowing even on the other side of the world, people have to deal with embarrassing, racist relatives. It's sadly a universal thing.

As the meal wrapped up, Jade and I headed outside to watch the fireworks in the distance. The top of the Changzhou Capitol Building was lit in bright yellow, standing guard over the neighborhood garden. Reflecting on what moments made me the happiest, it was small delights, like spending time with Jade, throwing snap poppers on the ground to watch them spark in the darkness.

After dinner, we headed back to a family friend's apartment where we were staying. The living room had lightly-patterned beige wallpaper, a beige refrigerator, white chairs with velvet maroon covers and little lace edges, and a gold pig figurine. The only picture on the wall was a print of two overweight Chinese boys laughing and dancing with cartoon snakes and coins.

"What are these?" I pointed at the picture.

"It is for prosperity. In feng shui the pig represents luck and good fortune," Jade said. What was the American equivalent? Maybe two women in yoga pants dancing around kale and a golden retriever. I liked the idea of putting reminders of your goals on your wall—a sort of lighthouse for what you want to bring more of in your life.

The following day, we headed to the Yancheng Chunqiu Amusement Park. Traveling with Jade's mother's high school best friends, we snuck in plastic bottles of yellow rice wine into the park and all got a bit tipsy. Seeing a descriptive placard, I leaned over a small boy to read the sign.

"Ahhh!" A little boy shrieked, jumping back in terror, seeing a white woman for the first time ever. As he ran to hide behind his parents, Jade's mother and her friends burst into laughter. I'm kind of glad Chinese kids had this reaction because children are often knee-height. My biggest fear in life was going to brunch, being drunk, and accidentally kneeing a kid in the face while heading to the bathroom.

Various types of food were available at the park including "pizza"—a pizza crust rolled into an ice cream cone shape filled with ground beef and corn, all topped with pepperoni and cheese. Not ready to further test my definition of pizza, I opted for something local, called "tang yuan," a sweet soup made of mijiu, water, egg-drop, and dried goji berries with black, sweet, dumpling balls filled with blue potato juice and white sticky rice dumplings with a yolk-ish inside.

On our last day, we headed to a neighboring city, Qidong, for the wedding of another relative. This was my chance to see what life had been like two generations ago. As we got closer, the streets changed from strip malls with fruit stands to intermittent houses and fields. As we drove along, the pattern became clear: a long row of houses, an open field, an irrigation ditch, an open field, a long row of houses, an irrigation ditch ... repeated over and over again. As we turned left into a lane, the consistent, equal portion of land assigned to each home became visible.[14] The lane was long enough that you had to squint to see the end of the row of houses. Some fields were farmed, and others were unused and covered in short, thick weeds. This was very different from the apartment complexes we visited the first night and likely what it used to be like for those families.

"We need to look like city bitches," Jade had said while we were getting ready for the wedding. Decked out in a nice dress, my grandmother's mink coat (the only time I wore it in China), my gold watch, and ridiculously long, blond hair extensions, I was ready to party.

Jade was forever attempting to make me look like Barbie. One time she even took me to get elephant hair lashes glued into my own lashes. They were so heavy that after a few days they started to point in different directions. Drunk one night, I ended up ripping them out, taking some of my own eyelashes and going a month with a chunk of eyelash missing. Another time, during my lunch break, I went with Jade to get my eyebrows dyed a darker shade, so I'd look like Cara Delevingne. Having never dyed blond hair before, Jade's hairdresser gave me neon green eyebrows. I looked like one of the rich people from *The Hunger Games*. Meanwhile Jade, everyone in the hair shop, and the hairdresser himself laughed hysterically at the hideous color. I had to go into the Chanel makeup section of a mall nearby and rub brown eyeliner on them before returning to the office.

At the wedding, I was diligently fulfilling my Barbie role. One of the tables was all old men, smoking and drinking.

"Say the thing I taught you," Jade said to me in a whisper, elbowing me in the ribs.

"Gōngxǐ fācái!" I said to the gentleman, holding up my glass.

The old men erupted into laughter. They spoke to each other in Chinese, trying to figure out how to respond.

"Cheese! Cheese!" one said, holding up his baijiu.

"Gānbēi!" I said back. This was the Chinese word for cheers, the only difference being that out of respect you have to down your entire glass. As I stumbled back to my table, one of the old men stood up to make a speech. Jade translated for me as he spoke.

"We are honored to have an American join us here today at this wedding and in our home." I listened politely as I filled my mouth with 'drunk shrimp,' which are live shrimp, twitching in an alcohol sauce. "We hope for great prosperity between our countries and between Xi Jinping and President Obama (the President at the time). We are both proud countries, and together we can do business and prosper."

"Gānbēi!" I said in response, followed by a room full of roaring laughter. I thanked them again for having me and felt lucky to have attended this joyous occasion.

As people ate, I took a moment to have some quiet outside. Compared to Shanghai, the dramatic quiet of this place shocked me. Only the sounds of birds chirping lightly. No honking horns, sirens, people yelling. In this sudden silence, I realized how much China had changed in the past three generations and also how far I'd come. If you had asked me even two years ago if I'd known I'd end up at a wedding in Qidong, I'd have said, "Qi what?" Who knew my trip to Paris at sixteen would end up like this a decade later. I'd gone from a girl who didn't even know what kind of beer she liked to one who enjoyed pork blood. I loved my new home. The food was amazing, the people lovely, and I was able to terrify children by my mere presence—I had no regrets about moving to China. It was shaping who I would become.

CHAPTER 11: SHAPOTOU DESERT

One Man Creates Fear of Many

One year earlier, Yichuan, China—Our international hotel in Yichuan, Shaanxi Province, with its cascading glass waterfall chandelier, high ceilings, and gold painted walls, was one of the most beautiful hotels I'd ever seen.

"This is a five-star hotel, but they're trying to make it four-star," our local sales rep, Qiang, said. "They were building a seven-star hotel next door." He pointed to a half-finished building wrapped in plastic. "Now, they're trying to make it four stars."

"Why would they try to make the hotels less nice?" I asked. More importantly, *how* do you downgrade a hotel? Do you remove all the beautiful marble bathroom countertops and replace them with cheap laminate? Maybe you replace the gold and pink, red-crowned crane wallpaper with shiplap, or the $600 chair in the corner with a white, plastic

IKEA chair. Maybe it's about absolutely destroying your customer service. "Carry your own bags, bitch," is the initial greeting as you enter the high-ceilinged hotel with its crystal chandelier on the way to reception.

"Hello, welcome to the Kempinski, I didn't know I'd be serving someone with pants as flowy as Kim Jung-Il visiting a cookie factory, but here we are," reception would say, "How can I *not* help you today?" Perhaps you tackle the food: the breakfast buffet is now a handful of Skittles, a wet cigarette, and a firm, go-get-'em tiger slap on the rump to get you started on your day.

He pointed to a large, Bauhaus-style—popular under communism—building facing the hotel. "See that? It's owned by the government. People visiting that building stay in these hotels. Because of austerity measures, government officials can no longer stay in above four-star hotels anymore." He leaned in. "But you should see the basement; it's all Lamborghinis." Once again, the rich had gone underground.

The hotels knew their guests and wanted to keep Daddy Government paying.

Why was I in a random city in northern China? After months of trying thousands of wines at tasting events, wine fairs, and trainings, I'd met a famous winemaker who worked at one of France's five First Growth Bordeaux estates who said things like, "Being a winemaker is like painting with nature. You have to control the elements and then combine them, like a chemist, in just the right way." After learning from winemakers from all over the world how to charm a crowd, tell stories, and take people on a journey, it was my turn.

Hosting my very first wine dinner meant I wouldn't be the handler for an export manager or famous winemaker. Instead, I'd be walking a dinner of predominantly Chinese locals—who didn't speak English—through an entire flight of wines, describing the flavor profiles, the origin stories, and more, like a real sommelier.

"This is all you have to say, repeat after me," Dong said. "Kàn, wén, shìyòng." Dong, a regional director, was in his forties, and on the shorter side with a sharp angular face. Very into physical and mental health, Dong would work out by swimming in the hotel pool every morning.

"Can, win, schlong."

"No: kàn, wén, shìyòng."

"Con, when, she yawns."

"Closer." He shook his head. I was very off. "This is to see, to smell, to taste the wine. If you can learn this one phrase, they will love you."

"Got it." I gulped. As a sign of respect, learning at least one phrase in the country you're visiting goes a long way.

The day after the banquet, we headed to visit some Chinese wineries in the region. Dong and I were traveling with our colleagues, Dove, who worked for our marketing team in the northern headquarters, and the regional sales rep, Qiang, who was tall, young, and wearing cerulean blue alligator shoes. Dove had slender, delicate features and long, fake, mesmerizing eyelashes that fluttered every time she laughed at the hotel general manager's jokes. His laughs got the biggest flutters mainly because they were fucking.

Our first stop was to visit a local winery owned by an international spirits company. On the way there, we went through agricultural areas with palm oil plants, Christmas trees, and a yard full of thousands of ducks that at one point blocked the street until a man with a stick got them to cross. Why did the chicken cross the road? Likely because there was a farmer with a stick chasing it. That's when we arrived at the vineyard. The vines spread for about half a mile before climbing up the base of a mountain. Unlike the dark brown with dried leaves on topsoil I normally saw in western vineyards, these vines sat in yellow sand.

Walking through the vineyards, the birds chirped in the distance and the air was much cleaner than in the city. The winery itself felt like a factory, with tall, clean interiors housing huge silver canisters for aging white wine. On the wall were framed photos. Wandering over, I squinted at one I couldn't quite make out. It looked like the Gobi Desert, the sand rippling from the wind.

"That's what this vineyard looked like when they bought it," Dong said.

I gasped at the difference.

"It was a big production. They took silt from the Yangtze River and dumped it in this desert." He pointed to the next photos, where tractors were dumping mud onto the desert sand. "It's so cold in the winter here, they have to braid the vines and bury them under the sand so they don't freeze."

Next, we headed to Silver Heights. They had a vineyard in the middle of the city where tourists could walk the vines, view the wine cellar, and do tastings without heading into the proper vineyard in the mountains.

Two red Tibetan Mountain dogs guarded the vineyard, and their barks were terrifying, but then a black Mastiff puppy ran up to us, its feet and ears too big for its body. A white man in his fifties stumbled after it. Dove gave him a hug.

"This is Thierry," she said. *Oh, he's French.*

"Salut," I said.

He motioned to us, and we followed him to the vineyard, the cellar, and then a table in the sun. He brought out an oversized bottle of Silver Heights wine and glasses. I was grateful to be sitting there, drinking wine with the Mastiff pup in my lap, licking my face.

Silver Heights is owned by Gao Yuan, one of the first Chinese wine-makers and one of the few female winemakers.[15] Gao also liked to be called Emma.[16] Since arriving, I'd noticed that some Chinese people went by their Chinese name while others went by an English name they were often told to pick while they were in elementary school. In America, kids aren't allowed to pick their names at this age mainly because they'd pick something like Skywalker or Lebron, so naturally here, I'd met a million Lebrons. Chinese is also a pictorial language, so from what Jade told me, people oftentimes choose very visual names.

"You can't be called Banana," an English teacher friend told me they told a student.

"But why? My friend's called Cherry," the kid explained.

My first Chinese tutor helped me choose a Chinese name: Fànxītíng, which sounds like "fancy thing" in English, which is an accurate descrip-tion of how I try to present myself. The first symbol is a generic last name, the second symbol represents hope, and the last symbol represents space. Apparently, she had done a significant amount of research and there was a bakery called "Christine's" that had the "xītíng" translation, so that was close enough to Kristen.

At first, she gave me a last symbol that meant "feminine form," but that made me visualize a vagina. I explained that although I appear very feminine, I want something more serious and less gendered. At this point in my life, I was starting to become less focused on dating and looking sexy to men and more about my career and my own money. I wanted my Chinese name to reflect that.

"I want to spread ideas," I told her. "You know, be a thought leader." I was reading a lot of Malcolm Gladwell at that point in my life. She probably thought I was farcical. Does my English name "Kristen" indicate I spread ideas? That's when she suggested the symbol "space." Later, I would be told the literal translation of my name was actually "Dream Gazebo."

"I am making your last name only one word because in Chinese, only royalty in ancient times had a two-word last name."

"Works for me." My two-word last name had also caused issues in America where some credit card companies and even the DMV were unable to have a space in the last name portion of their software or it would mess up their system. In the most attractive yearbook picture ever taken of me I was placed in the "N" section as "Kristen Nest."

Regardless, I loved my Chinese name. Every time people heard it, they'd stop, think for a moment, and then say, "Wow, so interesting ... and beautiful." While I assume that means it's good, to be fair, this is exactly how I responded when a Chinese woman introduced herself as "Juicy."

"Would anyone want to ride a camel tomorrow since we're near the Shapotou Desert?" I asked. I was hoping Dove would be down to come along.

"I have to head back to Beijing." She shrugged.

"I'm in," Dong said. At this point, I had traveled numerous times with a male colleague, and we'd been doing touristy stuff all day, seeing these wineries together, and he was married, so it seemed harmless enough. Plus, considering I didn't speak or read Chinese and was in a place where nothing was translated, I didn't even know how I was going to ride the camels if I wanted to go by myself. How would I buy a train ticket? Where would I buy a train ticket? Google Maps was blocked and even if it wasn't, all the names were in Chinese, which I couldn't read.

"Sounds good!" I said.

As we left the vineyard, I saw Emma in a room, overseeing an employee putting the signature red caps on newly bottled wines, already in crates ready for distribution.

After the vineyard, we went home, freshened up, then it was time for dinner. For the event, the entire restaurant had been shut down with one austere table in the center of the space. Without a lot of experience in public speaking, I nervously pulled the printed tasting notes out of my pocket to review one more time. Qiang started my introduction, which was all in Chinese. He paused and the room went silent. Dong motioned for me to start. Since I didn't understand the Chinese, I didn't know it was my time to start. Starting to sweat, my heart pounding, I rushed through my speech: "We're going to start with an Australian Cabernet Sauvignon from Barossa Valley. There are three steps to tasting wine: kàn, wén, shìyòng. First, you have to look at the color. Hold your glass to a tilt over the white paper and you can see—"

Qiang said something to Dong.

"Talk slower, and pause every few words, so Qiang has time to translate."

"Oh right."

"You're doing great." He gave me a thumbs up.

"Okay." I took a deep breath.

As the dinner progressed, I found my rhythm. Despite not being able to fully communicate with everyone, I could smile and at least make a connection that conveyed something along the lines of, "Thank you for being here, now please buy our wine." By the end, the evening was deemed a huge success. As I returned to my fancy room—my first time ever staying in a five-star turned four-star hotel—I was on a high. Fancy Thing Dream Gazebo had a work victory. I had proven to myself that I could make it anywhere, even on the other side of the world.

The next day, Dong and I headed to the dusty desert train station to travel to the Shapotou Desert. We'd stay one night, ride the camels in the morning, then head to our respective flights in Yinchuan—his back to Harbin and mine back to Shanghai.

On the train, Dong told me about Buddhism and the belief that good things come to good people. He showed me his prayer bead bracelet. He reminded me of one of the fitness freaks you might meet in Silicon Valley who is all about overall wellness. Outside, our train rolled along a dusty, auburn desert that reminded me of the empty plains in American cowboy films.

"I was thinking we could stay here," he said, showing me his phone. He flipped through photos of small cabins in the desert.

"Yeah sure, whatever's cheapest." On the company's dime, I would stay in a nice hotel, but in my spare time, I was fine sleeping on someone's crusty couch. After all, I wouldn't have been able to afford all my travel if I hadn't shared hotel rooms or stayed with people. That was the norm for me; I hardly ever paid for my own room.

Off the train, we stopped at a small restaurant and ate desert greens and candied potato chips while finishing off a bottle of South African Cabernet Sauvignon left over from the dinner. Since wine goes bad three to five days after you open a bottle, one of the best parts of my job was being able to bring these wines home for a second round of savoring. As wine oxidizes, its flavor changes. When a wine has gone bad, it's often because of too much oxidation, which will make it turn orange in color and taste like vinegar. However, oxidation can also work in your favor: good wines need to be aerated when they come out of the bottle. Otherwise, they taste too "young." That's why one to two hours in a decanter can help bring out the most flavor. Like everything having to do with wine, it's all about balance. I was here in the desert to experience my own work-life balance.

We checked into our hotel.

"We can just split the cost," I said as he spoke to the receptionist who then walked us to the cabin we'd be staying in. In front of us were two doors to two adjoining rooms. Not understanding what was being said, I waited for Dong to take the lead. The receptionist tried to open one of the rooms but had trouble with the keys, so she moved onto the second one, which immediately opened with the key card. I assumed that maybe she had opened the wrong room first, then realized we were staying in the right-side room, not the left. Well, one room with two queen-sized beds would certainly be "whatever's cheapest."

"Let me show you the place," Dong said. As we walked around, the entire place was little, wooden cabins. Couples took photos. In fact, it was only couples around us. Was this some kind of romantic escape?

"Take a photo here," Dong said as we waited for a couple to finish taking a photo in front of a lake. Feeling kind of uncomfortable, I took one. Something felt *off*, but I couldn't quite place what was wrong.

"Do you want to drink anything?" Dong asked as the waitress waited to take our order at the hotel restaurant.

"I'll probably just have a glass."

Dong relayed my message in Mandarin to the waitress. No one at this resort could speak English.

The waitress arrived with a full bottle of plum wine, which Dong started drinking like shots.

We sat and ate deep-fried desert flowers. Dong started to appear drunk. He seemed to argue with the waitress. She also looked at me as if something was wrong, but I could neither tell what was being said nor put my finger on exactly what didn't feel right. I stopped drinking. Dong was getting sloppy, and I couldn't tell if he was starting to try to hit on me.

"I am getting tired, let's turn in," I said and then insisted on paying half the check. Dong's words started to slur.

Back at the room, I put on my pajamas and slipped into my bed, turning away from Dong and pretending to be asleep. He climbed into his own bed. The room was uncomfortably silent.

"Kristen," Dong said, pausing for a moment, "I think I like you."

"That's inappropriate. We're coworkers," I said. *Oh fuck, here we go. Why'd he have to ruin this?*

I pretended to be asleep, but my whole body tightened. Hopefully that was that and we could pretend that he had never said anything. He got out of bed and headed out of the cabin. Soon, I heard the muffled sound of him on the phone.

I texted my rugby player roommates back in Shanghai, *So I'm in the desert to go ride the camels and my coworker just said he likes me.*

Cheeky perv, the British one messaged back.

[Laughing emoji], the Irish one responded.

Dong finished his call and walked back to his bed. Still facing the other direction, pretending to sleep, I heard him get back into his bed and hoped he would go to bed soon. The room fell silent as I continued to fake sleep, not moving an inch. As time passed, my tense muscles started to relax.

A rustling broke the silence behind me. The sheet flew off the back of me, and Dong crawled into bed behind me. Spooning my body in only his boxers, he reached to grab my arm, his fingers closing around my wrist.

I bolted out of bed—as in full speed sprang to my feet—and ran over to the light to turn it on. If I hadn't already been awake, what would have happened? Having clearly said his crush was inappropriate, why did he think it was okay to get in my bed when he thought I was asleep?

"That was not okay!" I screamed, standing next to the lamp, my heart pounding. Should I run for the door? Was he going to physically come after me? Where would I go? In the desert in the middle of nowhere where no one around me speaks English, would he try to attack me? My brain went straight into survival mode, mapping out how I could position myself to be safe and what I would do if I needed to make an exit.

To remove privacy from our space, I threw open the door to our room. "You need to leave!" I shouted and then walked away from the door so he could exit without getting near me. I stood again near the lamp so that you could see my form from outside and I could use it as a weapon if I needed to fight him off.

He climbed out of bed and slipped on his pants. "Where's the key?"

"What key? After what you did, I don't want you to have a key to this room."

"No, to the other room."

We had another room? He paid for two rooms and didn't tell me? I couldn't understand any of the conversations when we checked in. I dug through my luggage. "I don't have another key. Go ask reception, and do not come back."

He left and I locked the door and burst into tears. Lying on the sofa, tears streamed down my face, my chest still pounding. I called my friend, Laurie, who I worked with and who was also American, and I told her what happened. Jade was my best friend, but I was worried that she might tell other colleagues, and I didn't want any rumors to spread.

"You have to tell your boss," she said.

"I do?"

"It's your call how to handle this, but I think you do."

"Okay." At this point, it was the middle of the night, so I'd wait until the morning. I called a couple close friends in the U.S., and I cried over the phone. Because it was the middle of the night in China, it was the middle of the day for them. They comforted me, told me they were sorry this had happened, and wished they could help me, but with the distance and language barriers, there was nothing they could do. I had to figure this out on my own.

What if he still had a key to my room? Still too scared to sleep, I put a chair in front of the door, wedged under the doorknob so at least I'd know if he tried to enter. With the door secure, what was my next move?

In the bathroom, I looked at myself in the mirror. My skin was no longer glowing; instead of freckles, my skin had gaping dark holes. It was as if I'd cried every drop of water out of my body. The skin under my eyes was bloated and purple from sobbing and lack of sleep. The person staring back at me was a sad, weak version of myself. What should I do? Should I call off riding the camels and try to find my way back to Yichuan alone?

Before moving to China, when I had been trapped at home suffering from depression, I read an old book called *The Feeling Good Handbook* by David D. Burns, MD. The book talked about cognitive behavioral therapy and how to overcome trauma. I'd found it really helpful when I was getting over guys because it talks about how things that remind you of someone trigger your feelings about them. So, if you're getting over a guy, it's best to remove all contact with him as well as pictures together, etcetera, that might be around your house and remind you of him. Without triggers, your brain can forget about the feelings and move on. In this instance, how did I want to overcome a colleague that I thought I could trust trying to assault me? I didn't want to make the entire memory of this trip about this terrifying experience.

"Fuck it, I'm riding the camels," I said, alone in my room with all the lights on. I was going to bury these memories deep under new ones of me on top of a furry desert beast that could apparently spit through its teeth. The door secured, I lay in bed but set my alarm for early in the morning before Dong would be awake.

Despite trying to sleep, I got none, my heart still racing, scared that he might once again try to climb into my bed and grab my arms to pin me down at any moment. At five a.m., my alarm went off; I quietly packed everything in practical darkness—only using the bathroom light—and headed to the lobby. The receptionist, asleep on the lobby's pullout sofa, looked annoyed at being woken up so early, but when her eyes met mine, she knew something was up. Now, with the safety of someone else near, I texted Dong: *What you did last night was unacceptable. I am going to go ride the camels by myself today and then head back to the airport. I will do this alone.*

Looking up the word for taxi and popping it into my translation app, I showed it to the woman at the front desk.

I'm sorry. I'm coming, I'm coming, don't leave, Dong texted back.

Standing outside the lobby, I waited for the taxi in the pitch black. While I couldn't see anything, I could hear the receptionist behind me, which made me feel a little bit safer. Soon, through the darkness, I heard the wheels of his luggage scraping against the asphalt path. Dong appeared, holding the shoes I'd left on the banister, disheveled and still buttoning up his shirt.

"I'm sorry."

"What you did was inexcusable," I spat. A taxi appeared out of the darkness.

"I know, this is not about you. I am having problems and—"

"There are no excuses. Your behavior was unacceptable. I don't want to hear it."

"I know, I know, I—"

"I don't want to hear it," I repeated. When in Nairobi and wronged, I had trouble sticking up for myself. I had grown a lot since then; I knew what I wanted and was getting better at establishing boundaries.

"And what happened last night, I got drunk and don't remember," he said.

"You remember," I said. This was bullshit.

He nodded and turned to the driver, speaking with him in Chinese. After a moment, he returned to me as the driver put our luggage in the back. "We will go to the camels—"

"You are not riding the camels with me."

"I know, I know. I will not ride the camels, but you will ride the camels and then you will head back on the bus to Yichuan."

"Okay."

I climbed into the taxi.

For the trip, I looked out the window, but also tried to keep the corner of my eye trained on Dong and the driver. I couldn't understand what they had said to each other, and I absolutely didn't trust him. After all, I had trusted him to share a hotel room with me and look what he had done. Was I safe now? Adrenaline rushed through my body.

"I'm sorry about what happened. I am having trouble at home and ..." He put his hand on my knee.

"Do not touch me!" I screamed. The driver looked up at me through the rearview mirror, and I looked back, trying to convey distress in my eyes. He probably thought it was a lover's quarrel.

"Okay, okay," Dong said, holding his hands in the air. The driver said something, and Dong responded. The driver pulled over to the side of the road.

My heart thumped harder than a hummingbird's wings. We were in the middle of nowhere, surrounded by sand dunes. Why was he pulling over?! There were no buildings for miles. My eyes trained on the driver, I hoped this stranger had my back.

"We will pull over here to view the sunrise," Dong said. This man had the audacity to plan excursions when he had tried to assault me.

"I'm going over here. You are not coming with me," I said, pointing to one of the sand dunes. Giving way under my feet, it felt like I was drowning as I fought the endless grains of sand, struggling to climb the steep incline.

Once at the top, I peered at the sun peeking out over the dunes in the distance. It was one of the most beautiful views I had ever seen—miles and miles of auburn mountains, untouched by humans. A small black beetle climbed beside me. Despite all odds and the hardship of the desert, creatures had found a way to persevere.

I looked at the mound of sand next to me, to keep my eye on Dong.

"I am sorry," he had written in big letters on his sand dune.

This motherfucker. I told myself. I watched him stand back and snap a picture. My phone buzzed. On WeChat, the Chinese messaging app, he'd sent me a picture of his creation. As if this made anything better.

In this beautiful, peaceful place, I felt mixed emotions. Fear, adrenaline, exhaustion——my body was still processing what had happened. Why would he try to attack me? And like climbing in my bed was one thing, but the grabbing of the arm ... what would have happened if I had actually been asleep instead of pretending to be that way? The sun was high in the sky and Dong was back at the taxi. Time to bury those feelings deep.

In the taxi, we drove in silence to where the camels were. A rider and three camels were lined up.

"You are not coming," I repeated, seeing that there was one saddled up for him.

"I know, I know," Dong said as he stepped out of the car and spoke to the camel ... wrangler? Camel cowboy? Man of the camels? Let's go with the camel man. Seeing the camels, I was already starting to feel better. Sometimes travel is about running away from your problems, and if this involved going two miles an hour on a camel, I'd take it.

The camels looked at me. They did not care about me, my problems, or anything. This was a day at the office for them. As the shaggy brown one sat, I climbed on its back. The camel man called to it, yanking on the rope in its nose, and its spindly legs unfolded from under it as it slowly stood, me rocking back and forth on its back on its way up. They were like large, fuzzy dogs that seemed to hate everything.

The camels really had only one speed and that was slow. As they shifted their weight from leg to leg, it was like being in a rocking chair that moved sideways instead of back to front. We tottered along the sand dunes. To remember the experience and this moment, I took a selfie. Despite being physically on top, it was rock bottom.

The desert was peaceful. There were no people in sight except for my guide. I was yet again alone with a man. Did I need to be worried about the camel man? Did I need to be worried about every man? Were there factors I should keep in mind and evaluate to avoid an assault? Clearly marriage, professional ties, religious views—all of these hadn't stopped him. The one variable was alone time. Was it that I should never ever be alone with a man ever again? Is that on me, the woman, to keep to that rule? The camels slowly teetered along.

Soon we came to a tall dune with a little sled at the top. My guide secured these complacent beasts and then came to help me off. I flinched as he came close, not wanting any men near me. We were, after all, alone. Alas, I gave him my hand and climbed off.

Unable to speak to me, he hopped on the sled and motioned to it with his hands as if to say, "See this sled, you sit on it." He had no idea if I knew how to use a sled, even though I did it every winter in Connecticut. Kicking at the sand, he pushed himself off the edge of the dune and rode the sled down the hill. At the bottom, he hopped off, and put his hands in the air, jumping up and down as if to say, "See? This is *fun*. Not dangerous, but *fun!*"

I smirked. Not a full smile, just a little one. Climbing on the sled, I used my feet to lightly pushed off the edge of the dune. My hands in the air, my heart dropped as I slid down the mountain. It reminded me of being a kid in snow. My mom would give us a big metal mixing bowl from the kitchen and we'd ride it down the hill outside our house, over and over again until we'd fall flat out face first on black ice, laugh about it because kids are invincible, and do it all over again. My heart started to slow its rhythmic beat as a smile slid across my lips.

It was time to get back on the camels and head back to the real world. My camel snorted as I got on to make sure I knew he hated this job. As we meandered slowly over the dunes, led by the camel man, back to home base. I wondered: could I do trips like this in the future? Had my adventurous side put me in danger? Maybe I needed to stay on a less off-the-beaten path. I hated the idea that my gender would be a barrier to travel.

As we arrived back at base camp, Dong came out of the house, apparently having stayed to have tea with the camel owners. *What the fuck?* I'd hoped he'd leave me with the driver.

He ran towards me. "I worked it out, the driver will take you to get your bus ticket and the bus back to Yichuan. I will get my own transportation."

"Sounds good," I said.

As the driver headed on his way, he could not speak to me, but I could tell he knew something was wrong. At the bus station, he bought me a ticket, showed me to my bus, gave me a firm nod, and watched me get on to make sure I was all set.

As I watched the desert whiz by, I had to do the next scary step: call my boss. First, I messaged him on WeChat that something bad had happened and asked whether he was available to chat. Hopping on a call with him, I teared up as I relived the story. On a public bus, I tried not to sob too loudly, but it was not like anyone could understand me.

"Let me speak to Carolina, and we'll figure out the, next steps. Do you need me to change your flight or anything?" I felt grateful that our director was a woman.

"I think I'm good; the bus will arrive three hours before my flight, so it's fine."

As I stepped off the bus, my heart continued to race like my childhood hamster in her wheel. Would I see Dong here? Had my company relayed to him what I had told my boss? How would he react?

Once I landed in Shanghai, my boss called.

"I spoke with Carolina, and we think it's best you take tomorrow off. We also want to know how you would like the company to handle this situation."

What do I want? What did I want? I paused to think for a moment. Weren't companies supposed to have protocols for these sorts of things? I wanted to go back to life before this had happened. And I wanted to make sure this didn't happen to any other women at our company. After all, Dong was in a senior role. I'm sure there were women working under him or marketing team members like Dove who had been and would be traveling on business trips with him. What could I ask for? Could I sue them? I didn't really want to. I just wanted this to be in the past, and I didn't know what leverage I had here. After all, Dong was senior to me. How much income was he bringing in for the business? Likely more than me. From an employer's perspective, I was less valuable.

I took a deep breath. "At a minimum, I'd really like to not have to work with him again and if he is not getting fired, I'd like the company to think of how to make sure this doesn't happen again. I trust the company to handle it appropriately."

"Got it. And who knows about this?"

"Only Laurie and you," I said, referring to my American friend I'd called the night prior.

"Okay. We ask that you not tell anyone as we figure this out. You rest up tomorrow, and I'll be in touch."

"Thank you," I said, starting to tear up just saying it.

The next day, I stayed home.

"Feel better!" Jade messaged. I wished I could tell her. She was my best friend and we sat in back-to-back cubicles at the office, but I couldn't tell anyone. One lick of gossip and everyone would know. I didn't want to go into the office and have people look at me differently.

"What time can you meet tonight to discuss this?" Carolina messaged me on WeChat.

"Whenever it works for you. Can Laurie come?"

"What? No, this is a serious meeting. We have to prove this is not your fault. Bring your computer and let me know of a coffee shop near you."

Prove it was not my fault? Didn't my hysterical crying on the phone with Laurie and my boss prove that this wasn't made up?

That night, we sat in a Starbucks. Carolina rushed in, gave me a hug, and threw her bag down on the seat next to her.

"Men are the worst," she said, opening her laptop. I did the same.

"Okay, did you have any email correspondence with Dong?"

"Before I got there, I asked everyone if they wanted to visit the desert."

"It was not only addressed to Dong?"

"No, I'd never met him before. If you have IT check, you can see all the emails."

"We are keeping this quiet, so if you can just forward the emails to me, that's okay."

She had me walk her through every single interaction with Dong, having me relive the experience as she took notes.

"Now, at any point did he talk about his wife?"

Pausing, I thought for a moment. "No, he didn't. I feel so stupid, I saw the wedding ring and he talked all about how good things come to good people. I didn't realize he was interested in me."

"Stop." Carolina held up her hand. "Men are trash. Do not blame yourself. At my first job, one of the executives asked me to come have dinner in his hotel room, and I didn't even realize what he wanted. Do not blame yourself. But learn from this: it happened once, and it will happen again. This is part of being a woman in business."

Carolina was a bit unpredictable. When I had first arrived, she'd given me this advice: "You sometimes blush when you meet our CEO. You need to picture them taking a shit."

"Um, pardon?" My eyebrow twitched.

"If you picture him taking a shit, his fat rolls showing as he's hunched over, you'll never blush at authority again." She winked.

She'd likely gone through a lot of similar situations to the one I was experiencing now, which had built up her hatred of men. She'd gotten drunk a couple of times at company events and repeatedly yelled, "You're not listening to me because I'm a woman!" at our CEO. The real reason no one was listening to her was because she was so drunk, she'd forgotten she'd already repeated the same thing multiple times. I understood why she had these feelings. In this moment, she had my back. She was a fighter, and that's what I desperately needed.

The rest of the executive team who was consulted on this issue—my direct boss, the head of sales, the CEO, and the head of HR—were all men. If they had reviewed this situation without her, would they have said it was my fault for sharing a hotel room with him? If they were going to fire this man, would they be liable if he claimed I made it all up? Were they willing to take that risk? The CEO was in the process of trying to sell his company. The deal was worth millions. Could this have greater ramifications?

"Do you have any proof he did this?" Carolina asked. I thought for a moment and then scrolled through my WeChat.

"This," I said, holding up the 'I am sorry' he'd written on the dune. "In the morning, we went to see the sun rise over the dunes, and he wrote this."

She looked at the photo, "Great, send me that and screenshots of all text correspondence." She halted for a moment. "And after all this, you still rode the camels?"

"Not with him; I did it alone." I had forgotten in all the episodes of *Law & Order* I'd seen that they scrutinize a woman's every moment before and after the incident. Crying on the phone to my colleagues was not enough to prove the man had done what he'd done, but riding a camel shortly after was proof enough he didn't do it.

Assault happens when a perpetrator takes advantage of a moment of privacy. That moment of privacy makes it nearly impossible to get other people to corroborate your story. Women survivors are not only judged on their actions but on the actions of the man who committed the assault. In the moment, we are physically powerless and then in the aftermath, society puts us again in a position of zero control. To this day, I still keep the screenshots of his messages in a storage file. I'll nostalgically scroll through my drive, viewing old photos of my travels, and then my screenshot of his "I'm sorry" will pop up, and my stomach will drop. You never know when you'll need to defend yourself again. He messages me nearly every Chinese New Year a generic message wishing good prosperity, he likely forwards to every person in his phone. Still holding onto that text correspondence as proof, I haven't blocked him.

"I know this sounds weird, but I didn't want my only memories of the trip to be of this experience. I told myself this wasn't going to stop me from riding the camels," I said.

Carolina laughed and then her face turned serious. "Tomorrow, we have our head of HR flying to the Harbin office. He will meet with Dong outside the office and ask him to resign. I will let you know how it goes." She started to stand up but stopped. "But if we do it this way, I mean seriously, you can never ever tell anyone what happened. I mean no one."

"Thank you." I never told anyone until now. Nights and nights I'd spend with colleagues drunk at wine events, out at karaoke as friends, spending Christmas dinner together with our families so far away. My colleagues were my family in China, and this secret was for me alone.

The next few days at the office were weird in that I felt different and was overcoming what I'd been through, but nobody around me knew.

"Are you feeling better?" Jade asked. We'd told everyone I was out sick with a cold. She was asking me about me being sick, but what I was dealing with was more of an emotional trauma than a physical one. I processed the question.

"Yes, I think I got a cold while I was in the desert," I lied.

"The funniest thing happened," one of our South African brand ambassadors who lived full-time in Beijing would say to me on the phone a few days later. "You know, it's so strange. You know Dong? Well, he quit yesterday, and today I saw him at a wine event as if nothing happened. How can he quit one day and be fine the next? I will never understand how the Chinese do it!"

"That's so strange," I said, trying to act normal and continue with our call.

"Johnathan would like to speak with you," the CEO's executive assistant said, suddenly appearing at my desk. She motioned for me to follow her. I clenched my fists as I walked to his office. Was I in trouble? Did they change their mind about firing Dong? His assistant opened the door for me and I walked in, looking around the office. I'd only been in his office once or twice before. The CEO, a white Canadian man in his fifties, motioned for me to sit down in front of his desk. I squirmed in my seat.

"I wanted to say..." He took a deep breath. "When I started this company, with my father, and we chose to only work with family-owned wineries, I wanted to make a family here. And I know you're so far away from your family, and I am so sorry—"

Tears started to form in my eyes.

"No crying, no crying." He frantically waved his hands in front of him, the way men do when they have no idea how to handle a woman's tears. He had never married or had kids. "I wanted to say I am so sorry this happened to you, and we have taken care of it."

"Thank you," I said, bowing my head.

He stood up abruptly and motioned for the door, both of us happy to leave the awkwardness of it all. I'm glad the CEO took my complaint seriously, something that is sadly a rarity in most of these kinds of situations.

I wish that I could say that night hadn't changed me forever, but it had. Even now, after I've moved away and live on the other side of the world, I am always wary of when I exit from a public space to a private space with a man, analyzing if I trust that person enough to be there, looking for all my exits and if there was a weapon within reach. How can you tell which men are good and which are not? You can't ask the bad ones; they'll lie.

CHAPTER 12: GREECE

To Grexit or Not to Grexit

O ne year later, Shanghai, China—As I clung to the back of my taxi driver's seat, I noticed shards of safety glass trapped in between his chair and the sheet of plexiglass between him and the backseat passenger. In the middle of a typhoon, my taxi shook back and forth, the wind whipping past, as we drove across the North-South Elevated Road Bridge in Shanghai. Clearly, he had been in a recent accident, which did not quell my fear of the taxi careening off the bridge into the murky, violent waters of the Huangpu River. If I fell in, water encapsulating my taxi, I wondered how they would identify my body. The Chinese government didn't have my fingerprints and in a city of twenty-four million, how would they find someone who knew little ol' me? Would they put up posters that said, "This girl is missing" and then have the most hideous photo of me they could find, likely one a friend took on a night out. To be fair, I did look like a blond girl you'd see on a milk carton or missing in Aruba.

My stomach turned, not only from the rocking of the taxi, but also from heartbreak. A few months earlier, I had fallen in love with someone. His parents had met while his mother was motorcycling from Beijing to Italy. On her solo journey, she stayed in a monastery in Tibet. My date's grandfather told his father to approach this woman—whom he thought was a nun—and give her money for the church. When his father approached and found out she was not a nun, he started flirting with her, they wrote letters back and forth, and eventually they fell in love and he moved to join her in the UK.

I met *my* love on Tinder. Our first date was at a bar near my place with vaulted ceilings and mahogany floors; very Swiss Chalet vibes. Half-Nepalese and half-Scottish, Jampa grew up in the UK and had curly black hair, glasses with round frames, and a smattering of freckles—kind of like if Prince Eric was half-Asian. He was in China for a few months to teach English and learn Chinese. Apparently, many of his clients paid a premium because they wanted his British accent, feeling it was posh.

"So, the girl I tutor for thinks her boyfriend killed her dog."

"I'm sorry, what?"

"Apparently, the boyfriend hated her dog because it was very yappy. One day, it died abruptly. She thinks he poisoned it."

Normally I expect the guy to pay on the first date, but as he was a student and me a boss lady, at the end of the night we split the bill. Did I also mention he was really cute?

We were instantly drawn to each other. He was temporarily in Shanghai as a stopgap before going to architecture school in London. Our breakup was not one based on a loss of feelings but on the reality that we could no longer physically be together. When I returned to Shanghai after visiting Greece, he would have moved back to London, and I would be single yet again.

It appeared that Greece was also doing some soul-searching and mulling over a breakup, which at the time was referred to as "Grexit." If I put this in relationship terms, Greece was not very good at staying on top of their spending and couldn't pay their bills. This angered other countries in the European Union, such as Germany, which was very good at paying on time and had a great credit score. Why should the diligent partner work so hard for the fun partner to spend all their hard-earned cash? The question was, should Greece split from the E.U. or did the E.U.—with Germany leading the charge—believe that Greece could change and let them borrow some money to get out of their predicament? With the European Central Bank refusing to loan more funds to Grecian financial institutions, Greece had to shut down their banks. This happened to coincide with my trip.

"But why Greece?" The Chinese bank teller laughed as he withdrew a wad of Euros back in Shanghai.

"I planned this trip months ago; bad timing!" I wailed. The news was filled with stories of extremely low daily withdrawal limits[17] and a decision by referendum the Sunday before my arrival that Greece would reject austerity measures, which basically meant Greece was refusing to meet the demands to stay in its relationship with the rest of Europe.[18] This would mean a lot of sacrifice for the Greek people, and the Greek government going back significantly on its promises to them.

Rejecting austerity measures was very much an "F U!" middle finger to the "dictatorial overlord" of the European Union (mainly Germany). In Luxembourg, I had a Greek friend who was the butt of every joke. He was constantly chastised for his country's lack of economic due diligence.

This was the best joke with the biggest laugh at every party. Thus, I could understand why Greece might not feel very loved—or even welcome—as a respected part of Europe. Is your partner always calling you a deadbeat? Time to get rid of all that toxic energy, unless you need their help paying your rent?

With concerns about the government being shut down and citizens being unable to access capital, I was prepared to make a flail out of a sock I had filled with Euros if the going got rough on my trip. I even researched on Pinterest how to make yogurt out of yogurt if I needed my own food supply. Greek yogurt is high protein—perfect if I got trapped there and had to survive the drama of a Greek tragedy. Honestly, I had no idea what to expect, and I was a difficult traveler to please when my mind was spiraling over my ex.

When I arrived at the airport, I noticed that there were very few cars. Staring up at the terminal sign, I realized every single flight had been canceled except mine. Apparently my shitty, morally questionable, Russian discount airline had found the flooded runway to be a simple obstacle, not nearly treacherous enough to cancel. The airport was almost completely empty, adding to my loneliness.

To settle my anxiety, I stuffed my mouth with Burger King fries and sat alone looking out at the flooded runway. I leave early for the airport not because I have to, but because I'd rather eat at the airport bar, throwing back a craft beer, than having a panic attack in my apartment about whether I've packed enough underwear or not. When the beer is flowing, the underwear situation is unknowing. I thought about my time with Jampa two weeks ago.

On the fourth of July, I had put on a white tank top and a red and blue skirt, as well as my Daughters of the American Revolution pin I had recently inherited from my great-grandmother. I met Jampa for drinks at a place with tiki bar vibes, with a small dance floor next to a long mahogany bar. The owner had fastened a brass boat ladder on the bar so that you could climb up from the dance floor and shake your ass above the crowd. Three women were doing that as Journey blared across the club, while Jampa fastened an American flag around my neck like a cape. We headed to the dance floor.

"Just a small-town girl," Jampa said, fist-pumping.

I laughed, assuming he'd heard that watching *Jersey Shore*? I got down on one knee and pretended to air guitar along to the music as we danced together.

After a moment, Jampa grabbed my hand and led me to the bar, where he climbed up the brass ladder. He reached back to give me a hand. I looked up at him, a little nervous, but I couldn't resist his soft puppy-dog eyes. I climbed up to join him. I needed someone who was ride or die, ready to dance on a table with me or stay in to watch a show about people being murdered. The crowd cheered as he spun me, my American flag whooshing in my wake.

As we were swing dancing, twisting and turning and swooping beneath one another's arms, I felt so connected to him. It felt like a dream, like time slowed and everyone else at the bar disappeared. It was just the two of us, moving together in perfect harmony—just a small-town girl and a city boy about to take a midnight train, I mean plane, what about my plane?

A loudspeaker announcement at the airport shook me from my nostalgia. The pilot felt the storm had enough of a break for us to take off. I am not religious (or even Catholic), but I said many Hail Marys as the flight shook like a tiny tambourine in the pouring rain and typhoon winds.

In Athens, my budget hotel was north of the major districts, but only a twenty-minute walk from most of the main tourist attractions. Upon arriving at my stop, I realized I was in a rather rough area. There were a decent number of people with unhealthily skinny arms, face welts, and red eyes who looked like they might be on drugs. Shuffling to the well-lit roads, I kept my head down, making it to my hotel safely.

In the morning, it was time to play tourist and distract myself from being sad. At the corner, I purchased a Greek frappé—Nescafé with cream and sugar (like a frothy-minus-ice Frappuccino)—to carry with me. As a New Yorker, I understood the importance of looking busy, even if you were casually strolling through a city where no one was paying attention to you because grave things were happening in their own lives.

On the corner of the Parliament Building and Syntagma Square, I experienced my first Greek Crisis moment. On a pillar, someone had scribbled € = *a Swastika*. It was always intense seeing a swastika. That symbol never seemed to lose its punch. Reading the accompanying Greek scribble was unnecessary to understanding the very direct point being made here. Clearly, emotions were heated; Greece wanted more freedom to be itself. I realized this trip would be about tiptoeing around a country coming apart at the seams while I had my own, hardly as significant, existential crisis about the choices I'd made being a single woman who constantly moves and lives on the other side of the world from her hometown.

At this point, I'd had multiple relationships end because the guy moved back to his home country. Most expats had two-to-three-year contracts and then, like a timer going off, they headed on their way.

While Greece was considering breaking up with Germany, I was living a life that made any sort of commitment quite impossible.

I headed to Plaka, the central neighborhood for shopping and cafés. The main strip of tourist shops had the usual hustle and bustle, with shopkeepers out on the street, smiling gaily and offering help if you needed anything.

"Extra twenty percent off!" they bellowed through the shops' open doors.

"Thirty percent!" another would yell in response.

Most of the shopkeepers seemed at ease; overall, the tourist bubble kept this area seemingly prosperous. A few blocks off one of the main strips, it was like the Wild West right before a shootout.

Retail sales had declined since the June 29 implementation of capital controls. Locals were concerned about spending money, not knowing how long the controls would last. If you can't take your money out of the ATM, you probably can't go about spending your money on anything but that which is absolutely necessary.

Having walked enough for the day and dying in the heat, I headed for the National Garden. I admired the Greeks in their Sunday finest—white linen blowing in the wind. Despite the greater issues, everyone was enjoying their time together. Without its partner Eurozone, Greece still had the essentials: family, friends, and its local businesses.

In the park, as I wandered through the Jurassic foliage, I came upon a man on one of the more hidden paths. We were rather alone in this portion of the park, and he leered at me.

"You are pretty. I take picture." He gave me a creepy smile and lifted his crappy phone and stood in front of me, snapping a pic.

My lip curled; I didn't know how to respond to this.

"Leave me alone!" I yelled and walked away, stomping my shoes on the cream-colored gravel. What would he do with that picture? Cut a hole and stick his dick in it? Tell people I'm his girlfriend? Put it on his fridge and when people ask say, "I experienced love at first sight and it was so exhilarating, I took a picture of the woman without her consent and she screamed because I am likely a sexual predator and karma is a real thing that will likely land me in one of Dante's circles of hell after dying a cold death from an entire life alone." Okay, maybe not the last one—a girl can dream. I didn't like men having control over my feelings. The only thing I could do was try to suppress my reaction. After all, there was not much I could do to the creepy man. You can't just kick a man in the park.

This was extra upsetting because I was already in my own hell missing Jampa. I thought back to our third date, at a shooting range.

"There she is." Jampa smiled as I walked into the building. "You ready to shoot some guns?"

"Hell yeah!"

"Or as your folk like to say, 'Yeeeee hawww.'" He pretended to lasso me in, his thick black curls flying back as he cocked his head.

"Okay, I'm from Connecticut. I have never said that in my life," I said. A shooting range was not a normal place for a date in Shanghai, but since I was American, he wanted to do something "my people" loved.

"Did you bring your passport like I asked? Apparently, they won't hand you a gun unless they have your ID, which I mean fair enough. Sounds like that's more than in America?"

"They'll pretty much give anyone a gun in America." I handed my passport over. "Just don't look at it."

Jampa immediately opened it.

"No!" I yelled as he used his arm to hold me back.

He burst out laughing. "Oh my God, the braces!"

"Can we not?"

"But it's so cute!"

"Not cute, I had a snaggle tooth. It took pretty much all high school to straighten it out."

"It's adorable," Jampa said.

"And yours?" I asked.

After a small hesitation, he gave in and handed his over.

"Of course, you look perfect in yours." I rolled my eyes.

"Why, thank you." He cocked his head, beaming. "Alright, let me grab our guns and we're good to go."

The shooting range was deep underground and smelled old and musty. Unlike most places in Shanghai, here it felt like you could murder someone and potentially get away with it.

"Have you shot a gun before?" Jampa asked.

"Once." Traveling with some friends to New Hampshire, we bought a gun at Walmart, pulled over to a range on the side of the road, and shot at other things we'd bought at Walmart, the most memorable being a toy of Hello Kitty riding a wave. There was an old man at the range named Pete who smoked a pipe made of a corn cob. He let me borrow the shotgun he'd fitted for his eight-year-old niece by sawing off the backend and replacing it with a foam base. This stopped the kickback of the gun from dislocating her shoulder.

"If I teach you to use a gun, will you call me Daddy?" Jampa said, the corner of his mouth curling into a mischievous smile. We both laughed. "I'm just kidding, please *never* call me Daddy. I never understood that kink."

"I don't get it, either. It's a reminder that you're a relative, that you're old, and that you hypothetically changed their diapers," I said, counting these out on my hand. We looked into each other's eyes and giggled. There was such an ease with Jampa. My heart fluttered at everything he said, and even at the sight of him. He handed me the gun.

"Yes, please." I picked up a 9mm gun and pointed it at the target, safety still on. Compared to yet another date at a bar, this was rather exhilarating.

"Okay, first off, it's all about stance. May I?" Jampa asked. I nodded, and he stood behind me. "First, you need a wide stance."

He tapped the outer side of my lower thighs. That light tap caused my skin to prickle, as all the blood rushed from my head into my loins, which was probably something you don't want to happen while holding a gun. This was why shooting should not be sexy. Period. Yet, with him, it was the sexiest.

He put his arms around me to help steady me. "Now, point at the target and when you shoot, hold your breath so your aim stays straight." I could feel his breath against my neck. I held in my own, my heart pounding.

He stepped back. "Got it?"

I nodded. I would do anything for this man.

"You can take the safety off when you're ready."

Oh my God, he's so handsome, okay, focus, you have a fucking gun. I clicked off the safety. Pointing the gun, I held my breath and let out a full round. A rush of adrenaline came with each bullet that left the chamber. My entire body felt alive. After a few, I turned to Jampa. "I did it!"

"Let's see how you did."

I smiled as the target paper with a man's silhouette zipped towards us.

"Not bad," Jampa said, even though none of the bullets had hit the body. "I'm actually impressed at how well you missed."

"Thank you. I'm clearly a pro."

"You are my pro-tégée." He winked, pulling the paper off its clips and replacing it with a new one, sending it whirring back. He was a master of Dad jokes. Picking up the gun and loading it like a professional, he aimed and emptied his magazine.

I couldn't tell which was going faster: the bullets or my heartbeat.

After putting down the gun, he pressed the button, and the target paper came sputtering towards us again. Jampa took it off the clips. Every bullet had hit the center.

"Gonna hang this next to my apartment door. No better way to deter robbers," I said, taking his target paper and handing him mine.

While we were shooting guns in the bunker, it had started to rain. As we left, we kissed in the pouring rain, warm lips under an icy shower. Thinking about someone you love is almost like opening a little piece of candy. Pulling back the shiny layers of the wrapper, you get to the sweet, loving goodness inside.

Back alone in the park in Athens, I started to cry. Would I ever meet someone like him again? Why did my life choices have to get in the way? Why did strange men have to be creepy? I wiped away my tears with the backs of my hands aggressively. I didn't want my feelings and the creepy man to ruin my day alone. This was my first day of vacation! I had survived the solo flight through a typhoon to get here.

After heading up the hills from the garden, I bought baklava in a tiny local bakery because what better thing to soothe the soul than dripping honey deliciousness? My mind lingered back to Jampa. Pulling out my notebook, I scribbled some little jokes that related to our inside jokes: the note, "See you later, Alli—" and an alligator drinking a white Russian, his favorite drink. It made me feel better for a moment, his memory bringing back a rush of serotonin. Then I remembered: it was over. After I finished my baklava, I discovered a cemetery nearby on a map and decided to head over.

Admittedly, I can see why it'd be weird to decide, with honey-covered fingers, to visit a cemetery, but I always found peace in seeing how different societies treated their dead. While working as a theater critic in New York, I went to a performance in a creaky, faded yellow staircase of a historic church in Brooklyn. They had different actors performing the roles of various people they had interviewed who worked in the death industry or have had experience with death.[19] One was with a fisherman who saw the light while his leg was trapped in a rope that pulled him underwater, and according to his story, chose to walk away and stay alive. Another was a woman who spoke to the dead and had an out-of-body experience as a child where she met herself as an adult. Another guy, who worked in a morgue, explained how you have to stuff dead bodies' butts with stuff, kind of like bears hibernating in the winter, otherwise the dead bodies will explode out of their coffins after being put in the ground because their gastrointestinal fluids create a sort of butt bomb.

I am not sure if the latter is true, but I want to be cremated just in case. My mom wanted her cremated body to be sprinkled into the ocean. President Obama decided to throw Osama bin Laden's body out to sea so there would be no place for future followers to come and worship. The only thing connecting these two thoughts was the sea. My mother is a wonderful woman.

1st Athens Cemetery could rival Père Lachaise in Paris. If you don't share a joy of cemeteries, it's understandable that you wouldn't get this reference. Among the graves, there was an above-ground room where they have cremated remains stacked on top of each other on metal shelves, the kind you'd see at an office supply store. Each little box—the size of a scented candle—had a little placard photo of the deceased in faded sepia colors. I wondered who chose these special pictures. Some people had ones from when they were younger, others from when they were older and closer to death. They were probably shopping for their cremation spot and wanted a picture of themselves in that present moment, not one from their youth—at least this is my thinking. I'd want a sexy picture of myself to remember how great I looked in my prime. Maybe me sitting on a chair, naked, facing away from the camera, the top of my butt crack peeking out while I seductively looked over my shoulder, with a look that said, "I'm dead, bitch. Wanna fuck around and find out?"

The building had a downstairs with hundreds more cremated bodies in boxes. At first, I didn't think I was supposed to be down there, because there were garbage bags filled with dead roses sprawled out on the floor, but the shelves were set up on display for visitors. It must have been off hours.

There were young children (you could tell the age by their birth and death date range) with little butterflies and flowers drawn on their boxes. Some boxes were clearly a man and wife together while others were alone. Did they all know their neighbors in death or was it a random assortment of cremated bodies? Is there a cremation spot lottery? Who got to be upstairs, with the light shining through the windows, versus below, with the cement walls that gave off creepy basement vibes? More specifically, is there equality in death? This was not the best activity for someone feeling lonely, but it did get my mind off things. Afterward, I headed home, too sad to keep wandering. I wanted to get back to my hotel before sunset.

On my second day, I set out down Athinas, b-lining for the Acropolis before the hordes of other tourists descended. Around a corner, I came across a man in a blue shirt and bulletproof vest popping his head out of a store. Upon further inspection, I discovered he was private security hired to protect a money transfer shop. This was a definitive "Greek Crisis" moment and the first of many visible private security guards in bulletproof vests scattered all around the city.

I reached the Acropolis. My plan to avoid tourists was only half successful, but the early morning light gave a brilliant gold color to the sandy stone.

Democracy in all her glory, I thought, breathing in the fresh morning air as eagles soared and American flags waved in the back of my mind. I'm American, forgive me: the foundation of the values of my native home started here.[20] These towering columns upon a hill overlooked the entire capital—a reminder of what Greece stood for in the history of the modern world.

As I looked over the edge, my head tilted in contemplation. These structures were part of Greece's legacy—the root of many modern-day political systems. Had Greece lost touch with what really mattered? Perhaps Greece had looked a little too far out of itself and needed to turn its attention more inward? Was I projecting my own self-reflection onto Greece?

I decided to walk from the Acropolis to the Mediterranean Sea to see where this great city connected to the rest of the world. While I could see the sea from atop the hill, I should have recognized it was over a four-mile walk.

Romanticizing a great *Odyssey*-esque pilgrimage from the Acropolis to the port, the trip realistically should have been taken via taxi. Instead, this was the start of three hours of wandering through residential areas resulting in very few epiphanies other than that I was too stubborn for my own good by refusing to take a taxi to save a couple bucks and do it all on foot. The blisters made the experience even worse.

On my way, I happened upon a mobile phone and computer shop and entered to buy a phone cable. The shop gave off the vibe of some trendy startup or a poorly supervised Apple franchise. Every phone accessory you could ever imagine covered the round and white walls, and in the room were four bearded men feverishly typing on MacBooks, sharing a single table.

One of the gentlemen helped me find the appropriate cord. Handing him my cash, he opened the cashier till, which, although it gave out the appropriate "ding," as it opened, revealed itself to be completely empty. He called to his friends, who briefly looked up from their ferocious typing, shook their beards, then returned to their screens. Shrugging his shoulders, he pulled a tattered black wallet from his back pocket and handed me his own money as change. I wondered if using his own Euros was of great inconvenience to him, but he seemed unbothered.

Continuing on my journey, I entered an area called Flisvos Marina. With one main walking strip and shops that did not seem intended for tourists, this beach town seemed a little more somber than the main area in Athens. They had inexpensive cotton dresses and faux leather bags. Every shop had big, bright red "60% off" or "'70% off" signs in their windows.

Two people were chatting as I entered a shop. Seeing a potential customer, they jumped from their chairs and greeted me in Greek. They shifted their weight from foot to foot as I admired their clothes and bags. Feeling uncomfortable, I quickly left. It was too much pressure to buy, although I felt bad for not making a purchase.

Returning to the main strip, I noticed an ATM with a small cluster of people waiting in line. Everyone had the same expression: they looked off into the distance, folded their arms, and bit the inside of their cheeks. It was not a scared look, but the step before—thoroughly concerned.

Tired from my odyssey, I moved in slow zombie steps, dragging my legs to the water. I reached the sea after crossing the tram tracks, a boulevard, and going down a stairway, and practically threw my sore feet into the water.

As waves softly lapped the rocky shore, children giggled as they played in the sand. On the small beach connected to my stairwell, there was a spattering of middle-aged women in bright bikinis, their errand bags and tawny skin giving evidence of their visits being frequent. Laughing together, this outlet appeared to be a sanctuary where friends and family could enjoy a moment together, away from it all.

I was tired and hangry when my dream of reaching the port expired (Homer would have been disappointed). Perhaps I'd found what I had sought here on the beach where Greece reconnected with its true self.

Sitting with my tattered feet cleansed by the salty sea, I thought about my life choices and being single. The boyfriend I had had before Jampa had also moved away for work, and I had left the boyfriend before that when I moved to Shanghai. My boyfriend before that broke up with me because he knew I was leaving Luxembourg and the one before that, our relationship was cut short from my leaving New York. I didn't even know if I could technically call them boyfriends, because we hadn't labeled anything, mainly because the relationships were so short, travel plans getting in the way. Being an expat meant a lot of goodbyes and loose-end love interests. My own life choices would keep me single far longer than any of my friends back home. This was a decision I had made. I needed to get used to traveling alone and being alone. I had chosen this life.

Before heading back, I found a post office and mailed Jampa my little inside joke drawings and a cute postcard. Considering the entire government was shut down, I hoped they'd get to him. After all, who would pay this nice post person taking my card? Jampa would have to be another loose end love interest for now, another bro in a different country code.

Arriving at the tram station, I fed my money into the ticket machine, which it accepted, but no ticket came out. I tried again, but still no ticket appeared. Tired and frustrated, returning to a Neanderthal state out of pure exhaustion, I banged on the machine. A ten-year-old boy started yelling at me in Greek.

"I only speak English," I admitted, hanging my head. He paused for a moment.

"The train is free," he said with a little too much joy in telling someone older they're an idiot. "The banks are closed."

I thanked him with a nod.

On the tram, everyone seemed unfazed despite the collapse of their entire banking system. You can't expect the emotion of a Greek tragedy every time something bad happens. People have to keep going on with their lives. People are strong and resilient. Was this a pep-talk to Greece or myself?

At the metro where I transferred, I considered buying a ticket even though I didn't have to, because the Greek government needed the money more than I did. I decided that giving to the government is probably not the best bang for my buck if I'm trying to help the people of Greece. After all, the government got them into this mess.

Grabbing gelato around the corner from my hotel, I watched a woman high on drugs approach cars at the intersection, asking for money. She wore a pink striped sundress, and her arms swung as she wobbled from side to side, unable to maintain her balance. Most of the drivers listened to her and a few gave her coins. It was sad to see this woman struggle, but I was impressed by the generosity of the strangers, especially considering the daily limits on cash withdrawals.

That night, I headed to an outdoor cinema built in the 1920s by a hairdresser. It had a great view of the Acropolis lit up in the distance. On the walk over, just past Syntagma Square, I passed a line of police in riot gear, with plastic shields—which might still work in a testudo formation—and helmets. A few looked fearful.

At the outdoor theater, I peered up at the well-lit Acropolis, still shining gold, this time in the evening light, the red beams of the sunset nestled around its shadow. At the end of the film, I strolled down Kidathineon Street. The guy at the end of the street sold me Greek yogurt and offered to help me find a cab, knowing it would not be safe soon. Calling to the cabbies hanging just outside his shop, he asked me my address and shouted it to them. They turned in a huddle and then a younger cabby found an older one, repeating my address.

"He will take you," the younger cabby told me. "Five Euros?" he asked as he opened the door for me.

"Okay," I agreed. This was my chance to pay a little extra to help the old cabby off the meter.

My last day in Athens, I decided to wake up early again. Taking the metro, I got off at Evangelismo and headed up Ploutarhou Street. I opted to walk instead of taking the funicular to Ag Georgios, the highest point in Athens, atop Mount Lycabettus. There, I admired the whole city in all its glory, with the Acropolis in the foreground and the Mediterranean in the background. In ancient mythology, Mount Lycabettus was created by Athena after she dropped a mountain she was bringing to build the Acropolis. Now, it was a convenient perch to overlook the city.

I headed back to Ploutarhou to grab a coffee. My legs shook from three full days of nonstop walking. At the top of the street, I peered into a beautiful apartment, the open floor plan entirely visible from the open door. The whole apartment was white with glass, unmarked bottles of liquor on a mirrored table, sheepskins draped across the furniture of the back patio, and a picture of a naked woman was painted on one of the cabinets. The place reminded me of a bachelor pad you might see in a TV drama of a murdered politician who had secret orgies. A Shih Tzu slept on a white marble slab at the entrance. As I walked closer, the owner of the flat sat in his doorway in white pajamas, playing on an iPad. I wondered if I *should* take comfort in the knowledge that the bourgeois bohemians, per usual, were isolated from the throes of the economic crisis. I'd always wanted a sexy house like this, and Jampa, after all, was training to be an architect. It reminded me that friends from back home were saving up to buy houses with their spouses, while I was spending all that money on traveling. I wasn't making moves on a lot of those things we're told make us an "adult." I was grateful for my experiences, but did having them mean that I was sacrificing a traditional future?

On the corner of Aristippou Road and Ploutarhou Street, I bought a few iron bottle openers from a local artist. He explained that he made everything by hand and had been doing so for over ten years. He shared the history of each of his culturally significant bronze statues, which made me feel especially guilty as I bought the more hipster owl and mustached French sailor-looking bottle openers of no cultural significance, but that my friends would definitely prefer as gifts.

Down the street, I stopped for lunch at an Italian café with waiters in white shirts and black aprons. I liked this area far more than Plaka, since everyone there was Greek as opposed to tourists, making it a perfect perch for people watching. This neighborhood reminded me of Montmartre—where I used to go and eat oysters with Sam when we lived in Paris—because it was lush and built on a slope. The restaurants were more formal places to be "seen", much like the Upper East Side in New York City. The women wore white, high-waisted, flowing, flared pants and platform heels. The men had leather briefcases. This was far removed from the Greek Crisis.

As I sipped my fancy coffee and munched on a prosciutto sandwich, tears started to form in my eyes. Greece was so peaceful and beautiful. It had its own culture and wanted to respect that. Yes, it was part of the European Union, but that didn't mean it should give up its *raison d'être*. It was strong, independent, and admittedly a bit stubborn. Once again, I was projecting, and mad at myself. I had chosen myself over love, over career stability, over saving money to buy a home. That was hard to live with, at times.

Shoving my fresh sandwich back in my mouth, water welled in my eyes. Greece and I were one and the same, we were on our own journeys, figuring out the best path for ourselves, even if that meant being alone. I hoped the Greek Crisis would not spread and more parts of Athens would not end up like my hotel's neighborhood. In the wake of all

Athens' hard work, I made a wish for the site of the foundation of modern-day democracy to not crumble any further.

Early the next morning, I headed to Kefalonia, an island where I would meet two girlfriends to take a weeklong trip together on a yacht. As my taxi drove from the airport through the island, I played a sad game: "Is it a Greek ruin or a Greek Crisis unfinished building?" Abandoned foundations of buildings that were unable to be financed looked a lot like ancient Greek ruins.

I was the first to arrive outside our Airbnb. In the early morning light, I found a group of sheep, munching away on the grass. Their coats and the wheat rippled in the breeze, shining gold. There was no one in sight. I did the only rational thing: I chased the sheep. No one was there to tell me that I couldn't. As they ran from me, I laughed. My bare feet felt good on the fresh earth.

After checking into my Airbnb, I headed to the beach where I unexpectedly met a stranger who will be referred to as Charles from Bristol. He wore a black Speedo and was sunburned to a crispy savannah red, his bald head making him look like a cooked hot dog.

Charles was fascinatingly boring. He came to this same island and this same beach for two weeks every year. The beach was rather secluded. He knew no one there, and returned every year for his time on the beach alone. While going there annually sounded relaxing, I preferred being thrown into something completely unfamiliar every time I vacationed.

I made up a fake backstory for Charles to reimagine why he went there every year. My backstory was: Charles was secretly a spy. He could not share any of the excitement of his life because it was classified. He came to Kefalonia every year to get away from everyone and go completely off grid to decompress from his wild and crazy life as a double agent.

Charles used his vacation days annually to travel just like me, but he returned to that beautiful cove to spend time alone. Clearly, Charles felt content being alone. I had spent my trip worrying about being single, when alternatively, I could be grateful for and embrace the life I had created. After all, I was spending next week on a yacht with my friends. There were perks to a life of adventure. It was not that I was choosing between love, stability, and financial success versus a life on the road, I was choosing to have them in stages. Instead of putting money into a mortgage, my money went to sitting on a beach off the coast of Greece. Instead of pouring my heart into a man I loved, I was pouring time into figuring out who I was, so that one day, when the timing was right, I was ready to fully love and commit to a partner.

Maybe years from now, when I was a completely different person, I would return to Kefalonia and find Charles on that very same beach, burned up, enjoying the only sun he gets every year when he's away from his cubicle (or secret life as a spy). More likely, I will never see him again.

He—and Greece—had reminded me: my life was absurdly exciting and wonderful. I had sacrificed a traditional life and Greece was going through a tough time, but we weren't dead yet. I still had a ton of excitement and pleasure and life ahead of me. More history to be made. I could get to all that important stuff later. I would never regret these moments—sticking my feet in the Mediterranean, shooting guns in Shanghai, eating baklava in a cemetery. For me, these delectable moments were worth giving up a traditional life.

CHAPTER 13:
MEDITERRANEAN SEA

Who Knew Yachting Meant Swimming in Poo

Two days later, Kefalonia, Greece—The main premise of Jean-Paul Sartre's *Huis Clos*, "No Exit," is "L'enfer, c'est les autres" or in English, "Hell is other people." I learned this the hard way: on a yacht in the Mediterranean. I'd like to add a caveat that anyone who quotes French philosophers and casually throws around yachting is likely insufferable. That was something I was deeply grappling with at this point in my life. Being an expat, a lot of my time was spent with well-educated people, often with high incomes and privileged backgrounds. I had also met many English language teachers who had found by working abroad, they were oftentimes paid more than teachers in the U.S.

208

I had a theater teacher friend who got paid triple her usual salary while living in China. In the U.S. people would say, "What valuable skills do kids learn in theater? We should cut the budget and put it into math and science." In China, they saw English-speaking theater classes as a chance for their Chinese children to learn Western mannerisms and how to convey emotion in a Western way. That way, their children could work abroad. I was also adopting foreign mannerisms. I had already started to use a lot of British phrases, picked up from all the British men I had dated, and from being around people who had been taught British English as their second language.

Living abroad was beyond the grasp of most people and, having lived in New Canaan—one of the richest towns in America—and Luxembourg—one of the wealthiest countries per capita in the world—and now Shanghai—the richest city in China—I was starting to become, for lack of a better word, a douchebag.

From my childhood I had some grounding and empathy for people who were considered "outsiders," so that's not to say that I was a difficult person, but I was slowly jet-setting from snobby to snobbier to snobbiest. In New Canaan, my family was always the town trash, or as people more politely called it, "Townies." Townies were the poor people who lived close enough to walk into town.

On my side of the tracks, to keep us entertained cheaply, my mom would take us to play in the rivers behind people's homes. The first step in this process was walking to the very back of a cul de sac and then eyeing each house, trying to decide which one was the least likely to arrest us for trespassing. Then, we'd sneak down the edge of someone's well-groomed lawn, past their back patio with a hot tub or pool, and slip into the water in our bikinis with our fishing nets to chase after minnows and crawfish to our hearts' content. It was so much fun. Maybe I also loved graveyards because that was another location where we'd play.

There was also that one time in high school when I was babysitting, and I opened the door to find two police officers. My mind raced. Had the parents died in a crash on their way home and I—a teenager—would have to raise these two kids on my own?

"Hi, little lady, do you know that man over there?" one of the cops asked, pointing to my dad's beat-up second-hand SUV parked nearby on the street. On his weekends with me, he parked outside to take me to his place after I was finished at work. The cops, seeing his old truck in between all the mansions, must have been concerned when he said something along the lines of, "I'm waiting for a teenage girl to come out of that house over there." I explained that he was my dad.

"Oh my God, are our kids okay?" The parents that I was babysitting for screamed as they ran out of their car, having just come home from dinner to cop cars outside their home.

"Just a mix-up," the officer said. I tried to smile politely, not wanting to lose my job. Since my parents didn't hang out with any other parents in our town, I'd found the job through our high school job center, where people would call in and leave notes for any high schoolers looking to make extra cash.

I came from that place, and as an adult who could afford to take absurd trips, I craved being on a yacht. After all, my dream since childhood had been to be an international business lady. Still living in Shanghai but having switched jobs since working in the wine industry, I was now Global Content Marketing Manager at an international luxury company, overseeing global campaigns with models we'd handpicked and flown in from all over the world. More importantly, for the first time in my career, I was a boss. I had hired and trained a full-time writer as well as a number of contractors. I had had many shitty bosses in the past, so this was my chance to start to formulate the version of "the man" I wanted to be. Did I want to haze those below me, did I want to be their friend, or did I want to be something in between that evoked some sort of healthy work environment? This was my chance to do some good while getting paid more.

With my new wealth, I could buy frivolous things like a designer handbag, but every time it came time to click "add to cart," it felt ridiculous to spend that money on something so unnecessary. Calculating how many hours of work it took to afford it made it feel less exciting. My time felt more valuable. However, I had found a Lululemon hookup at the fabric market. While there, a Chinese woman with her cap pulled down over her face whispered to me, "Lululemon?"

She looked both directions and opened her jacket to reveal a bright purple, slim-fit zip-up, new with tags. I followed her back to her stall where in a hidden cabinet she had stacks and stacks of workout clothes, tags still on. She definitely knew someone at their official factory in China, so I was wearing real Lululemon even if I was paying half the price. It felt like I had made it, or more specifically, like I didn't have any children of my own, so why not put my money toward spending a week playing an adult child? Men do this type of shit all the time, so why can't I be a wo-man child myself and get drunk on a boat? In other words: if men can be toxic, why can't I? I aspired to be insufferable, at least in my free time.

I'd heard about this thing called "Yacht Week," where a bunch of young European professionals met up in the Mediterranean and traveled around on a fleet of yachts. It was basically a bunch of beautiful, rich, young, drunk people with sexy accents partying together.

"My friend from college is organizing his own yachting trip to raise funds for his charity. The charity takes underage men who would normally go to jail, and instead sticks them on a boat together and they compete in a race across the Atlantic. To raise funds and since a donor donated a boat in Spain, he is doing back-to-back weeklong trips across the Mediterranean. Should be a lot of fun," a colleague explained after I told her I was looking for yachting options.

Looking at their website, I discovered it was considerably more reasonably priced for a yacht trip—$650 for the whole week—and as an added bonus, my payment would go towards their charity to help incarcerated youth. Messaging a few friends, I convinced, Evelyn, who I had known since high school, and Neirmeen, who I had met while living in Luxembourg, to come with me for the week as I travelled from Greece to Montenegro.

To kick off our adventure, we met with the group who had just spent the past week on the yacht. They sat at a table together, eyes glazed over, as if they had just returned from a war; they were sleep-deprived and bummed out, as if someone had beaten their souls out of them. It was not what I had expected after a week of yachting.

"The motor almost fell off," one of them told me. He didn't make eye contact, but instead looked off into the distance, as if he'd been trapped on Noah's Ark and not allowed to swat at the two sole mosquitoes trying to survive the flood.

"What?"

"The motor wasn't hooked on properly, so it almost fell off the boat. We had to spend three days at a marina getting it fixed."

"Three days!" another person screamed, as if this trauma was still too fresh to process. This was unsettling, but maybe it was an extenuating circumstance? We were going to be on a yacht!

As last week's group headed to the airport, my group slowly arrived. The trip would include: a hippie in her sixties—the mother of a friend of the guy who ran the charity; a couple in their thirties who had just had a baby and were on their honeymoon (they left the baby back home); Logan—our captain, and the founder of the charity; two deck hands; a college student from two weeks ago who ended up never leaving after his trip and who I'll call Sea Dog; Niermeen, Evelyn, and me. Other than my friends and I, everyone was from Florida.

While I had pictured a week trapped on a boat with sultry, tan Europeans, I was instead on one with a bunch of Floridians, who didn't seem to really have ever left Florida. Even worse, the people in charge of this little floating piece of wood, our itinerary, feeding us—were all college guys in their early twenties.

If you don't know a lot about Florida, my best advice would be to Google "Florida Man" and the day and month of your birthday. Whatever headline—or more likely headlines—come up should accurately sum up Florida and how it is a unique corner of the earth and the schlong of America. It has the wrong kind of big dick energy.

Through my travels, I've met many Europeans who, used to the scale of Europe, think that you can ride a train from one side of the U.S. to the other in about a day. They don't realize how large our country truly is. With that scale comes many different types of Americans and the opportunity for different local cultures to form. People from the East Coast may not know a lot of Southerners, or people from the West don't know a lot of Easterners. In my experience, I didn't know how good tacos could truly be until I visited L.A., and I didn't know how good white gravy on biscuits could be until I went to New Orleans. I knew more about Shanghainese food and culture than I did anything about Florida. The week on the yacht together would be a weeklong crash course on their culture, beliefs, and customs.

When you picture a yacht, you probably imagine paparazzi pictures of Elon Musk shirtless somewhere or Paris Hilton throwing Veuve Clicquot pillows up in the air while smiling. A yacht is technically any boat longer than forty feet and, in this case, we were on a sixty-five-foot sailing yacht. This meant that the entire top of the boat was a bunch of sails and thick ropes you could pull on to get places, not a helipad or a nice vignette to have breakfast. Below deck, where all ten of us would be living, was about the size of a two-bedroom New York City apartment, with no A/C, a limited water supply, and a toilet with a pump motor. Very quickly, we realized that the experience was going to be more like camping than pretending to be Jeff Bezos.

The couple on their honeymoon was given a private room. Niermeen, Evelyn, and I would all sleep on a triangular downstairs bed in the hull, the hippie would sleep on the cushions in the living room area, and Logan, his crew, and Sea Dog would sleep on the top of the boat, which had a hammock, a small, cushioned seating area, and a bag for the mainsail.

As we left port, drinks were flowing. We were so excited to be at sea. With cocktails in hand, Niermeen, Evelyn, and I sat at the bow of the ship in our bikinis and sunglasses, looking out at the rich, blue waters as the sun started to set and turned the sky a playful splash of auburn, orange peel, and cherry blossom. Within the hour, I would lose four out of the five pairs of sunglasses I'd brought, after forgetting that they were on my head and repeatedly jumping into the sea.

"We have a surprise for you," Logan said, handing us more alcohol as he tossed his thick, golden brown beard. The guys were definitely trying to get us drunk to see whom they could sleep with. "Look." He pointed as the boat slunk around a cove and a beach with a giant shipwreck came into view.

For the night, we would be mooring at Navagio, a cove off the coast of Zakynthos island, which had the most famous shipwreck in Greece. Grounded in the 1980s, legend has it that the 1937 Scottish coaster, *Panagiotis*, was carrying contraband cigarettes for the Italian mafia when it got lost in a storm and ran aground. It looked like a rusty, steel skeleton with a huge crack in the middle. I jumped into the sea to swim to shore. I held my cocktail over my head, but it immediately filled with seawater.

"We're going to have a firepit right there," Logan said as he loaded our dingy up with lumber, enough alcohol for a whole ship of pirates, and some sandwich supplies.

"Are you sure we're allowed to?" I asked, with only my head above the water. It didn't seem like the Greek authorities would be too cool with a bunch of Americans lighting a huge bonfire next to their most famous shipwreck.

"It's fine," Logan said. I swam away. I couldn't question the captain. For context, sailing can go from fun to deadly very quickly. The big base of the mast in the center of the boat is called the "boom." A common sailor joke is that it is called this because if you turn quickly, that thing can shoot across the boat at ninety-five mph, and "Boom!" knock someone unconscious and throw them into the sea. On boats, there is a very clear hierarchy to be followed for the safety of everyone aboard. I had recently become a boss, but I'd be spending this vacation with a boss of my own.

As we sat together around the fire, I admired how the flames lit up the red steel of the ship. It reminded me of when I lived in the mining town Esch-sur-Alzette in Luxembourg. The mountains on my morning hikes were the same red, filled with the iron ore used to make ships like the one next to us. A couple of people from other boats joined us around the fire, passing bottles of rum around like pirates. On a high from our first day at sea, everyone got trashed. As I swam back to the boat to sleep, I saw Sea Dog and Evelyn peeking off the stern of another ship. Their heads bobbed in and out of the sea as they made seal noises while jumping straight up out of the water. Above them, a yacht owner with a Tupperware bowl of pasta in the crook of one elbow dangled pasta on a fork over their heads, as if feeding fish to seals.

In the morning, a loud boat filled with tourists entered the harbor and woke me. I headed up to the top of the boat, and it was empty. What had happened last night?

To check the shore, I dove into the water. A guide with a microphone walked along the white sand, a group of tourists following him.

"That's not supposed to be there," he said, kicking at the soot leftover from our fire. I doubted that you could normally have a fire here, but with Grexit going on, many of the government officials who normally patrolled this area were probably furloughed.

"Navagio is the most famous beach on Zakynthos, famous for this shipwreck from the 1980s," the guide said, motioning to the boat. The tourists looked on.

"Water!" Sea Dog said, stumbling from the wreckage, his hair flowing in every direction and ash from the fire streaked across his face as his skinny legs fought their way through the sand. "I need water!"

The tourists shrieked in horror as Sea Dog tripped in the sand, falling at the feet of the guide. He looked like he was trapped here from his own shipwreck. The tourists whispered, worried for this stranger.

"Please give me water. I'm so hungover."

A Spanish dad slowly stepped forward, handing him a bottle, which he chugged immediately.

"That's not part of the tour, we're going to keep moving," the guide said, stepping over Sea Dog and continuing down the beach. Part of me felt embarrassed that we were causing such a ruckus at a historical site, but part of me loved every moment of it. After all, it's not like the debauchery was hurting anyone, except maybe our own livers.

Over the next few days, we island-hopped around Greece, seeing varying ancient cities with cobblestone streets, castles, and eating all the gyros we could sink our teeth into. The days would start by waking up and hopping off the back of the boat. A coffee in one hand, I'd balance on a pool noodle and look out at the pristine sea or the edge of a castle off in the distance. Then, Niermeen, Evelyn, and I would wander through the streets and stop in a plaza for lunch and an Aperol Spritz, or two, or three. In the evenings, we'd all hop back on the boat and try to let the rocking of the sea lull us to sleep. Being surrounded by my friends, experiencing new cities, and enjoying the peace of nature were magical. By day three, things started to change.

"Remind me when we're at sea to empty the sewage tank," Logan said to a deckhand at one of the docks. On boats, there's a valve that holds in all the poo, pee, and sea-friendly toilet paper you use on a ship. If every ship emptied at port, the bays would be filled with sewage, attracting sharks and other scavengers and making the docks wreak. Boaters have to remember to empty out at sea, but a lot of general ship maintenance best practices were being forgotten.

The men who were responsible for us had made some miscalculations. First, they had spent far too much money on booze at the start of the week, so despite online saying our trip was all-inclusive, we needed to buy our own food, water, and more. Second, they had miscalculated the distance and time it would take to get from Greece to Montenegro, and because we'd gone in the opposite direction on the first night to see the shipwreck, we'd lost a day at sea and added to the number of miles we needed to travel. This meant that the days of wandering in small Greek towns were over. To get to Montenegro in time to make our flights, we had to spend three days nonstop at sea. We'd also be traveling by Albania, which Logan had researched and read was extremely corrupt. If we tried to moor, they might try to throw us in jail or extort us. We would not be able to touch land for three days. When we signed up for the trip, it was not communicated to us that half our week off would leave us trapped, unable to do any activities, in order to get to our flights home on time. Then there was the third problem.

"I have an announcement. We are low on water, so if you need to shower or pee, give me a holler, I'll stop the boat, and you can do both at the same time," Logan announced. When you live on a boat, despite being surrounded by water, your boat can only hold a certain amount of fresh, clean water to drink, pee into, and wash your hands and dishes with. This water is purchased at ports, which we wouldn't be at for three days.

Lastly, there had been a crumbling of camaraderie on the ship, mainly because college-aged men are, as a complete generalization, idiots. One of our deckhands had sex in the cabin where Evelyn, Niermeen, and I were staying while we were at shore. We got back to the boat and discovered that not only did we need new sheets, but there had been an opportunity for all our valuables to be stolen because a stranger had been in our room without us knowing in advance. Furthermore, the couple on their honeymoon had thought they were spending a romantic week together on a luxury yacht and had not realized their trip would be more like sharing a campsite with a bunch of drunk strangers. This had led to constant bickering between them, as well as fighting with Logan.

As a general rule, it's always better to "under promise and over deliver" when running a business, but the expectations of those going into Yacht Week and the reality of an experience where we couldn't shower or pee, had to buy our own food and drinks, and soon half of our "week on the water" would be spent trapped at sea unable to touch land, had people angry. Those angry people were now trapped together in a tiny floating vessel, unable to walk away or "find space" when things got heated. Under an unforgiving sun, everything was heated. Before our long trek along the coast of Albania, we had one last night in a basin together.

As we left the choppy Mediterranean Sea and entered the wind-protected cove, our boat glided across smooth, calm waters. The cove was on a small island and only accessible by boat. The people who could physically get there were people were predominantly millionaires, their families, and their staff. I was surrounded by successful bosses. There were some smaller, private boats and then your mega yachts with helipads and whatnot. Donated to the charity, our boat had a beautiful navy-blue hull that our twenty-year-old captain designed with signatures of all the donors to the charity. Instead of a regular name like "My Second Wife" or "Actin' Knotty" that you saw on most ships, ours was called "#ATSEAFORRIGHTS," the slogan for the charity. While the passion Logan had for helping rehabilitate incarcerated men was endearing, in this setting, our boat entering the harbor was basically the equivalent of a trailer RV pulling up to a country club.

To make it worse, "Chicken Fried" by Zac Brown Band blared while Logan and the hippie swing-danced on the front of our boat as we entered port. While the other yachters were delicately sipping their Sancerre sauvignon blanc as the sun set, they stared, their jaws dropping as our boat entered their private slice of heaven.

"Why are they such fans of chicken?" Niermeen, the only European on our boat, asked as the song played. This is not how you were supposed to behave in the upper echelons of European society. As the deckhands docked our boat, Logan continued to play loud country music, including "Wagon Wheel" by Darius Rucker.

"They're all looking at us," Niermeen said.

"I know," I said, watching our neighbors in the cove. A guy ran down the back of the mega yacht in the harbor. He left the big ship, hopping onto a small cream-colored tender with cream leather seats tied to the back. Full speed, he sped across the calm water to our boat.

"Turn the fucking music down, you assholes!" he said in a thick Italian accent.

"You don't like our music, well it's a free country!" Logan screamed. While Greece was also free and the global model for democracy, it was not the country Logan was referring to.

"Can't you see you are disrupting our calm evening?" he snapped back, his linen shirt blowing in the breeze.

"Fuck you!" the honeymooning wife screamed. At this point, she had made it very clear that she hated Logan, but when it came to a rich European calling us out, her Floridian roots came out and she was standing by her countrymen. The Italian sped off, his middle finger in the air.

While my younger self would have tried to chameleon my way into schmoozing with the affluent boat owners around me, I was having much more fun with my rowdy crew. Even so, Niermeen and I looked at each other. While we didn't agree with how the Italian handled things, we could understand how we were in the wrong. After all, this was a shared space. I think Evelyn agreed on this point, but she had started fucking Logan everywhere: in the sail bag, in the sea at the front of the ship, in the dingy. Her trip would end with her spending a day wandering around Rome looking for UTI medication so she wouldn't be in inscrutable pain on her flight back to New York.

"You want fancy? We can do fancy!" Logan screamed after the Italian before disappearing below deck. The music went quiet for a moment.

The Dutch family on the boat nearest to us stopped staring and went back to doing their laundry—hanging bright orange sheets up on a clothing line. Then, as loud as Logan could increase the volume on his speakers, Mozart started playing. No one messed with us after that.

In the inlet, there was a small public beach with picnic tables, a public restroom, and a small, covered area. That night, all the boats headed over to this area to have a little party, and we joined after dinner. The party was very family-friendly, mainly with adults over forty and children under ten, putting our group solidly in the middle. Having not showered in days, I bee-lined to the public restroom.

"Can you use hand soap as shampoo?" I asked Evelyn as I flipped my entire head of hair into the sink, filling my hands from the soap dispenser. If I could have, I would have fit my arms and legs in the sink to wash off the three-day layer of sunblock, salt, and sand that had accumulated on them, making me feel like a sticky, sugar donut. Because I was so pale, my summer look was Communion wafer. You could see through my skin. I could dissolve on your tongue and in your pool.

Mothers shielded their children's eyes as they walked past me to help their young kids use the restroom. While I had come on this trip as a sort of celebration for becoming a bougie corporate boss, I was starting to embrace the Florida lifestyle. It was being forced on me. To dress up "fancy" for our night with all the other yachts, Logan had put on a tweed jacket with no shirt, Evelyn had on a flowery dress over her white bikini with her initials written in sailing flags, and I was wearing a frilly, blue sundress. All the other families were fully clothed in convervative attire you'd wear to a country club: polos and khakis or cocktail dresses.

As I walked out of the bathroom, I flipped my wet hair; it felt like a greasy mullet as it slapped against the back of my neck. Some of those around me grimaced, having no idea why my hair was suddenly wet. Still, we all danced to Greek songs that none of us could understand. Despite the obstacles, a generous portion of Captain Morgan on our part and likely a good Nebbiolo for the other yachters, our differences were put aside for the sake of a good old party.

A conga line formed led by Logan. As we danced, the German dad behind me wasn't putting his hands on my shoulders like everyone else.

"Put your hands right here!" I said, pointing to my shoulders. I assumed maybe he didn't know what a conga line was.

"Danke, don't need to touch," he said, politely. Instead, he stood behind me, hovering his hands a few inches above my shoulders to avoid contact.

Wow, I'm fucking gross.

As the party raged on, I walked out onto the beach, then swam to a floating dock slightly offshore. From there, I watched the party in front of me, people from different nationalities dancing under one roof. I thought about this trip and who I wanted to become. For lack of a better word, I was my hometown's trash and the cove's trash, but did I want to be fancy like the Italian in the mega yacht? If I was going to be a boss, was making money my only goal, or would I consider my employees in the decisions I made?

It was kind of fun being trash. I was moving up in the world, starting to build assets of my own, and could hypothetically buy real designer clothes, but did I want that? Would nice things make me happy? I knew a shower would. Reflecting on my happiest moments over the previous year, most of them were simple joys—biting into a juicy dumpling, feeling the water on my toes, watching the sun set next to a good friend. Becoming worldly and sophisticated was exciting, but using big words or saying things like, "I don't eat lemon pepper chicken, only *yuzu* chicken?" as one might if they were used to the fine life didn't really make me feel like I was a better person. If anything, living abroad had made me use more basic English because for most of the people around me, English wasn't their first language. How I chose to communicate with people could be inclusive or exclusive. This was a *choice*.

I had met "citizens of the world" that were pretentious and had used their status to lock themselves in bubbles away from the reality and hardships of the world. Was my purpose to sell luxury products? I was really good at it. Maybe being a good boss was another goal. That was definitely something I could work on. Sometimes I would get too passionate about my work and bring emotions into the office that didn't need to be there.

As I traveled more slowly, my feet dragging, and I entered adulthood with a fancy job, managing others, who did I want to be? Alone on the dock, I thought back to my childhood, playing barefoot in the rivers behind people's homes. There was so much joy in the freedom of not caring or even knowing what others would think of you—finding excitement in a water bug or, as you overturned a rock, a blue crawfish, its claws up in fighter mode.

I watched everyone dance, this little moment suspended in a secluded cove in the darkness of night, only the stars and I as witnesses. As I found success, did I want it to keep me in a bubble? I wondered if the people from the mega yacht were joining in on tonight's festivities or if they had decided to pass. I didn't see the Italian guy who had screamed at us. Probably best, since we wouldn't want a fight to break out in front of the kids. The moment reminded me how grateful I was for the life I'd chosen.

The rest of our trip was a nightmare. Like those adrift, we were trapped. The summer sun beat down on us and we only had a small amount of shaded space at the back of the boat, because it was too warm to stay inside the boat. It also reeked of pee down there because if we had to pee, we weren't allowed to flush, in order to conserve water. They did allow us to flush if we pooped. In that small pocket of shade with a breeze, we were trapped with our group of people who hated each other. The honeymoon had been ruined, and none of us wanted to be there.

I sat at the back of the boat with my feet in the water. "I've Got Friends in Low Places" by Garth Brooks played in the background. I hate country music, I felt trapped and conflicted, and Sartre was right. No internet, no phone, and reading a book made me seasick—this was my hell. I imagined letting myself fall face-first into the water, weightless in the thick saltiness. The boat would keep on without me and no one would notice that I was gone. Maybe that would be better than having to listen to that southern twang.

"Time to make a pee stop," one of the deckhands said as the boat slowed. We all jumped off the sides into the cool water. As I sat on a pool noodle, a small, brown, log the size of a Snickers bar floated by.

"Is that a shit?" I said. Another one floated by.

"Oh sorry, one sec," the deck hand disappeared below deck before returning. "I had to switch the bathroom valve closed again, I forgot." He giggled.

Swimming in shit, I did not giggle. I didn't even get mad. I already knew this trip had gone to shit and getting angry wasn't going to change anything.

That night, we gathered around the back of the ship, telling horror stories to pass the time.

"I mean we used the pull-out method forever and then finally, we got pregnant," the honeymoon wife said. At that time, I was not ready to have kids mainly because I wanted to spend my days being a boat hoe and kids couldn't float. It was extremely impressive that so many women had made new people. All I could make was microwaveable mac and cheese. Even in that case, I could have made a band called "Hot Bowl Cold Dish," which would be ballads for all the times I had pulled food out of the microwave early.

"So, then we got married," her husband said, throwing his arms in the air. They both laughed. The bickering all the time made sense.

"Let's go skinny dipping!" Logan said. This time everyone got naked and climbed in. Because I'd heard Sea Dog say, "Maybe we'll get to see Kristen's huge tits," a moment before, I decided to keep my clothes on. I was also still traumatized by the whole swimming in our own feces thing.

As the group climbed back on the ship, Evelyn shrieked in pain.

Her toe had gotten caught in between the fiberglass of the boat and the wood of the ladder as Sea Dog had put his weight on to climb up. The hippie mother of the ship sprang into action. As the ship's grill rocked softly in the waves, she, completely drunk, hovered over its open flame, trying to hold steady a needle to sterilize it.

"Are you sure this is a good idea? We've all been drinking!" Evelyn cried, a little nervous at how excited the hippie, a former nurse, was to use her skills on her foot despite being naked, wrapped in a towel, and intoxicated.

"Here, drink more," Logan said, shoving a whiskey bottle into Evelyn's hand.

The hippie held firm on Evelyn's foot, the needle in her other hand, "We have to alleviate the pressure."

I have a phobia of needles, so I looked the other way as I held Evelyn's hand for emotional support. Our hippie pushed the needle through Evelyn's toenail to drain the pool of blood below. The whole emergency surgery killed the friendly vibe.

Evelyn, Niermeen, and I peeled off from the group, sitting at the front of the boat.

"Did you hear that whole thing about the pull-out method?" Nier-meen said.

"Yes," I said.

"Is that normal in America?"

"I hope not," I said. "But I have highly educated friends in New York who also told me they do it. We were only taught abstinence in school." I pointed to Evelyn and me.

"Don't even get me started." Evelyn shook her head. She had other things on her mind. "I'm getting old, and how am I supposed to go to the Hamptons and find my future husband without a big toenail?" She started to cry.

"We'll figure this out," I told her, putting her hand in mine. "Maybe get a good pedicure when we get back?"

"But what if my toenail falls off? I mean who wants to see a big toe without a toenail? I'll never be able to wear open-toe sandals again!" She looked me straight in the eyes, her eyebrows furrowed. "No man is going to want to marry me if I'm missing a big toe!" She was spiraling.

That night it was too warm and stinky in our room, so I lay an outdoor pillow on the upper shell of the ship to sleep. In the middle of the night, we were hit by a storm. Rain poured down on me while the front of the boat plunged up and down in the waves. Water poured over the sides, spraying me. No one else was in sight. Off in the distance, I could see the moon glowing red. It was huge and touching the water. I had heard the old sailing phrase, "Red sky at night, sailor's delight. Red sky in the morning, sailor's warning." What in the hell was three a.m.? Should I be worried? If I fell off the boat, I would be dead. With the large waves and no one around, there's no way anyone would find me.

When I was nine, I was swimming in the Atlantic off the coast of Fire Island right before a big storm. Suddenly, the waves started coming faster and faster. Desperately fighting to keep my tiny head above water, my thin arms thrashed in the heavy, salt water. Every moment I got a fresh breath of air, I'd be thrown under another oncoming wave. Luckily, a sixty-five-year-old lifeguard named George saved me, but I would not return to the sea for a year after, still scared from that day.

Alone, I stared at the moon. To this day, I still wonder if I was hallucinating or if it was all a bad dream. I'd never seen the moon so large and close to the horizon. It felt like I could step off the ship and walk into it, as if entering the gates of hell. I could have gone downstairs to shelter, but instead, I sat there, letting the waves and rain wash over me. It felt like some sort of rebirth, like nature was reminding me that life is short and fragile. It was for me to decide what I wanted to do with my time here. Yes, I had career success, but was I happy? Was life all about selling luxury products to make more money to buy myself nice things, most likely more luxury products? My work did pay for me to do trips like this. At least at my job I was learning how to be someone's boss, which was a new experience and a chance for me to think about how I wanted to treat others.

I walked to the very front of the boat, out onto the metal spindly edge at the front of the jib, and I stared into the devil moon, almost challenging it. *Take me, I dare you!* I still had a lot of living to do.

The next day, we had our last day and night on the water. No one else had seen the devil moon, but they had felt the storm. While at sea, Logan let us take turns sailing the boat. A Greek beer in one hand, the steering wheel in the other, it felt good letting the wind on the sail direct me. I might have been swimming in shit the day before, but this was a new day.

The next morning, moored off the coast of Montenegro, we were woken up early by a port guard on a microphone, zooming around our boat and screaming, "It is illegal to moor off the coast of Montenegro! You will be imprisoned if you do not follow me to the port authority."

Every country has its own laws, and apparently in Montenegro, you could not check your boat in in the morning, which is what Logan had assumed. Instead, you had to check in immediately when you arrived, even if that was two a.m.

Montenegro is around the size of my home state of Connecticut and home to about 670k people. For those in the mega-rich superyacht community, the country is known for its $200 million port, which has space for huge yachts, a swim club with an infinity pool, and a long downtown promenade. When the port project was started in 2010, many were against it.

"This country is for sale," said Vanja Calovic, the head of Mans, a corruption watchdog affiliated with Transparency International. "Montenegro is selling everything it has, and I am just not sure what the country is getting out of all this."[21] However, the government was already well-known for their corruption, having allowed many questionable businessmen to live there and do business who had had to flee their home countries. A year later, you'd have Nat Rothschild, whose family owns Louis Vuitton, and an investor in the port, throwing a million-dollar fortieth birthday party for himself there.[22] Was increased income inequality the future world I wanted? Was buying a Louis Vuitton bucket bag supporting the rich becoming richer? Was there a better way I could spend my money, maybe on small businesses? I saw that how we choose to spend our money shapes the future of the world we live in, and maybe I was right to not buy myself a designer handbag even if I could afford it. Having more responsibility at the office meant I'd have more disposable income, but it also meant being frequently stressed and having less free time to enjoy traveling and spending time with friends.

While we had avoided Albania because of corruption, we had clearly not dodged it here. The port authorities hauled Logan off and put him in a jail cell for the morning, but we were told not to worry.

First, we went and showered in the public restrooms on the dock. This was not the public restroom you might find at a public beach with, "Will suck dick for French Fries," chiseled into the bathroom stalls. This was an exclusive spa-level bathroom. The shampoo and body wash smelled like lavender as I rinsed off days' worth of built-up grime. Eucalyptus leaves hung from the waterfall shower head. I never wanted to leave the scalding water. The stalls had bountiful toilet paper. I even hid some in my bag to take back to our boat.

Next, we wandered down the main promenade, Evelyn's entire foot wrapped in gauze, as we strolled past a bunch of luxury designer brand shops and size zero women in flowing dresses walking with bald, heavyset older men in designer clothes. The strip felt like a cookie-cutter fancy outlet mall. We searched for some food. I wanted local food, not over-priced, generic Italian food.

We walked one street behind the main strip and the city was completely different. The main strip's luxury contractors had removed the old cobblestone walkways and buildings with flowers flowing from their balconies and replaced them with generic sheet rock tiles and beige stucco. The uniqueness of the former was so much more mesmerizing. Imagine having all the money in the world and to attract you, people spend millions to make every location you go to look exactly the same. Haven't we watched influencers on social media standing in front of their large mansions with their designer handbags, fake lips, and extensions? When I was in the thick of that, it felt so foreign, so fake, like everyone was reaching for some ideal level of wealth that was never attainable and had diminishing returns on happiness.

We found a bakery with €1.25 spinach pastries and more. There were blue-collar men and women there, and no designer clothes. As we walked farther past the promenade, we came across a beach, where an older woman knitted clothing while tanning. We sat in the sun, feeling its warmth against our bronzed skin. When I got back to Shanghai, the sun would be blocked by all the pollutants in the air.

As we got back to the ship, Evelyn ran to hug Logan, as he'd luckily gotten out of jail after paying a nearly thousand-euros fine. He had lost practically all the money he was supposed to make for his charity for our week of the trip. On top of that, the nearby laundromat had threatened to call the cops on him after he'd refused to pay €250 to wash the boat cushions, as he hadn't asked the price before having them cleaned. On their boat with a microphone in hand, the laundromat's staff blocked us from leaving the port until Logan finally paid.

Soon, I was back in Shanghai, on solid ground, taking this experience in stride as I thought about what kind of "captain" I wanted to be at work, how I wanted to spend my money, and who I wanted to become. When my theater teacher friend told me that the local English-speaking theater might go under, I happily went to their fundraising performance. To raise money, you could pay 100 RMB (around fifteen dollars) to buy the cast shots as they performed *Macbeth*. In this private event in the dimly lit, attic theater with a vaulted roof and catering chairs, I saw an Irishman, heavyset with a ginger beard, slowly spinning while reciting Shakespeare, bottomless with his penis shoved in between his legs. It was hard to faze me, and no amount of money could buy that experience. It was priceless, and I was back home.

CHAPTER 14: LOVE LOST IN JAPAN

Sexcation with an Old Flame

Four months later, Osaka, Japan—A Japanese woman in a navy skirt suit with a microphone followed by a camera crew ran up to me just outside of customs. "Miss, we are a local Japanese TV show, can we ask you a few questions?"

"I guess so?" *Shit, I am so late, where am I?* My flight from Shanghai had just landed.

"Miss, why did you come to Japan?" She held the mic up to me, the camera lens pointed my way, the red recording light blinking, awaiting my reply.

"For sex," is what I couldn't say. *Shit! What is an appropriate answer for a Japanese news show?* I stood up straight. "I really love *Memoirs of a Geisha*. It's such a beautiful book and I read it ages ago and had to visit Japan."

She smiled politely at me as if this were an acceptable answer, which it was not. The best reason I could come up with was an overhyped book from the '90s?

"Thank you, miss," she said with a soft nod to wrap up the interview, clearly realizing that I was an idiot.

Sprinting down the airport corridor, my backpack flopping, I looked for Baron. Baron and I had met two years ago in East Hampton, Long Island, a community where bankers go to blow off steam in the summer. We had a mutual friend who said we would have beds (we slept on the floor), and it'd be free (a $500 tab by the end of the weekend). Baron and I instantly connected and two years later, he'd hit me up to come explore Japan with him. He was also one of the most attractive guys I'd ever hooked up with. In fact, he was so gorgeous, my brain shut off every time I tried to speak to him. There was not enough blood left in my brain to form sentences.

"Where have you been?" he called, spotting me before I had even noticed him, flustered as I was.

"A local news station interviewed me."

"What? Why?"

"Why I'm visiting Japan—why are you?"

"Because Goldman Sachs legally requires me to take days off each year. Listen, the next train is leaving in five minutes. We have to get your ticket; you're so late!" He paused, then using his muscular arms, he pulled me in for a hug. He pulled me away, looked at me for a moment, and gave me a deep kiss. Blood flowed from my brain down to my loins. "God, it's great to see you," he added.

"You, yes," I said in a daze.

"Hurry, let's get you your ticket." He had to practically shake me back to life. We rushed to catch our train and then headed to The Ritz.

"Hello Mr. and Mrs. Mengue," the steward greeted us as we walked in. Having never been to a Ritz Carlton before let alone been called by a man's last name, I was pretty much living the dream that all my friends from my hometown wanted. Was I the same me that Baron had met in the Hamptons?

It had been years since I'd been home other than to visit my family, and I'd traveled all over the world, yet seeing him reminded me of my old life and the ambitions for women that came with it. Working in banking, he made an unfathomable amount of money more than I did. My mom had always taught me that I could be whatever I wanted to be, but I had rarely actually seen that. It was always women working hard at the mid-levels, and men at the top. Sadly, most of the most senior women I had met through my travels were either single or had marital issues relating to their busy work lives. This meant that I had a very binary view of "success." I could marry a rich man and have a nice house or marry a poor man and always worry about money. The idea that I could be successful, spend my own money, and have a healthy relationship with a man unintimidated by my success seemed impossible. Soon I would be hitting my three-year mark of living in Shanghai, the moment when many expats decided to return home.

The steward put "Mr. & Mrs. Mengue" labels on all our luggage to bring up to the room. Baron thought it was funny hearing his Cameroonian last name pronounced as if he was of Asian descent. The thought of being called by the last name of a man I hardly knew made me blush.

The summer I met Baron, I was working as a theater critic for a magazine. I was sent to cover Caryl Churchill's *Serious Money*, which recounts the financial climate in London in the late 80s post-Margaret Thatcher's Big Bang. The satire follows bankers after the death of a colleague, and the characters prioritize wealth as the ultimate thrill and achievement. In the lobby, waiting for the performance to begin, I sat next to a woman in her sixties with a facelift, cheek implants, lip fillers, and enough diamonds to sink the *Titanic*.

"Women like us can do a lot for the arts," she said in a soft, deep voice.

"Yes, I love writing about these shows," I said.

"I always loved the theater, and I bring my husband and his friends to shows, convincing them to invest in the arts. And that's how we keep the arts alive; we find people to invest."

Was she suggesting I use my body to marry someone rich and then convince them to invest their money in the arts, making that my life mission? I looked at her blankly.

"I know a nice man, he's in real estate development. He just went through a divorce, but he's the sweetest man. Can I give him your number?"

"Okay," I said, even though I should have said, "I am moving to Shanghai in a month," or, "I'm not whoring myself for theatre."

I Googled the man to see what he looked like, but all I could find was a YouTube video on how to manage the plumbing in your rental investment property. He wasn't in the video; there was just the voice of a man in his forties with a strong New Jersey accent. When he did call, I politely told him that I was moving to China and that was the end of that. The woman's words stuck with me. She took a look at me and expected me to marry rich.

The Ritz hotel room in Osaka was rather frumpy. The drapes and bed sheets were dark floral patterns, which reminded me of the Holiday Inn, but with more ruffles. British old money would have loved this decor, but I couldn't see anyone under sixty-five thinking it was the bomb.

"How are you doing, Mrs. Mengue?" He laughed, pulling my shirt over my head. Laying back on the bed as he removed his clothes, I watched as he neatly folded them on the chair. *Did he fold his clothes before sex when we were in New York?* I honestly couldn't remember. He kissed me again and then folded his underwear. The folding was really taking me out of the moment. The scratchy floral sheets made my back itch, but I tried to stay focused.

The next morning, we headed up to the lounge for the buffet, reading the *Financial Times* while overlooking the city. The stock market was good. Wonderful. I smelled great, having slathered the free, high-end vanilla bean body lotion from the bathroom all over my body. I dabbed more clotted cream on my scone.

"What do you want to do today?" he asked.

"Wander," I responded, still unable to communicate more than one word at a time. Maybe this was coming off as mysterious? Honestly, this was how I traveled: showing up completely unprepared and ready for the city to take me on a unique adventure. My everyday life required Excel spreadsheets, planning, and being organized. For me, travel was about having the freedom to do whatever you wanted.

"Did you do any research before we got here?"

"No ..."

"Don't worry, my coworker's wife made a whole spreadsheet from when they visited." He pulled up the Excel file with hourly scheduled activities. This was my nightmare.

"We could see Himeji, the oldest castle in Japan?"

"Okay!"

We finished our breakfast and headed for the train.

"Take a picture of me, the only tall Black guy surrounded by tiny Asians," he asked in the train station. I took a picture.

"You can't really tell," he responded, looking at the photo.

I climbed up some stairs to get a better angle and took another.

"Let's try later," he said after reviewing it. Visualizing what he wanted, I didn't think I could capture it on a crappy cell phone camera. We headed for the train.

"Hmm?" I asked, leaning over his shoulder, looking at his book, *The Short and Tragic Life of Robert Peace: A Brilliant Young Man Who Left Newark for the Ivy League* by Jeff Hobbs.

"It's a fascinating story about this guy who grew up on the streets, got a scholarship to Yale, and still got gunned down. It's a good read about violence in the Black community. What are you reading?" he asked, pointing to my iPad.

"*Bernie's Desire.*"

"Oh, what's that about?" He leaned in, expecting it was a fresh new take on this progressive presidential candidate.

"A naïve, New York refugee from the one percent decides to spend the weekend in Vermont, only to join a sex cult run by Jane and Bernie Sanders." I gulped. "Romance novel." The book was hilarious, framing Bernie Sanders as a sexual prophet ready to educate the upper class on the beautiful simplicity of being—and boning—a working man (and woman).

"Oh." His head jerked back as if he'd just smelled a turd.

"Socialist puns!" I defended my choice.

Exiting the train station, you could see Himeji Castle off in the distance, perfectly centered on a long road of tourist shops. Walking this would not have taken much time, except that upon arriving in Japan, I discovered my Chinese debit card didn't work at any ATMs. This had never happened to me before. Part of my "hop on a plane" philosophy was never taking out cash in advance and always just getting it from the ATM in the airport.

Along this winding road, I insisted on stopping at every convenience store to try to see if my debit card worked. After a few days, I felt bad that I couldn't pay for anything. My mom always taught me, "Don't let men pay for things because then you'll feel you owe them something." Regardless of what I owed him, over the trip, I felt as if I'd accrued a massive debt. Baron didn't seem to mind, and he had significantly more money than I did, but I felt like a bit of a mooch. I had a credit card but couldn't withdraw any cash.

"I'll pay, it's fine." Baron was a bit annoyed at this point. On top of constantly stopping to check if my debit card would work, the castle also ended up being extremely disappointing. It was a few stories high, but every floor looked the same: an old room with holes to shoot arrows out of. It was more of a military base—no furniture from a specific time, crazy outfits, stories about the king's harem. At least the koi pond had some two-foot-long, spattered gold and yellow fish, gasping for bits of food as a man in a cream linen shirt fed them. Their bodies seemed so graceful and pristine, while their wide-open mouths seemed desperate.

On the way home, we stopped in Kobe for a Kobe beef dinner, which I paid for on my credit card while Baron was in the bathroom.

"You didn't have to do that." He sounded genuinely disappointed. I hadn't paid for anything else, but even that small cost gave me anxiety. It wasn't a lot for him, but it was a lot for me. We lived in two different worlds, and his smelled like hand-poured luxury candles while mine smelled like public transportation. The first time I'd slept over at his place in New York, in the morning, he said, "Stay as long as you like," and as a freelance writer at the time subletting an apartment with no A/C in the dead heat of a New York summer, I wondered if the next time I stayed over, I should bring my laptop and spend the whole day working in his huge air-conditioned apartment off Gramercy. Luckily, in Japan, public transportation is really nice, but it isn't in New York, what Baron—and I, formerly—called home and where I assumed I would return after China.

"I honestly don't know if I want to be a banker's wife in Manhattan or move back to Connecticut," Evelyn, an executive assistant, told me the last time I visited New York from Shanghai. She took another huge slurp of her fishbowl margarita. Luckily, her toenail had grown back since our yachting adventure.

"If you don't have kids and don't have a job, what are you going to do all day?" I was genuinely curious.

"Probably do charity work or, I don't know, drink wine," she responded, taking another sip. That is what her mother did. To make this dream come true, Evelyn would match with guys on Tinder and once their full name was revealed, look them up on LinkedIn to see if they worked in finance or, were at least on enough of a career path to help her meet her lifelong career goal of being a rich man's wife. Baron was one of those men, yet I felt ashamed for not paying for anything and not doing any research in advance. Did his paying for everything mean we should enjoy our trip only in the way he wanted? In my mind, we weren't co-pilots: he was the pilot, and I was a flight attendant. It was a test run of the life the old me would have wanted.

On the train back to the hotel, we stopped again to try to get a picture of him as the only Black guy. I took the picture. I knew it wasn't good.

"You're not doing it right. Whatever, I have a headache, let's get home. Can you figure out directions?"

At that point, my Chinese SIM wasn't working. He handed me his phone, and I pulled up directions to walk back to the hotel. The GPS was not very accurate, so we went the wrong way for only a block.

"Why did you have us go in the wrong direction?" he screamed at me.

"Sorry!"

"You can't do anything right!"

We walked in silence. I felt impotent. I hadn't planned anything for this trip, couldn't pay for anything, and couldn't even form sentences. Things had not gone as planned—I'm not perfect. Sometimes, things go wrong when you travel. This is what I should have said to him. My own insecurities around him—feeling less attractive, wealthy, and articulate, and that being a good "housewife" meant "only speak when spoken to"–had led to me not feeling comfortable speaking up. I grew up where part of the film *Stepford Wives* was filmed, a movie based on a satirical book where the husbands replace their strong, independent, smart housewives with more subservient, "perfect" robots. I was also trying to enjoy this trip, which meant doing things differently than he wanted me to. I felt like I was free-falling into my old life.

At the hotel, he still wasn't feeling well, so we only ventured out for a quick dinner.

"I want to go to this restaurant I heard about where you eat in stalls." He searched for it on his phone.

The restaurant was long and narrow. On one side were mini booths lined in bamboo, dividers in between each, and a red stool at front. He and I took booths next to each other but could not speak due to the divider in between. After filling out a piece of paper, you slipped it under a sliding bamboo door in front of you and once your food was ready, the door opened and two hands placed a bowl of steaming ramen through the slat. Zero human interaction.

As we sat in our separate stalls, it reminded me of our predicament. We lived in two separate worlds, both geographically and financially. He wasn't a bad person; this was an internal struggle of new me and old me and revisiting what future I wanted. Upon reflection, the world I was from seemed to be a place I could no longer fit into. If he came home from a long day at work, I don't think Baron would be happy with me asking, "Oh, can you take care of the kids and cook tonight? I have my writing class." I would have to give all that up to plan Excel spreadsheets, ensuring that during our time to "relax," I was "go, go, go" so my kids and my husband could get the best out of their trip. Where would that leave room for me, my career, and my creative projects? I had dreams and goals, and with this guy, my career would be devoting myself to his happiness and maintaining our status within an elite group, like the koi, trapped in a pond surrounded by opulence and yet desperately seeking more. Did I need to fit myself into my old societal pond? I was no longer the girl in a second-hand dress on the outskirts of town. Regardless, the thick, warm broth of the ramen was comforting.

"That was so good," he said as we left.

"I know," I said, half-smiling.

That night, we stayed in. In separate beds, he watched sports recaps while I read my Bernie romance novel. I came to this trip exhausted and ready to blow off some steam with some rip-your-clothes-off—not fold them into a nice pile—sex with a love interest from my life in New York, a place I thought that I would return to after Shanghai. Instead, only Bernie was making me feel the burn. The trip was bringing up so many reminders of the life I had in New York and why I'd decided to leave. Trapped living in little sardine boxes stacked on top of each other, everyone gossiping over champagne brunch about the new coffee roast they discovered from Ollantaytambo, Peru—it was a competition to show off their wealth.

I didn't want to play that game anymore.

CHAPTER 15: SHANGHAI

I Found HPV in a Hopeless Place

One year later, Shanghai, China—As part of a preventative health measure, the company I worked for in Shanghai had a free health checkup for all employees. The results were not what I'd hoped for.

"Your vagina is Clean Level II," Ingrid, my Danish friend and colleague said.

"Clean Level II?" I repeated. Ingrid could read the test results written in Mandarin, while I could only speak it at a basic level.

She looked shocked and laughed, "Yeah, they ranked our vaginas!" She looked at our two results, "I'm also Clean Level II. Clean Level I means you have a clean Lady V. I guess we're sluts!" She cracked up. What was this scale based on? Was Clean Level I Virgin Mary Clean, while Clean Level V was Ron Jeremy Clean?

After sheepishly consulting with my Mandarin tutor that night about my unclean, bearded clam, she suggested I go to the gynecologist. Ingrid and I headed over a few days later.

After entering the huge hospital, we were instructed to take numbers. For about $150, you could go to the premium section a few floors higher, but we didn't think that was necessary and headed to the non-rich-people section of the hospital. As we entered the waiting room, an open space with hundreds of chairs, there was a large group already waiting, and above us, on the wall, numbers indicated when you would be called in for your checkup. We squinted at the sign: there were over 700 people in front of us in line to see gynecologists.

During the Cultural Revolution, Mao Zedong promised universal healthcare, even in rural areas. In the 1960s and 1970s, these "barefoot doctors" would travel around the country, helping to treat the sick and were the foundation of China's present medical system. The system was abolished in the 1980s, but based on my experience in 2016, there still seemed to be a lack of doctors, considering China's population of 1.39 billion.

"The one-child policy is to help protect the people of China. If the population kept growing, there wouldn't be enough doctors to take care of everyone," my Mandarin tutor later explained.

"But don't you think it's unfair for the government to tell you that you can only have one child?" I asked.

"No, they are trying to protect me. What if I had a child and there weren't enough doctors if my baby was sick? Or not enough food to feed everyone in China. There are too many people." Historically, that had been true.

With 700 people in the queue in front of me, the strain on China's medical system still seemed quite apparent. Ingrid and I walked to Starbucks and gossiped about who might have sullied our meat curtains.

After three hours of waiting, Ingrid, in Mandarin, asked how much longer. It turned out that there was only one gynecologist who spoke English, so they let us cut the line to meet with him. After getting in the stirrups for an inspection, I waited with Ingrid as the doctor tested the little swabs of our respective juice boxes.

Once the results were in, he called us back into the room and motioned for Ingrid to sit as I stood in the open doorway.

"Your test results are fine. No problems."

"That's it?" Ingrid checked.

"Yes."

"Great!" She jumped up with a smile. Perhaps the test knew she'd once slept with a man visiting Shanghai on a layover? I took her place in the seat as she waited in the open doorway.

He stared at me with a curled lip as if I were trash. "You have HPV; you get this from sexual intercourse." I had followed the guidelines in *All the Rules: Time-Tested Secrets for Capturing the Heart of Mr. Right* too closely, resulting in a dry spell my first year in Shanghai, and I had only slept with a few men since, and I had been exclusive with most of them. I'd *still* contracted HPV and probably from an Irishman! In the doctor's eyes, I was a nasty slut, bringing disease into his country. I sat in shock as strangers passed by just outside the open doorway behind him.

"HPV?" I whisper-screamed, looking around the room in shock, confusion, and embarrassment. Level II Clean ranged from Ingrid's "you're totally fine" to having a sexually transmitted infection? Shouldn't there be more levels than only Level I and Level II?

I turned to Ingrid. "Doesn't everyone have HPV? I got the vaccine when I was a kid! Can you help translate?"

Ingrid translated to the doctor, who gave her a longer explanation in Mandarin. Then he looked me straight in the eyes, his lip curling as if I shouldn't be shocked at the results of my "inappropriate" actions and said in English, "There are over a hundred strains of HPV. You could die."

"What? Die? From HPV?" I exclaimed.

The doctor tilted his head for a minute, thinking, and then looked at Ingrid, speaking to her in Mandarin.

Ingrid translated: "You may have gotten vaccines for the top strains in the US, but there are hundreds of strains of HPV, and some of them could give you cancer. He suggests you get a biopsy of your cervix."

"But it's not HIV, so why can I die?" I asked, my brow furrowed with confusion. I felt fine, but I might have a deadly disease? Maybe I was finally being punished for my sins. But which one? Stealing unicorn stickers from the toy store when I was six? Forgetting to wipe down the elliptical after a sweaty workout? Maybe it was from wearing white after Labor Day!

"There are cancerous types of HPV. You need a biopsy to see," the doctor explained curtly.

I felt like a zombie after I left the hospital, and walked back to the office in the severely polluted, foggy Shanghai air. Once I got home, I turned on my internet settings to get around China's firewall and frantically searched. For HPV, the average global mortality rate is 6.9%.[23] Cervical cancer is the third leading cause of cancer deaths in women and the second most common type of cancer to result in death in women aged fifteen to forty-four worldwide.[24] I couldn't find anything about twenty-six-year-old women being at high risk for HPV-related death. That night, I couldn't sleep. Shouldn't you take everything a doctor tells you seriously? My appointment for a biopsy loomed over me. It would be another week before I'd have more information.

"This stops the pain," the doctor explained once I climbed into the stirrups after waiting an hour for my biopsy appointment to begin. She held up a cotton swab with gel on it. Then, she slipped the cold gel inside me, and we waited a few minutes before she continued with the procedure.

As the doctor cut pieces off my cervix with little scissors, I watched a huge cockroach climb up the pole behind her. My snatch might be Level II Clean, but they couldn't keep out these creatures that flourished in humid climates. The doctor peered into my humid climate.

"Keep the gauze in until tomorrow," she instructed when she was done with the procedure.

They refused to test my biopsy until I had paid, so I headed downstairs to the cashier. I walked past hundreds of patients, my little, clear jar of cervix bits in hand.

After paying, I walked back upstairs, past hundreds more people, the jar full of my cervix visible to all, and dropped it off at the testing station. It cost $250, a quarter of my rent, to have them chop up my cervix. I did not want to even fathom what this would have cost in America. I headed back downstairs to get medication to take home.

The man in the medication room took my receipt and returned with multiple boxes of pills. Today, I can't remember the exact number he told me to take, but it was something like six pills every few hours to prevent myself from bleeding to death. I weighed 115 lbs; there was no way I needed to take that many pills. If these were to cause blood clotting, I was going to become one giant clot.

"Maybe they give the same number of pills to everyone?" Ingrid ventured.

"Great, I'm being told to take as many pills as an overweight man," I replied.

That night, I stuffed my underwear with extra paper, took less than half the pills, and hugged myself as I tried to sleep, a huge wad of bloody gauze still in my penis fly trap. What would they find in my biopsy? What if it was deadly like the doctor said? What if they had done it wrong, and I couldn't have kids? The huge cockroach wasn't reassuring. For the next week, I hardly slept, shaken by the whole experience and worried about whether the surgery itself could cause long-term damage or if the results would confirm that I might die any day now.

A week later, I returned to the hospital. In the waiting room, I tapped my foot on the floor anxiously. Who knew what the results would say? A nurse came out of the results room and looked at the name before her. She called another nurse to look at it, unsure how to pronounce the foreign name.

"Uhh." They scanned the waiting room. I was the only foreigner. "You!" They pointed to me. I took a deep breath, clenched my fists, and followed the doctor into the checkup room. A woman in a white lab coat sat in front of an old, cream-colored computer. She typed on the keyboard, pulling up my file. A huge, blown-up picture of my cervix appeared on the screen. She clicked a button and then handed me a paper copy of the blown-up image. Oh great—a souvenir! Maybe someday I could show my grandchildren—if I could still have them. They'll be so proud of their Nana.

"You have the cancer HPV," she said. "The strain you have, HPV-16, is very likely to give you cancer."

"What?"

"See the dots on your cervix? It is the cancer kind." I squinted at my print-out. She was right; there were white dots.

"Am I going to die of cancer?" I covered my face with my hands.

"If untreated, you have a 99.9% chance of dying of cancer."

"I am pretty much guaranteed to die?!"

"Yes."

Speechless, I stared at her. I was alone in a country with only a rudimentary grasp of the language. I hadn't asked Ingrid to come because it was a workday, and I wasn't expecting to be told I would surely die.

"What is the treatment?"

"I can give you medication, but the best way is to burn the dots off with lasers." She pointed to my cervix's portrait.

"*You want to laser my cervix?!*" My heart throbbed within me. Was this a sick joke? It felt like an *Austin Powers* film, but instead of sharks with laser beams on their heads, they wanted to go into my cave of wonders with laser beams to fight the dreaded human papillomavirus.

"It is the best way," she said.

I sat in the chair in shock. Finally, I decided.

"I will start the medication but wait on the lasers."

Over the next two weeks, I took the treatment. Each night before bed, while lying flat, I squeezed a syringe full of shiny, cold gel into my hoo-hah. I couldn't read the instructions in Mandarin, but the name had "alpha" in it, allowing me to Google studies on the treatment. Everything I found said it hadn't been proven clinically effective.

During this time, I'd lie awake in bed with a fever from the medicine, wondering if my life would end soon or if this was all a sick joke. Some moments I was sure I was going to die and wondered if I should tell my family. Others, I just giggled, thinking this was what expats called "China problems"—just one of those nonsensical things that happens when you live in China but never understand because of the language and cultural barriers. I didn't want to worry my family if it was unnecessary. They were concerned enough about me living on the other side of the globe and if this was a "China problem" they wouldn't understand what that meant. Would this make me infertile? I wanted to have kids someday. Could this take the gift of motherhood away from me? Not only was I emotionally distraught, but I was also physically drained.

During the day, while sitting at my desk at work, I'd suddenly get a fever and feel completely exhausted. Was this because of the medication or because I was potentially dying of cancer?

Years later, after returning to the U.S., a nurse friend told me that she thought the medicine was a form of chemotherapy. According to research I've done since, HPV 16 and 18 account for seventy percent of all cervical cancers worldwide.[25] There are vaccines for these, and since I had the three HPV shots while I was in high school, I was confused about how I still got it, since those strains must have been covered. For a little context, chemotherapy has a very low success rate. It's often given as more of a "Hail Mary" last attempt to cure cancer when all hope is lost.

"You can't live this stressed, and that medicine, something's wrong with it, don't take it," Ingrid told me after another day watching me grow more and more exhausted next to her at work.

"I'm going home in two weeks for Thanksgiving. I'll see a doctor in the U.S. then."

I wasn't sure what else to do. In the meantime, I kept taking the alpha medicine and dealing with its symptoms. Every day, I felt anxious, with no idea what was going on in my body.

Home in New York, embarrassed, I didn't tell my family that I might be dying from a sexually transmitted infection. Instead, I booked a routine checkup with my gyno.

"Here's a picture of my cervix that they took from a biopsy." I rushed at him in my surgical gown as soon as he entered the exam room, thrusting the printed image from China into his hands. "They told me I'm going to die of cancer!"

"What?" My gyno held the picture up. "Yeah, I have no idea what to do with this, we don't take pictures like this."

"They said I have the cancerous HPV and I'm going to *die*."

"You're twenty-six—pretty much all sexually active women your age get HPV at some point. We don't even test for it," he explained. "If you aren't stressed, it should go away in six months."

"But they said I'm going to die!" How could I possibly not be stressed?

"Maybe if you were in your fifties, then a cancerous form could be serious, but you're healthy and twenty-six! You're fine!"

"How are you going to treat it?"

"It doesn't need to be treated. It'll go away on its own, probably in six months." He looked at me as if this wasn't a big deal.

As I left the doctor's office, I was shocked and relieved, but also angry that I went through so much stress and turmoil over nothing. More importantly, what the hell had I been putting in my pink taco? I'll never know.

On my way back to China, I sipped my airport Pumpkin Spice Latte, which, in my mind, tastes like America, and I looked out the window of the plane. I accepted that I will never know what I had been putting in my hot pocket and from then on, I'd avoid going to the doctor.

There is no test to detect if men have HPV, although the Irishman who I thought gave me HPV did go to the doctor in Shanghai after I told him and said they shoved a huge needle up his dick. One might call this karma. Regardless, every time I had sex afterward, I was significantly more hesitant. A little thought in the back of my mind chirps, *Will this kill me?* Quite the turn off.

A year later, there'd be an episode of *Broad City* where Ilana Glazer proudly stated: "Of course I have HPV. I'd almost be embarrassed not to have HPV at this point." When I told a friend from North Dakota about the experience, she had said her American gyno had treated her like a slut when she'd once asked for an STI test, which is why she switched to going to Planned Parenthood, because those doctors didn't judge her. Years later, another friend from Florida told me that when she was in her mid-twenties, diagnosed with HPV, her doctor also told her to laser her cervix. When she did, she could smell the burning. Why is there so much disparity in how to treat HPV? According to studies, gender bias is a major issue in healthcare and research of diseases that only affect women are underfunded compared to those that affect men.[26] The patriarchy strikes again!

"China problems" like these wore down my love of the country. As an outsider, sometimes the little things became so difficult to navigate in a language and culture completely different from my own. While I loved the career and personal growth challenges the country provided, these other experiences became exhausting. They seemed like a waste of time and energy that could be put toward my ambitions and long-term goals. On top of the pollution building up in my lungs, the stress was very bad for my physical and mental health.

Chapter 16: San Francisco

Is It a Dream (Job) or a Nightmare?

O ne year earlier, Shanghai, China—My first day at a new job is like my first day at school. I put on that fresh outfit I spent days thinking about, enough makeup to completely transform my face's entire DNA structure while still trying to appear natural, and those new heels that will cause massive blisters. Like how a new car smell fades, though, sometimes you realize that "new opportunity" that you thought would "change your life" is new shit, different toilet.

While still at the wine company, a headhunter reached out and told me about a new role leading the digital marketing strategy at a startup, run by Steven, an American tech bro. Steven promised that I could run my own team, that the company had a flat, collaborative, everyone-has-good-ideas structure, and with the headquarters in Shanghai but most sales occurring in the US, I could oversee global campaigns.

My primary objective was to one day oversee global strategy while managing an international team, which is why I chose to major in International Affairs and Economics in college. This job promised that. It felt like I'd reach the goal I'd been striving for my whole life.

Immediately, I put everything I had into the work. Being a boss and overseeing global implementation were two exciting new challenges. I wanted to prove to myself that I could be a successful executive leader. Growing up, my aunt was the most successful woman I knew. Having quickly risen to the top at an international beauty company, she made well over six figures. She was my idol. I even adopted some of her mannerisms in how I communicated, such as slowing down, lowering my voice, and using my hands when I spoke in business settings to convey a level of calming, even-keeled confidence. However, this perspective on how to behave at work differed from my experience at this new job.

The founder, an engineer and rumored former Albanian mob boss, had started the vibrating scalp massager division through money he'd made via his other invention: sex toys. Coming from a conservative background, I'd never used a sex toy before. How did I get my first one? I won it at the office holiday party.

"You see people search 'butt plug' on Google. But since we're a premium butt plug, we call ourselves a 'prostate massager' on the product page and use butt plug wording in our blog posts. That way, we can capture the search engine optimization traffic while maintaining our premium brand," the head of content for the sex toy company explained to me in a casual tone, likely having used the word "butt plug" already a hundred times that day. I looked through the walls of the glass conference room, still adjusting to the fact that these conversations were now part of my workday.

As I put my whole self into the work, I started to question whether I aligned with the "vision" of the firm. Firstly, to get free PR for the sex toys, they'd make up statistics like, "69% of left-handed people say they have better sex." Hundreds of press outlets would create clickbait headlines based on this "survey conducted on our site," when really, it was something a bunch of marketing executives made up in the conference room.

"Feel free to do a survey like this, but I don't want my name on it," I told Steven, to his dismay. I lived off statistics, only napping for twenty to twenty-six minutes because any longer you enter REM cycle; chugging a coffee pre-nap since while you're sleeping, your body more effectively absorbs the caffeine; using the researched-backed seven-minute workout to stay fit. Nearly every moment of my day was designed around optimal energy use and efficiency. What if someone like me truly believed the hand they used to write their name was destroying their sex life? Should I start masturbating with my other hand?

Despite the hundreds of vloggers we'd paid to rave about our items, it had started to become clear that the product didn't really work. In addition, we'd put on the packaging "according to clinical trials," but I soon learned that this meant a study done with only twenty-three people. While that was the norm in the beauty industry, such a small trial size would have never been acceptable in an academic setting. Then there was the fact that the packaging said, "Swedish by design," to emphasize our luxury branding, but the only thing Swedish about the company was the founder's ex-wife. Leadership labeled these tactics as "smart marketing," but to me, they were lies.

While I had finally reached the point in my career that I had dreamed of since I was a child, I hated going to work every day. I hadn't realized that being a manager might mean going against my own values. What value did I bring to the world? Using lies to convince women like me to buy expensive products that didn't work? Were all the long hours working late worth it? Why was having my dream job not making me happy? The excitement of management was leading and inspiring people and creating a good work environment. I thought a manager could help make people's lives better, but what if it involved telling people to do things that I believed were bad?

Despite selling our product to women, the majority of leadership roles within the company were filled by men. As they say, "A fish rots from the head down" and, as such, I'd started to lose faith in our leadership, but I was also part of it. When the cabinets at my desk broke, they gave me new ones. Inside, I discovered smutty magazines with the founder's handwritten notes, like "Cashmere stocking," or "Velvet whips," as he brainstormed new products. The magazines were clearly old, with faded pages and models with blown-out, bleached blonde hair. It was inspiring to see his initial ideas from long ago ... until I looked in the drawer underneath and found a cobalt blue, ruched, silk size zero dress with a big 1980s poof on one side. Praying it was something his daughter might have worn to prom, I thought that it was more likely from one of the women he was sleeping with. After all, at that time, rumor had it that he was cheating on his wife with the head of sales. I was putting my entire self into this job, but for what? To make rich scumbag liars even more rich? Have you ever met your company's senior leadership team and said to yourself, "I'm making money for these people?"

"I don't understand when people say you need work-life balance. If you love your job, it shouldn't feel like work," Steven would proudly say when the leadership team conducted brainstorming sessions in his office. Hustle culture was basically gift-wrapping bad mental health and saying it was a lifestyle choice. In Europe, August was your vacation month. Do whatever you need to recharge. In America, it was more like you should work yourself to death, we're tracking your OKRs![27] You can go to Coachella when you're sixty-five!

The toxic work environment led to a high turnover rate. Other employees, hired a few months before, were quitting right and left. They also fired a developer while he was in a taxi on the way to the airport for a two-week vacation.

This left me, the wonderful team I managed, and some other stragglers, such as the Russian developer who, sitting behind me, would message me, "Your hair looks beautiful today." My skin crawled, knowing that he was admiring the back of my head. He also considered me a "strong businesswoman" and to try to show me that he was an ally to women, would send me blogs called, "How to be a boss babe," with a Q-Tip thin woman in a business suit and sky-high heels as the logo. I knew I needed to quit my job because message notification noises haunted my dreams. I wanted my dreams to be haunted like they were before: by ghosts and ghouls, not developer bros in gray Patagonia vests.

"Made me think of you," he would write with the message.

While I was partially able to shield my team from this and keep them from quitting, I was making a lot of excuses for a company that I no longer believed in. As a manager, that was part of my job. With the exit of talent, those of us left had to handle the responsibilities of our departed colleagues on top of our own jobs.

Despite numerous video calls where he claimed that this was untrue, it also started to become clear that Steven—whose Shanghai office had the highest turnover rate of anywhere I'd ever worked—wanted to move the office to San Francisco, where he suddenly disappeared to for months. What this meant on my end was having to manage a girl he hired named Savannah, who lived in San Francisco and wrote copy in a tone that seemed to be designed for 12-year-old girls discovering their mothers' lipstick for the first time. Meanwhile, the people who bought our luxury product were mainly in their late twenties and thirties—an age where they had the disposable income to afford it.

This and other first impressions were not ones that gave me faith in the quality of the new hires. For example, a new colleague had said, "I don't like working with timelines" and I am very impressed that they set boundaries so early on. My concerns were amplified when we saw the first campaign out of the new office, one that they had intentionally made without the help of the Shanghai "headquarter" office.

"It's called 'Beauty and Brains,'" Steven said. "Because, like our products, women can have both." They slowly walked us through their presentation as my team and I sat in silence, completely shocked.

"What do you think?" he asked when the presentation was over, leaning forward in his swivel chair, eyes lit up, with a big smile on his face.

"If our products have 'beauty' and 'brains' and we're comparing our customers to our products. Do you see how suggesting women are like a physical object could be seen as objectification?" I asked, trying to articulate my rage.

"No, but it's not saying women can only be smart or pretty. We're saying they can be both," Steven projected back, as if this was a novel idea. I knew Savannah had signed off on this.

"We don't need to tell women that. They already know that," Chloe, my head writer, scoffed, visibly and vocally angry. I put my hand up, not visible on video call, trying to keep the conversation from getting too heated, even though I felt the same way. It was so fucked up, but how do you explain this to a man who thinks he knows what women want? As a manager, it was my job to try to convince him of what was best, but at some point, go with whatever he wanted. He was the boss; I was supposed to follow his strategic vision—even if it was sexist.

"I think what we're trying to say is that this type of commentary is what men say about women, but women don't need to be told that they can be intelligent and beautiful; they already know that. To assume they don't is speaking down to them."

"But we're saying women can have it all!" Steven said, completely missing the point. Many companies use social movements in their marketing campaigns to increase their capitalist success. This was the norm. However, feminist messaging is usually nuanced because it's written by women to sell to women. This was written by a man and approved by his younger, brand-new female colleague.

I typed into my laptop. "If you Google 'beauty and brains,' all the articles are written by men and show models who are 'surprisingly smart.' That phrase is really focusing on beauty and acting as if it's a 'surprise' that attractive women can be smart."

"I think what they are trying to say is that this could be misinterpreted in a way that could lead to bad press," our Head of PR said diplomatically, calling my team a "they" as if she wasn't taking a side on the idea. She was very good at playing office politics.

The meeting ended without resolution. This campaign would be the first out of the San Francisco office. Steven was so proud to unveil it. He could then pitch its success to the founder, calling it a "win" and justify the office move to San Francisco, which had higher overhead and office space costs, leaving the Shanghai office in the dust.

If we hadn't spoken up, it could have been a chance for them to shoot themselves in the foot, but my name and any posts my team wrote meant *our* names would be all over it. We were not ready to sacrifice our careers and reputations.

"Why would you disrupt my happy place?" I whispered to myself after getting a work email on the weekend. This gig had already taken a toll on my mental health. I worked long hours and hated my job. Before moving to Shanghai, while working as a writer in New York, I'd worked on a book on sexism in the workplace. It made me feel sick to be asked to become the face and commit my own time to push messaging that spoke down to women.

It was around then that I was invited to visit the San Francisco office and meet the new team, most likely to be asked if I wanted to move there. It seemed to be a very popular dream for many people all over the world to work in San Francisco. It was the natural next step in climbing the corporate ladder. I questioned if living the dream I had had since I was a child even made me happy. Did I still want this life?

During my trip, I stayed in a hotel near the office. The sun shone over the clean streets as I walked through San Francisco. I hadn't been to America for a while, so I figured I'd get a bacon, egg, and cheese sandwich—a habit I'd picked up while working in New York. The first place I went only had avocado croissants. The next place had açaí bowls. After visiting a few more places, I discovered that none of them had them, not even a greasy grilled cheese! What was this healthy hellscape? If the American dream involved giving up delicious food, I was out. I'd heard of "food deserts," a place where it was difficult to buy affordable or quality fresh food. San Francisco was some other kind of food desert: one that lacked bodegas. It felt like the city took the idea of being a healthier person to a whole new level. It was a competition. Everyone was trying to one-up each other about how much they could make the world a better place.

Giving up, I came across a coffee truck parked on the fake grass of a plaza. A long line had formed, so I figured it must be good.

"Mint mojito iced coffee, please," the person in line before me said. I gawked; it wasn't happy hour. Regardless, I should trust the locals to know what was good.

"Hi! I'd like an iced ..." I paused. "Mint mojito? There's no alcohol in that? I'm going to work." It was only eight a.m.

He laughed. "No, it's really good, you'll like it."

"Okay, great!" I smiled. What was this place? I'd officially entered the global headquarters for capitalism. Here, you must buy whatever is trendy at all cost.

My coffee cup in hand, I headed to the office. The coffee was fine, although the cocktail flavor made me want to leave work, not head to it. Then again, the mentality here was that you loved your work so much, why would you ever want to leave? Your life *is* your work.

After security checked me in at the front desk of the office building, I headed up the elevator.

"I love Johnnie's!" a guy in a gingham button down in the elevator said, referring to the name of the food truck on my cup.

"Oh, thanks!" I said as if I was the owner of Johnnie's Coffee.

Once I checked into the lobby, I sat on a sofa and waited for a colleague to come get me. A young woman came in and addressed the front desk administrator.

"Hey, do you have walking desks?"

I blinked so hard that I was worried I might fall off the couch.

"What?" the admin asked.

"Like a standing desk but with a treadmill?"

The admin was silent for a moment. Walking for eight hours? That sounded like corporate torture.

"No," the admin responded, "but that sounds awesome! We do have biking desks, where you can pedal to power your laptop." Was this how people in San Francisco viewed their work, like they're changing the world through getting people to buy things they don't even need.

"Kristen? Oh my God, it's like, so great to meet you!" Savannah said, giving me a hug and shaking me from my thoughts. She was shorter than she appeared on our video calls and her dark brown hair had the sheen of fake extensions. "Oh my God, you got Johnnie's? I'm, like, obsessed. It's like you're meant to be here!"

Why in the name of late-stage capitalism are people so enthralled by this coffee? Maybe I should be working for Johnnie's.

"So great to finally meet you in person!" I said, faking a smile. As she introduced me to the office, I realized that Steven's hiring practices here were likely similar to in Shanghai: lowballing everyone on their salaries while promising great opportunity in a fast growth environment. In San Francisco, wages were high, and everyone promised that. If you're not offering a lot, you're getting the b-team. To put this into perspective: imagine the most annoying and worthless person in your office. That was this place.

They also shared the office with a guy I vaguely knew from Shanghai, who had moved here to make an American version of China's WeChat app. He was the kind of person who started every conversation by somehow weaving in how he went to Harvard. Despite having graduated nearly a decade earlier, he still told everyone he went there within five minutes of meeting them.

Steven showed me that the office had free beer and table tennis, perks that I didn't care about if it meant hardly getting paid enough to live in one of the most expensive cities in the world. A woman even came around with a little cart, offering everyone cupcakes. The office felt like a daycare for adults. It was designed to keep you at work. Why would anyone want that?

"We're only here temporarily, though," he said. "I'm looking for a permanent office."

As he looked around the packed coworking space, he had trouble finding a free private conference room, but once we did, he sat me down, and pitched me on joining his team there. The hair on my arms rose. This was supposed to be one of those exciting moments in my career. Didn't most people want a fancy job in San Francisco? If I took it, all my friends and family would be so proud of me. I would have come from feeling like a loser only three years ago living with my mom to working for a global company in the most innovative city in the world. The roommates who told me, "You're going to move to Shanghai without a job? You'll never make it," and the others who had discouraged me from taking an alternative career path, I could prove them all wrong!

I felt nauseous even thinking about taking the job. The lies, employees being taken advantage of, the lack of respect for each other, our customers, and women ... it was so not *me*.

"While this is a great opportunity and it's so exciting to see what you've built here, I'm not ready to leave Shanghai."

His eyes grew in size as he sat back in his chair, as if taking a physical blow.

That night, Steven offered to take the office to happy hour. We headed to a place with a beautiful art deco vibe, where all the men were in gingham shirts and gray Patagonia vests. Had they planned their outfits? Was San Francisco fraternity culture post-college? In college, we're committed to learning about all these wonders-art, history, and literature. Then we graduate and as adults we find out how to use Google Sheets, proper etiquette in messaging, and some men ain't worth shit. It reminded me of the bro culture of my hometown. Would this be my dating pool? People whose parents paid their rent but were now trying to "make it on their own" by starting their own businesses selling something like shorts with waterproof zipper pockets, perfect for yachting. Where were all the women? From the book I'd worked on prior to moving to Shanghai, I knew that there were fewer women founders because society systemically deterred them from being able to start businesses. As I sipped my cocktail, I hoped I'd made the right decision.

Back in Shanghai, I watched the office crumble around me as I tried to find purpose since I was no longer getting it from my job. Some ways to make it seem like you're working hard: act stressed, walk fast, wear a blazer. My job had boiled down to mainly video calls with the San Francisco office. People who don't look at themselves on video calls are serial killers. To myself I'm like, "Who is that lil cutie over there and why do they look so tired?"

I started not having to go into the office, and when I did, I'd take two-hour lunches, leaving around 11:15 a.m., while everyone else went at twelve. As long as I returned by one p.m., no one would know. Despite doing the bare minimum, no one seemed to notice or care. I felt numb and without purpose, and I could hardly convince myself to get out of bed in the morning. I decided to try to fill my free time to start to feel alive again.

Luckily, back in Shanghai, I had been accepted into an accelerator program for entrepreneurs and started taking improv and doing standup in the evenings. My schedule was completely packed. Both of these activities made me so happy.

I was exhausted. While these were fun, getting on stage and learning these new skills took a ton of energy and my job involved so much politics that it was also sucking the energy out of me. Every moment I worked, I felt sick, like I was forcing myself to eat insects. Even so, it was my safety net.

Then, Chloe got a job offer. I was her boss, but I was also her friend, and she felt comfortable enough to ask me for advice on if she should take it. This was one of those situations where I had to choose between being a good manager or a good person and I chose the latter. The writing was on the wall; this office would shutter.

While telling Chloe to take the job supported my values, it also made me feel like a failure. In working so hard to become a manager, I was not doing that job well. Finally, it came time for the call I knew would come.

"I'm getting fired, yes?" I asked the PR exec via video call.

"The office is moving, and Shanghai will close."

"That's what I thought."

The meeting went as I had expected. I handled it gracefully and afterwards was handed a severance package, which I signed, and then had to later get a lawyer involved because the amount promised—written in English—was lower than the legal minimum in China. I should have known they'd do me dirty.

I had to find a visa to stay in Shanghai, all while my mind was foggy from the constant stress, lack of sleep, and exhaustion.

It was at that point that my landlord notified my roommate and me that he had sold our apartment. Because most expats live in Shanghai for two-to-three-year work contracts and I was on year three, multiple friends I'd had since first moving there had decided to move back to their home countries over the previous few months. My friends, job, home, visa—the entire life I'd built for myself was all gone in a matter of weeks. Don't you love how when something bad happens, the universe is always like, "Let's make two other bad things happen and make it a shit sandwich?" I was like, please stop making shitty sandwiches. I had already ate one from the convenience store that day. Everything that had tied me to Shanghai was gone, and I'd recently rejected my one ticket back to the US. I had nothing.

I felt so stupid for not thinking through saying no to their offer. Why did I make my life so difficult? Couldn't I have taken the easy road for once? It had been handed to me on a silver platter, and I had said no. As I lay in bed feeling depressed, my deep sadness reminded me of when I lived at home before Shanghai. I felt like a loser, but at least before I had had my family.

Depressed, with no job to go to, I woke every morning, weighed down by my choices, unable to get up. You could have called me 007: zero fucks given, zero cares in the world, seven breakdowns a day because it was all a lie. I was filled with anxiety. I hated myself; I couldn't even look in the mirror without being filled with rage. The bitch I saw staring back at me was stupid, stubborn, and difficult. I didn't trust her. How could I? Look where my decisions had gotten me.

Past me had made these decisions so current me could be happy. I had had a job, but it was a crutch. The paycheck was making me stay in a bad situation. I was being forced to recreate my life in a way that brought me joy. The present felt hopeless, but it was not like it was the first time I'd been in a tough situation. I'd gotten myself out of many of them. I could trust the bitch looking back at me. She had proven she was resourceful in the past. I had to have faith.

Luckily, Ingrid found a startup that needed a copywriter. The Chinese founder offered to sponsor my visa. He was doing me a huge favor and was a genuinely good person. My reputation as a good, kind, easy-to-work-with person meant other good people wanted to help me. Even if I hated myself at this point, my friends still in Shanghai loved me. I was so grateful for that. Relying on my reputation, I was finding more people who shared my values.

I had the most time-sensitive issue worked out, so what did I want for myself? Still depressed, I started to go to coffee shops every day to work on starting my own business, and I performed improv and standup on stage at night.

I hadn't wanted to give everything up, but it was forced on me. At least I had more time for comedy. As for the apartment hunt, I decided to find a two-bedroom and rent out the second room on Airbnb. That would help me cover rent and I'd heard of people running very profitable Airbnb businesses. I knew enough Chinese to scout with local agents, who offered cheaper rent than if you tried to find it in ways normally marketed to expats.

Finally, I found a centrally located apartment within walking distance of the comedy club and a cute coffee shop. Not sure what was next, I signed the lease and, with Ingrid's help, painted the place a bright, clean white. Spending my days camped at the coffee shop, I looked for potential copywriting clients, for more apartments to build my Airbnb business, and writing jokes for my standup sets.

I had always thought that you had to climb the corporate ladder to be successful, but I had been forced to explore being my own boss (and was starting to enjoy it!). Even so, every day was absolutely terrifying, taking so many risks with only a little savings and severance to hold me over. It was one of the roughest times in my life, but I had to believe in myself and push for the life I wanted. If I hadn't, I wouldn't have my life today.

As for the San Francisco office, within six months, my replacement quit, returning to the job she had before, and within a year, the entire division closed.

While it hurts to even think about that time of my life, I don't regret it. The months I'd spent on comedy and working on my entrepreneurial endeavors were emotional and filled with constant failure, but they were foundational to creating a life that sparked joy. I also learned so many skills I use to run my business today. Ingrid and Chloe remain two of my closest friends. Messaging daily despite our differing time zones, we always go to each other for advice on dating, work, or to share a good meme. I no longer regret taking the hard road.

Chapter 17: A Tsunami of Poo

Donald Trump Becomes President

Five months later, Shanghai, China—It was supposed to be a day of celebration. I walked into brunch at an American restaurant in Shanghai. The venue had fifty packed tables, flowing beer, and the 2016 Presidential Election vote count was displayed on huge sports-size projector TVs around the room. It was a staple of the expat community, and I had been there many times before for Halloween parties, World Cup matches, and this time, the broadcast of not a sports match, but as many Americans saw it, a competition between the red and blue team.

I found my friends, some from the startup I had left, and I waved at another table—all the friends who I used to work with in the wine industry— and another—my friends from the comedy club—and on the far rim, my former rugby player roommates with their team. Most of the Americans living in Shanghai were there. With the time difference, we'd all taken the day off work and gathered for breakfast to watch the votes roll in. This room was nearly entirely Democrats. Donald Trump was on the rise, and most of those I knew living abroad saw him as a threat to our national security and an embarrassment to our country. Most of those I grew up with saw him as not great, but better than Hillary. For them, Hillary was the pillar of a corrupt establishment, inefficient policy, but also, did I mention her emails?

Growing up, everyone around me was Republican, me included. Despite being a suburb of New York City, my district, Fairfield County, was the last Republican district in New England. It was a town full of wealthy executives and bankers who moved from the city for Connecticut's lush forests and lower taxes. Anyone who thought differently had trouble fitting in.

One year I had a history teacher who was French and a former ballerina. He taught us in the plier pose, the back foot horizontal with the front foot pressed firmly in a perpendicular position, and he would get into screaming matches with students a quarter his age over things like universal healthcare, income inequality, and more. He quit because he couldn't take, as he put it, "teaching sheeple," and our final exam had the question: "Who is the worst President of all time?"

1. George Bush, II

2. George Bush, Junior

3. The Second Bush

4. The man who got us into Iraq

Did I mention that Ann Coulter had graduated from my high school? She learned all her beliefs in the same place I did. My town was also very Christian. In a town of 20,000-people we had Presbyterian, Baptist, Congregational, Episcopalian, Christian Science, Catholic, and Mormon churches. To keep that many clean and running, I'm sure you can imagine how much money was being donated. Along those lines, they believed money for the poor should be the choice of individuals, not the fiscally irresponsible government, which meant funneling donations through churches (and the favorable tax credit that came along with this choice).

Overall, the towns' views were very much about helping families, treating others the way you wanted to be treated, loving thy neighbor, abstinence only, if you smoke weed one time you'll become a heroin addict, and most importantly, low taxes. On the social side, this became more nuanced and oftentimes aligned with which church you attended.

"They did a test on me, and I have an off-the-chart IQ, but I have ADD," I'd had friends say to me, their parents' pressure causing them to spin into extreme anxiety disorders and, later on, constantly smoking weed. They couldn't take the pressure of their parents not understanding why they weren't getting grades as good as their classmates'. "Keeping up with the Joneses" wasn't possible if the parents had to admit to their friends that their kid had failed math, or even "worse," had a learning "disorder."

The Mormon girls in my high school class often wore skirts that went to their ankles. One time, a high school girl was caught sitting on a bed in her high school boyfriend's room, and the next day, her family had shipped her off to a private boarding school in Utah.

"It's so curious how all the kids you went to high school with waited until after graduation to come out as gay," a lesbian classmate's mother told her in shock.

"Isn't it obvious why?" my friend asked. "Because our town was terrible. We'd get bullied."

At the country club, most servers were people of color, and most guests were white. My best friend Patricia's family was one of the only Black families in our town. She explained to me how her brother—who drove a Lexus—was constantly pulled over, the cops running his plates to see if the vehicle was stolen. It didn't seem like a coincidence that this happened more regularly to her family than to any of our white friends.

With all these types of things happening, it created more of an exodus from the community than internal change and reflection. As everyone tried desperately to fit in for their own survival, these stories were whispered and swept under the rug instead of being given the soul-searching thought and actionable change they deserved. The community wouldn't change, and if you didn't like how you were treated, it was your choice whether to leave. As those who were "othered" understandably decided to leave, the community became more uniform—more white, more Christian, more condensed Campbell's cream of mushroom soup. Without experiences of how life could be elsewhere or an understanding of how others lived, the empathy towards those who were different declined. To those who were accepted, it felt like a loving community. For those who were not accepted, it felt like a quick kick out of the nest at a time when they were developing as people and needed love the most. It was a self-fulfilling bubble that wealth, watching Fox News, and reading the *Wall Street Journal* didn't appear to fix. Those inside the community felt loved, while those who left learned that the world is unloving and had to find a way on their own, sometimes disowned and cut off. According to a recent study, more than one in four Americans over the age of eighteen are estranged from a family member.[28]

My parents were staunch Democrats while my grandparents were avid Republicans. A bit of a mix, I was fiscally conservative but socially liberal. My views could be distilled down to two guiding principles:

1. Treat others the way you want to be treated: don't be an asshole, and advocate for everyone to be treated equally and with mutual respect.

2. Mind your business: if living a certain way makes someone else happier and doesn't hurt anybody, they should be allowed to do it. You should be able to make your own choices about whom you love, your body, and your money.

As I started to travel the world, those two guiding principles remained the same, but some of my other views started to soften. I found myself challenging a lot of the principles I had learned growing up. In America, we were taught that if you work hard, everyone can succeed. Republicans saw the need to create a social safety net as unnecessary because with freewill, anyone could rise from poverty. That was the American dream and the responsibility of the individual, not the state.

While my family was in the poor part of town, my version of poverty was about as watered down as a Natty Light, having lived in a safe neighborhood with a great public school system, and my grandparents paying for after school activities, offering themselves as free childcare, and more. My parents have always been there as a safety net, taking me in as I figured out my next move. Before moving from Ohio to Connecticut to be near my grandparents, I remember when my parents could hardly afford food.

"I don't want to eat hamburgers again tonight," I cried to my mom at age four. We ate them every night for two weeks. Have you ever thought about how a cheeseburger is like eating a female cow covered in her own baby cow food (milk)?

"We can't afford more," she said, teary-eyed. "Here, let me add more ketchup." Maybe this is why as an adult I hate ketchup? Even after the big move, I remember nights where dinner was blocks of cheese on crackers, which is maybe also why I hate Triscuits.

As I grew up, I started to realize, why would I want anyone—especially children—to go through anything like I had experienced, let alone anything worse? Republicans made it sound like this is the way it works, and it was impossible to—on a macro level—change things or reduce poverty. This was the responsibility of the individual.

In meeting people from all over the world, I learned how other countries had tackled income inequality. It wasn't a necessary evil. Things could be better even with a similar level of taxation (oftentimes taxing corporations more and individuals at an equal tax rate or less). A lot of the Republicans in power seemed to be actively creating policy that hurt those in need. This went against my principles and didn't feel like the Christian theology I had learned while going through Confirmation.

In economics classes in college, I learned how lower regulation, open borders, and pro-trade policies helped "all ships rise." In other words, everyone specializing in what they're good at does not mean nations are competing against each other, but building a bigger "pie" of economic wealth and opportunity. However, working in corporate jobs, I'd also learned that many leaders give zero fucks about their neighbors and that regulation is necessary to stop companies from lying and doing awful things that hurt people. In China, melamine, a chemical used in making plastics, was added to baby formula to reduce the apparent level of protein, but resulted in babies getting sick.[29] Greedy people could not be trusted to regulate themselves. I learned how tax havens worked while living in Luxembourg. It was not like companies did what was right.

As I changed and was surrounded by more progressive, open people, the overall views of the Republican party started to shift in the opposite direction. More of the moderates, like me, started to get pushed out of the party and replaced with extremists. When Trump came front and center and started talking about the "Muslim ban" and other policies, this completely contradicted my guiding principles. Everyone around me in China was very liberal, but when I spoke to my friends from my hometown, they seemed distraught, hating Trump, but hating Hillary more.

In Shanghai, everyone assumed it would be a celebration of Trump losing. We gathered around pancakes and beer flights, ready to watch the stupid man with the funny hair get what he deserved. Luckily, I could take the day off and spend the morning getting drunk. Since getting fired, my day job was now entrepreneurial: renting out apartments from Chinese landlords, having a designer redecorate them, and putting them on Airbnb. I sat and drank a hefeweizen, when I got a text from my cleaning lady that a toilet in one of my units was clogged and no matter what she tried, she couldn't fix it. While I spoke basic Mandarin, it was sometimes easier to come over and have a look.

"Be right back, don't let them take my beer," I told my friends. I headed a few blocks over to check out the issue. Even if we used the plunger or flushed, murky water remained in the toilet. I called the landlord. While landlords are known for being the worst, this one and I got along really well. I even went to his daughter's nail salon to support her business. He didn't speak any English and as one of the only foreigners he knew, he loved the foreign exchange whenever we met, stumbling through discussions on diplomacy despite his lack of English and my very minimal Mandarin. Years later, throughout the COVID-19 pandemic, we'd still message each other, sharing our experiences. As we spoke that day, I had a guest on the train, heading to Shanghai to spend the night in that very apartment. The landlord said he could come in an hour and a bit, so I headed back to brunch.

"What happened?" I asked, sitting down in front of my warm beer.

"It's getting pretty close," Ingrid said. The air in the room had shifted. Instead of pure jubilance, there was a light tension.

"Trump won Iowa, but Hillary won Nevada," Chloe added. "It looks like they're almost done counting Pennsylvania." There was still excitement in the air, but everyone started to feel on edge. What was seen as a slam dunk for Hillary didn't appear that way anymore. I sipped my beer. I was not sure how to feel. Surely, he wouldn't win? We watched the screens and discussed all the scenarios about who could win what state and how that could impact the results.

My phone buzzed. My landlord had arrived. It turns out the toilet was a special type, similar to the ones used in boats, and could clog easily. It had to be replaced, but first, we had to clean it out. As I pulled the back of the toilet off of the wall, as if in slow motion, a tsunami wave of sloshing, watered-down fecal matter—from hundreds of Airbnb guests-crashed across the floor of the bathroom. As it hit the far wall, it rippled the same way the ocean does when the tide comes in. The landlord laughed hysterically as I gagged at the smell, trying to keep my composure to mop up the mess. As the landlord fixed the toilet, I messaged my guest apologizing profusely, explained the unexpected issue and that the entire apartment smelled terrible, and offered a full refund. Despite suggesting he find alternative accommodation, he insisted it was fine.

"What's going on?" I said when I sat back down, the waiter having taken my beer. Chloe had her hands on top of her head, a look of lifeless shock in her face.

"Trump might win."

"*What*?" I motioned for the waiter and ordered another beer. I needed it.

"A couple county races are still unsure, but they're calling that Trump has won." I looked around the room; dread was growing on everyone's faces and some people were even crying. It was like getting slammed by a truck. No one had expected this outcome. In our little, protected bubble as expats on the other side of the world, we had been shielded from the reality of what America had become.

"How could this happen?" a French guy a few seats down asked.

"I don't know," I whispered. I couldn't speak this truth, and I didn't have an answer.

"We need another drink," Ingrid said as we slowly left brunch to head to another bar. The next few hours were spent drinking and connecting with friends in other countries.

"How do I explain this to my kids?" my aunt asked, calling me on the phone.

I was supposed to be on stage that night at an open mic, but after texting the club, the owner understood, and said it was fine for me to skip—something I had never done before.

As I headed home, I processed what this meant. Even in that moment, I didn't fathom the nonstop hatred and vileness that would happen over the next few years every day with Trump on the news. My only thought was how disconnected I felt from my home. The America I had lived in and loved no longer existed. My fellow Americans—including close friends from my childhood—had chosen a racist, misogynistic man to lead them. Their vision of America included one in which we turned our backs on immigrants in need, took away rights for women, and pushed beliefs that your neighbor had to earn the right to survive and prosper. This new view—chosen by Americans for America—was so cruel and against my own beliefs. How could I ever return to that? Did I even have a "home" country anymore?

As I walked home that evening, I passed a pet shop. In the window, a hamster sat in its little wheel, its tiny legs powering it in circles and circles. I had desperately wanted a hamster as a kid, and my mom had said I could have one as long as I earned the money for it myself. Determined, I sat outside with a hot chocolate stand, in six inches of snow, with a sign my mom had written, dictated by me: "I am selling hot chocolate with marshmallows in it for 50 cents." I'd drawn a picture with brown and yellow markers as a visual. I sat hunched over in a wicker chair, a huge turquoise thermos in front of me with a stack of Styrofoam cups and a bag of extra-large marshmallows. Living in Columbus, Ohio's suburbs at the time before I'd moved to Connecticut, there was little traffic on our street, so I sat there for hours, our old German shepherd, Jenna, lying next to me in the snow so I "wouldn't get kidnapped." I still remember the cold in my bones, but also the excitement as my mom counted up my coins and announced that I had enough to buy a hamster. It would aptly be named: Hamsty. That was my first business ever, and now I had one that involved shoveling shit into a bucket while I discovered that my country was also going to shit.

More than anything, my drunk self wanted to buy the little hamster in the window, and very delicately hold it in my hands, stroking its little furry body, praying that I could go back in time. I would give anything to go back to kind neighbors buying hot cocoa from me. Then my phone chirped.

"The entire place smells like shit," the Airbnb guest texted me. Like I had, he ignored the repeated warnings, out of hope, had experienced an awful surprise.

CHAPTER 18: RETURNING STATESIDE

Deciding to Move to Los Angeles

Two months earlier, Shanghai, China— "Speaking of boobs, here's Kristen Van Nest!" a white male comedian introduced me. I walked on stage and grabbed the mic. I stared out at an audience, my first stand-up audience ever, that had just been instructed to think about my private parts.

"I call them Big Papa and Biggie Smalls; same person, different sizes," I blurted, now both terrified and objectified at once. Honestly, I would prefer not to talk about my privates on stage. At the moment, I was shocked, but afterward, I was enraged at being put in that situation by a stranger with a mic. How dare he use my body to make *his* joke, let alone an awful one?

Luckily, I'd won over the audience. Adrenaline filled my body, that addictive rush. I had to have more. I performed on stage four to five nights a week while living in Shanghai.

My life in Shanghai had started to suck. With many of my friends' expat contracts ending, they had moved away, so I dove headfirst into the comedy scene.

Unfortunately, the comedy clubs were owned by men, run by men, and predominantly promoting men, so there were very few women I could look up to while I performed each night or even talk to about what I was experiencing. Soon, I had reached a glass ceiling.

"She only won because she's hot," male comedians would complain about very talented female peers if they won any showcases or competitions. Sadly, usually, sexist comedy performed well.

"A woman wearing sexy clothes and not wanting to get raped is kind of like me taping dollar bills to my body and not expecting anyone to rob me," a comedian said one night. That joke *killed*.

On my improv team, I also felt stuck. The only place to perform improv in Shanghai was a school run by this man in his fifties. His entire mindset was still trapped in the '90s, which is probably when he left America. At his theater, I distinctly remember watching a musical improv about a farmer fighting with Monsanto to keep his farm while falling in love with the "most beautiful stripper at the local strip club." The poor female performer—a sassy woman in her fifties—was forced into playing a stripper, having to "yes and" all his jokes about how she was so dumb, kept losing her keys in her voluptuous breasts, and tolerated other physical comedy about her looks. These were my only options for improv.

It was soul crushing feeling alone, isolated, and discouraged, but where would I go and what did I actually want? I had left my corporate job to run my own business and was doing comedy regularly, my other passion, but I was still unhappy.

Having settled enough in Shanghai to commit to an animal that would live another twenty years, I decided to adopt a street kitty, Nala, named after the best Disney princess. I always made things work, so I'd find a way out of this funk. It was just a funk, right?

Luckily, I had a family Christmas trip coming up to visit L.A. with my brother and dad. Curious to experience the comedy scene in another city, I signed up for a week-long improv class. Taking a class while on vacation may seem strange, but at the time, I would have honestly given a leg to just *see* women perform jokes to a crowd with even a handful of women in it. A few male stand-up comedians from Shanghai had forayed there and described open mic nights as terrifying make-or-break career moments—an agent might change your life in an instant or you'd have a "never make it in this town again, kid" moment. They'd return claiming their career was "ruined" because they bombed on some comedy podcast. My favorite category of podcast was "inspirational." I loved hearing from people whose parents were famous, telling people to "work hard." You would not believe how they inspired me to pour myself another drink.

Looking back, why the hell would an agent waste their time at an open mic night when they could go to a paid show to see curated, better talent? Open mics are for beginners to try out new stuff, not a place to be "discovered." Even so, I wanted to experience the city firsthand. What was it *really* like? Did all agents have mid-Atlantic accents?

I didn't know what to expect on my first day of improv class. The school seemed pretty plain. The walls had scratches on them, as if someone had been trapped in there for months and tried to claw their way out. They were really from the wooden chairs chipping the paint after years of use being grabbed and thrown into the center of the room for a performance.

"Can someone come up in front of the class and tell a one-minute monologue? We'll then make scenes from their story," my teacher instructed. A smaller girl with soft brown curls volunteered. I was unsure of her age; she acted like she was in her mid-twenties but looked thirteen or fourteen. It turned out that she had a rare condition known as Fabry disease, where you look like a child even as an adult.

"I was on a date and the waiter asked my date if I was his daughter. My date blushed and said, 'Yes, she is my daughter.' 'Why did you lie?' I asked him, and he said he was embarrassed. Embarrassed? I told him to go fuck himself! This is how I look; I'm not ashamed!"

Having never met someone with Fabry disease before, I was amazed by how brave she was. On dates in Shanghai, I'd always try to impress the guy, and on my terrible dates, I never spoke up. I'd just drink more then sprint away when it was time for the kiss at the end of the night. From the start of her date, this girl in my improv class stood her ground. She knew who she was and was proudly that person. Her real self.

During our class break, she told me she was determined to be a performer and refused to let her condition stop her. She was then Ariel at Disneyland. That's right, a full-time Disney princess! She wasn't the only one: Mulan was in my class, too!

Did I want to be a princess?

I was more of a jester, but much like in a Disney film, you could be whatever you wanted in L.A. The skies were the limit!

That night, I had drinks in the dreamy pinks and oranges of a California sunset with my high school friend, who I was staying with for the week.

"I moved here because I couldn't be gay in our hometown," he admitted to me as we sat with an assortment of Hollywood characters, including a celebrity's daughter who performed as Ursula on Disney cruises—I had no idea why everyone I knew worked for Disney. "Last time I was home, I was walking down Main Street with my mother, and she said, 'Uncuff your pants.' 'Why?' 'Because you look too gay.' In L.A., I don't have to hide who I am."

That night at one a.m., still awake due to jet lag, I got a call from an Airbnb guest, an Italian businessman. I'd mentioned in multiple emails that I was on vacation and to call my friend who was managing everything. He felt he needed to contact me directly. The internet wasn't working, and he needed it fixed right away. I explained that someone would come by the next morning.

"On Airbnb, it says this is a four-star place, and if this was a four-star hotel, they would have someone immediately come fix this," he began, hinting he'd give me a bad review. I'd watched so many people stick to their guns over the last few days that his threats weren't going to work.

"Sir, hotels have 80-100 rooms in one building, so hiring a full-time IT guy makes sense. This is an Airbnb down a back alleyway. You're paying $20 a night and a four-star hotel would be around $100 a night. Do you see how that is an unreasonable analogy? Also, I am in Los Angeles on vacation, it's one a.m. here, and I still took your call. Can you take a moment to process the level of customer service you're asking for and what I'm giving you?" I was done apologizing for craziness. No one in L.A. apologized for nonsense.

"Okay, you're right, I'm sorry." Did he just apologize *to me*? I was in shock. This had never happened before. As I lay awake, I realized that despite crafting a life that yes, on paper, fit my goals, Shanghai no longer made me happy. According to an article in *Business Insider*, you're the average of the top five people you spend the most time with[30]. In other words, who you let into your close inner circle shapes who you become, your beliefs, and your success. By that logic, I was the average of five very pale misogynists complaining about their Asian wives.

With many of my friends gone, I was very much an outsider despite calling Shanghai my "home." Both personally and professionally, a significant amount of my time was spent sucking up to people, whether guests or comedy club owners. To make my life work, I couldn't be myself. In the smog, I couldn't flourish. In the sunny openness of L.A., I could. The only barrier: giving up everything I'd created for myself and starting over on the opposite side of the world. So, that's what I did. I got Nala vaccinated, hopped on a flight, and soon we were living in L.A.

After only six months living there, I could see the difference already. While in Shanghai, I was often terrified to try new material onstage, wanting to give only trusted performances to the male club owners who booked weekend lineups. Here, even on my Instagram, I was no longer afraid to be myself. Before moving, every picture was of a nice scenic view or architecture, without me visible. Now, I could freely improvise on stage and filled my Instagram with videos of me performing funny characters. What if someone didn't like them? Who cared! I had stepped out from the shadows to be my full self. I joined an all-women improv team—who knew women could be funny? I let loose, without worrying about what people thought of me.

"Play a really gross character," my improv teacher instructed.

As we started a scene, I slouched my shoulders, pushed out my belly, and spoke in a nasal voice.

"I heard you got rats; I'm your exterminator."

"Wow, it looks like you haven't showered," my scene partner said.

"It's so the rats feel comfortable with me." I crouched as low as I could on the ground and called to the make-believe rat, "Come here, ratty, ratty." My classmates giggled. I motioned as if the rat appeared and crawled up my sleeve to perch on my shoulder. Making a hacking noise, I thought back to how much it smelled as I cleaned up the tsunami of poo from the plumbing accident that I had dealt with on the day Trump was elected President.

"He's smelling my breath: once you tame the king rat, all the others will follow." I stuck my tongue out, to, naturally, make out with the king rat. I bathed in the laughter. Maybe I didn't want to be a princess. Maybe my true calling was to be a hilarious, disgusting exterminator who swaps spit with sewer rodents. Perhaps being a comedian who once had HPV would suffice. I'd finally found a city that embraced the weird, even depended on it, where I could truly be myself and pursue my passion.

Once again, I finally felt at home.

CHAPTER 19: LONG DISTANCE LOVE

Impossible to Be at Home in Someone's Arms

Five months earlier, London, UK—Being in London felt weird. The last time I'd been here, I was visiting Jampa. We stayed in his flat in Shoreditch, visited his childhood home in Bath, and took a road trip to his mother's homeland: Scotland. We hiked the woods in between fields filled with black and white sheep and their baby lambs, and the corpse of a fox that'd been shot in the head trying to eat the latter. We took boat rides on Loch Lomond, drank cocktails in smokey glass bird cages in basement pubs in Edinburgh, and held each other tight at night to stay warm in the cute Airbnb we rented together on the edge of the Loch. That was the thing. We only saw each other on vacations, during the good times. In between, we survived off memes. It's not like I could text him, "You up? I need someone to cry with. What, vulnerability is supposed to be sexy!"

This time, I was in London for a wedding that was not mine.

Juste, a former wine colleague of mine, stood up at the altar with Alorec, her soon-to-be husband, while the minister, an American, read them their nuptials in an art deco church in Little Venice, London.

Despite Jampa and I breaking up when I headed to Athens, the little drawings I had sent him kept the chapter we intended to close, open. Our relationship was like hanging on to a fantasy. No matter how hard you closed your eyes and pictured a unicorn, putting a toilet paper roll on the forehead of a horse would never make it the same thing. We loved each other deeply, but his career path chained him to the UK and my career in comedy meant I needed to be in L.A. We could never live in the same place. We each had to choose ourselves and our dreams and that meant ending our relationship, even if we loved each other. Love could not conquer all.

My friend's long-term boyfriend and I chatted with the minister at the reception after the service. Also American, he had previously skateboarded with a famous American skateboarder, and having been Protestant before converting to Catholicism, he was one of few priests who was married with six children.

"Many of us met in China; we all lived over there together," my friend's boyfriend told him.

"The Chinese come over because they're smart and go to all our schools, unlike the Muslims who come over and bomb everything," he said. I watched my friend's boyfriend's face as he processed this comment. I could visibly see the gears turning in his mind as he switched from "What a curious man" to "Oh my God, I am talking to a racist."

"I need to get another drink," my friend's boyfriend said. I nodded and followed him.

That evening, I sat between one friend in a serious relationship and another who had recently started dating the man who would a few years later become her husband.

"Everyone thinks we've been together longer," she said happily, as I threw back another glass of white wine.

Listen, divorce is okay. Breaking up is okay. Starting over is okay. Moving on is okay. Saying no is okay. Being alone is okay. What is not okay is being the only single person at a wedding. It was a nightmare. It's better to pretend that your pet raccoon ate rat poison, or any other excuse you can think of, to avoid a night of two joining in holy matrimony, while all the couples around you look wistfully into each other's eyes, and you look deeply into the bottom of your Italian wedding soup. At my funeral, can they throw a bouquet and whoever catches it is the next to die?

"Excuse me for a second," I said as I wiped some wine from my lips, held back tears, and stood up from the table.

I sat outside on the mossy, damp, ancient cobblestone steps in the back alley of the chapel, and tears poured down my face. I scrolled through Instagram, and I saw yet another "pop the bubbly I'm getting a hubby." It filled me with a completely unnecessary level of disgust and rage. Just call him a hubbly! Go for the full rhyme!

It seemed like everyone was getting hitched. I thought of Jampa. Within the past year, he'd flown to New York and met my family. We stood on the front porch of my grandparents' house on Fire Island. We bicycled through town, and I showed him where I almost drowned, where I caught fish, where I caught a tortoise. We went into New York City, walked along the High Line, and took a selfie together. Our relationship had spanned three continents and two years of messaging each other every other day.

The breakup felt like déjà vu of when Sam broke up with me. I was back, living at my mother's, sitting on the floor in the bathroom for privacy, the computer propped up on the toilet, as Jampa stumbled through a break-up he didn't want but knew he had to have.

"I know we could see other people, but I haven't been," he admitted. While I had been seeing other people during our open, long-distance relationship, I was not emotionally open to anyone else. If anything, all the other men reinforced how singular my feelings were for Jampa.

Then, I was back in his city, this time without him. Sipping on my glass of wine, it was a little salty as my tears, mascara, and lost sense of self mixed with it. With no relationship and no job, had I made any progress? It felt like my life was cyclical, but was I actually progressing? I felt stupid. Maybe I was falling down and picking myself up over and over again and getting nowhere. At least I was learning things? With every difficulty, I learned what I did and didn't want in my life. With every plane ride, I met new people and saw how they lived, giving me inspiration and courage to make bold choices. Those risky choices meant high highs and low lows. At that moment, I was small crystal tartrates at the bottom of a wine bottle low.

In Korean culture, there's a concept called inyeon, which is a belief that sometimes, people are connected through intangible forces. We can know people from past lives, and through each existence, we are re-united with them. Our "person," the person that we love the most deeply, might not be the right person for *this* life. I loved Jampa, but in this existence, we could not be together. Our love for each other was critical. I needed to love someone and have someone love me back, as hard to believe this level of love was even possible. I needed that to feel that I could love myself that deeply, not only for a man to love me that hard. Jampa wasn't the only one I loved and who loved me back.

There was a reason I was there: to see my friends from all over the world. In fact, instead of a cake, Juste had made a pyramid of cupcakes, each one with the flag of the country of whichever guest it represented. If I had known this earlier, I would have only eaten one American flag cupcake instead of five. This would be one of my few chances to see these friends, especially all of us together. Even though Jampa wasn't there, I didn't need him.

I wasn't a young girl anymore. I was a grown ass woman who had traveled the world, I had unique experiences, had learned from any failures, and was getting to know who I was and that she was someone who could be loved. The following day, I would be in Kazakhstan! I had gotten through tough times before, and once again, I needed to believe in myself, trust in the process, and remember that hard, high-risk choices came with amazing rewards. I was in no way back to where I had started nearly a decade ago. I was a completely new person, with no reason to be sitting here, crying over a boy. I chugged my wine. Time to get out there and be my badass self.

I headed back inside, and I saw all the Lithuanians in a circle, doing some kind of traditional dance. They raised their arms together and then interlocked them, shaking their legs in the center of the circle.

"Everyone's barefoot!" I yelled to some other friends, rubbing the mascara streaks from my cheeks. Kicking off my shoes, I ran to join the Lithuanians, and immediately stepped on broken glass. Leaving a snail trail of blood on the floor, I was committed to nothing keeping me down. I had to cheer myself up. Wrapping toilet paper around my foot like a mummy, I joined in on the dance, which was followed by the *Macarena*. I scrunched a napkin between my toes to control the bleeding. I didn't have Jampa, but I had friends and my adventurous, resilient self. Through my travels, I'd learned that was enough.

CHAPTER 20:
KAZAKHSTAN

Out with the Old, in with the New

O ne week later, Astana, Kazakhstan—Astana is the Kazakh word for "Capital City." The city's main street's name means "Main Street." The main square's name means "Round Square." The land is flat as far as the eye can see and the city was rather empty of people, the government having built it to replace the former capital of Almaty. The whole city was a bit of a rush job.

Why was I in Kazakhstan? Great question. A Fulbright friend had called me up a few months earlier and said, "Kristen, this is going to sound like a cult, but I went last year and it's this excellent program run by Germans in which they pay for top American and European future leaders to travel to an off-the-beaten-path country and discuss geopolitical issues. Want me to recommend you?"

Let me be clear: if anyone ever wants to pay me to travel and listen to my own voice, I will wholeheartedly accept. A wealthy Jewish German banker had to flee Germany during WWII for the United States. Upon returning to his home country after the war, he committed to building a bridge between Germany and other parts of the Western world. To do so, he set up a program where, once a year, up-and-coming foreign government and business leaders from other Western countries could connect with German government officials. That way, if there was another war, there would be relationships in place to help Germany—and most importantly, its people—gain the support they needed from abroad. The Fulbright was created for similar reasons. The underlying principle was that understanding how your friends and your adversaries think is worth more than a thousand tanks. As I had seen for myself through my travels, sometimes relationships go sour not because of intentions but because of miscommunications caused by cultural differences.

The conference was about forty percent German and ten percent Austrian. The rest of us were from elsewhere in Europe and the US. It was about a third women, the majority of which were American, while most of the Germans were men.

"This is such a boys club," one of the German women who worked at the United Nations complained. "Most of the events I go to commit to fifty-fifty men versus women."

"Really?" I asked. The other American woman and I looked at each other in shock. "Most of the events we go to are about 10% women." Outside the mandates of the UN, the world was still a boys' club.

When I'd been invited to the program, I was about to move back to my mom's studio apartment from Shanghai. This meant a good six months unemployed, living with my mom and step-dad on a pullout sofa in a nook of their living room (there was not even a wall). During my departure from China and arrival in the US, I had started my own business sourcing cat-themed jewelry from China and using my digital marketing background to sell this to the US market online, mainly through Amazon. My company name was EVERY DAY IS CATURDAY. My plan at the time was to try to make this my main income while pursuing my comedy career in L.A.

"They want people with Chinese experience, so I think you can get it," my friend said. That is how I, an unemployed American living on my parents' pull-out sofa, ended up at a conference with other Americans who started every conversation with, "The views I am about to share are not those of the US government, but my personal views."

I would respond, "The views I am about to share are not those of the US government, but those of a comedian. Oh ... You don't know that English word? It's like a professional clown, but worse, because you usually don't get paid."

"I thought EVERY DAY IS CATURDAY was a typo," one of the head speechwriters for Angela Merkel, the Chancellor of Germany at the time, told me while laughing. His comment was on my written affiliation in the brochure, where my profile sat, right in between a commander in the German Air Force and an elected North Dakota State Representative.

"No. It's my livelihood," I said. Weddings *and* conferences were so fun! After this experience, I decided not to mention my cat-themed jewelry business in my official introduction.

"Hi," I said, hesitantly taking the mic. A mic usually felt natural in my hand, but I was normally performing in front of drunk people, not future leaders of the world.

"My name is Kristen Van Nest. Prior to this, I lived in China working in the wine and beauty industry." I had mulled this over in my head and this seemed pretty sexy. "And now I'm ... a comedian."

The room gasped. It was like a sudden wave of exasperated breaths, all released at once. No one had done this when anyone else spoke. I had changed my path from corporate ladder climbing to one more entrepreneurial and creative, and saying it out loud felt like a coming out. Or at least, I had been trying to hop off that ladder for a while and had finally committed to getting off forever. At that moment, in a room full of government officials selected as likely to be the next leaders of our world, I was brave enough to announce that my new career path was one where I'd make considerably less and likely have to live with six roommates in North Hollywood where they make porn.

However, my perfectly crafted introduction was a mistake. If anyone was lost for words during the conference, their go-to conversation topic was asking me to perform stand-up for them. I explained that jokes about dick pics were probably the least appropriate thing for a government conference. Forever a self-promoting saleswoman, this was followed by me scrolling them through the cat jewelry website that I had built from scratch.

"Yes, those are my hands wearing the jewelry," I'd say before showing them my hands for comparison. I had taken the photos, SEO-optimized the site, and built it all on my own.

To say that I was experiencing imposter syndrome was an understatement. Every moment at the conference made my skin crawl. Trying to impress all those people was like committing social gymnastics, when I didn't have much going on in my own life. Once again in one of my "loser" periods living back at home figuring myself out, I'd come from a wedding where all my friends had found love and new careers, and the most exciting thing that I had going on was gift-wrapping cat rings on the floor of my mom and stepdad's studio apartment.

Feeling like you don't belong at conferences is common for women. Studies show that many women suffer from impostor syndrome.[31] Even though I was able to hold my own during conversations, I still didn't feel I belonged.

"There are two emotions that drive people: hope and fear. Obama leads with hope, Trump leads with fear," I said, ending a monologue on foreign policy that made me feel like Erin Brockovich.

Using my experience in stand-up, I added dramatic pauses as the room waited with bated breath. I was unsure if I was good at diplomacy, but at least I was good at entertaining people. I was whatever the authentic version of a diplomat was, if that even exists. Even so, I felt like I didn't belong there until I showed my knowledge and skillful diplomacy during our group discussions. I was elected a "Chairman" to run a breakout room module, so for a two-hour period, I had authority over a Commander in the German Air Force—not bad for an unemployed cat lady.

We spent the following day touring the main tourist attractions in Astana. Built on oil money, the city would have looked modern when it was built in 1997. It had sand-colored, boxy, concrete exteriors, industrial materials, and highly metallic, rounded accents. Like Von Dutch biker hats, it had been so trendy that it went out-of-date almost immediately.

"She knows she needs to cover her head, right?" A German man told another German man while pointing at me. The man's choice to not speak to me directly felt particularly appropriate considering the circumstances. We had entered a clean, white mosque, and all the women had been asked to put on turquoise robes.

Muttering to myself, I covered my head and admired the intricately painted patterns and gold leaf on the inside of the mosque. Entering the next room, all the men could walk into one room, while the women, with our turquoise hoods on, stood in the corner, a barrier indicating women could not go any further. The men looked back at us, laughing.

While in Almaty the week prior, one of the locals told me, "Many people did not know that our country even existed until *Borat*. We hate the '–stan' in our country's name. I wish we were called, 'Kazakhlandia.' Everyone assumes we are like Afghanistan and are too scared to travel here."

She was right. Sadly, one could argue Americans learn geography according to where we've bombed. This also explains why Afghanistan was the most well-known of all the "-stans."

"Muslim men would pay top dollar to rape a beautiful Christian like you," a relative had said to me when I said I was going to Kazakhstan. To avoid these kinds of conversations, I had stopped telling my family about my travels, but since I was living at home, it was almost unavoidable.

Thus far, Kazakhstan seemed safe and, like America, had a wide variety of levels of religious beliefs. While I had to wear a shawl in the mosque, no one wore burkinis when I had spent a spa day in Almaty. I did see a man whip himself with some brush in a steam room and then jump into an ice bath, a tradition that I was told is very common in Russia. A taxi driver texted me after my trip that he was "good at massage," but that has nothing to do with religion and more to do with the fact that there are scumbags everywhere you travel.

Finishing up our morning tour of Astana, we went to lunch.

"The restaurant is on the twenty-fifth floor. There is only a small elevator that can fit ten people at a time. It was not a good idea to pick a restaurant on the twenty-fifth floor, but this was not my decision," our Kazakh guide shared over the bus loudspeaker.

The restaurant was up to Western standards, if not too modern. To use the bathroom faucet, you had to turn a square dial side to side instead of up, resulting in me, with my hands covered in soap, having to ask the coatrack attendant how to turn on the water, dripping soap all over the restaurant because life is hard.

"Ahhhh!" I screamed, jumping back after walking around a corner and running into a mannequin wearing traditional nomadic Kazakh garb. While attractive from afar, a few inches from your face, a life-size doll in bright red silk is quite terrifying. These were positioned around the restaurant to emphasize the traditional cuisine they served.

After admiring the view, we headed to the Museum of the First President of the Republic. President Nazarbayev, at age seventy-six, was increasingly focused on his legacy, including having his face plastered on billboards all across his country and the creation of this library. It made me think of my own legacy. After all, I'd quit my fancy global executive job because it felt like I wasn't adding anything to this world. Making people laugh felt more fulfilling. I'd also helped find forever homes for a bunch of stray cats in Shanghai. That should count for something!

The library looked like a giant eyeball and cost five billion dollars to make.[32] In the US, you need to be dead or leave office to have a Presidential library, but as a dictator, hell, it's your birthday; why not gift yourself your own library!

The library was the epitome of questionable, which is maybe why they took our phones away upon entry. Inside the golf ball, one side looked like the Guggenheim with white walls in different floors all the way up. The other side was a huge window, open to the blue skies above.

"This is the direction of the future," the guide explained, pointing to the window. The future has a direction?

"Please do not step on the carpet; disabled children will play there tomorrow," the guide said, scolding one of my group for accidentally stepping on the rug. We all looked at each other, perplexed. This place was full of surprises.

One floor had all the books gifted to Nazarbayev, with Bill Clinton's book front and center. Another floor had all the books "written" by Nazarbayev. Some covers even had him in a pondering pose with yellow lighting, giving off a romantic vibe. I would have titled them: "One Night with Nazarbayev." He must have worked on these at night, under candlelight, writing these extensive pieces of literature for his country. Or in the words of Borat, the fake diplomat they never wanted, "Not!"

Another floor had all the gifts given to him, such as a gold and ivory pen from a Swiss banker or a dope ass clock from Russia. It seemed to highlight that corruption was alive and well. Perhaps it was a hint to touring dignitaries that they should also gift lavishly, like shaking the collection plate in front of someone at church.

Hungover from karaoke the night prior, we were ready to head back to the hotel.

"Are you sure you don't want to visit the university?" the Kazakh guide asked.

"We are tired and some people are feeling sick," a leader of our group explained.

"You sure? They really should visit our university."

"*No.* We *are* canceling it."

The Kazahk guide held up the bus's mic, "You really should visit Nazarbayev University ... but you have been refused. Nazarbayev University has over 3,700 students ..."

"Is that a mall?" an older German barked, looking out the bus window.

"Yes. And the University is named after President Nazarbayev. They asked him if he wanted it named—"

"Is that a Starbucks?" a Millennial asked.

"Yes."

"They have a Starbucks!"

"... the government wanted to honor him by naming it after him, so they asked our dear Pres—"

"Is that a hospital?"

"Yes, it is a chain hospital. A very good hospital. If you have problems with drugs, blah blah blah, they will help you," the guide snapped. Clearly, she was fed up with us and thought that hospitals came in chains like McDonald's.

That evening was spent at a local Ambassador's home. Albeit with a beautiful view of Presidential Park, the ambassador's apartment was surprisingly small. He explained that it was because in the winter there are many feet of snow, so living in a big home became a hassle, while in apartment could stay warm and cozy. From his balcony, we watched the sun set over the city, a warm egg yolk orange drifting below the skyline.

On the way out, some people exited through the wrong floor and entered a locked garden of a high security ambassadorial apartment complex and were unable to get out.

"They are locked in the garden!" I heard repeatedly in heavily accented English for the next thirty minutes, as a bunch of Germans ran around screaming, trying to find someone with a key.

The next day, we attended the Europe Day celebration. I asked the Europeans what this meant, and they had no idea. I Googled "Europe Day Kazakhstan" and found a picture from the previous year of an Asian woman picking up European Union flag pamphlets from an outdoor table. When you zoomed into the background there was someone dressed in a onesie as a spotted black and white dog. This picture was the only link I could find on Europe Day in Kazakhstan, with no description attached.

The introductory concert was exactly what you'd expect from a Europe Day concert: one song from each European country, mixed so as not to offend anyone with a specific order. As I had learned, the European Union was about equality and mutual respect. This was the constant, unwavering message put out by the institution. During the songs, short videos were played in the background. One was of Brussels, with lots of zoom-ins on the dick of the statue of the little child peeing. Another was of vines growing, with yellow and black butterflies bursting out, the kind of thing you might find on the cover of a Romanian young adult romance novel. The last was of purple and pink ink dripping and swirling on a white background; this is the exact packaging of the sex toy company that I had worked for with bright fluids gushing on the boxes of their vibrators. Kazakhstan had made Europe seem so sexy! Scheisse!

As I watched, I realized that maybe I did deserve to be here. After all, I had visited many of the countries displayed on the screen, taken a class on the creation of European Union at the Sorbonne in Paris, and had visited all the major E.U. institutions while living in Luxembourg as a Fulbright Scholar. My life was a bit dismal at the moment, but I had learned so much through my travels and could qualify as a citizen of the world.

Afterward, there was a reception with decent food. As we palled around, we met ambassadors from a number of countries.

One, a bald man in his fifties, was wearing a fancy watch.

"How long have you been in Kazakhstan?" I asked. Years of living abroad and attending networking events had made me a master of boring conversation.

"Four months. Before that, I was stationed in Syria for the last three years."

"Wow, this must feel like a vacation, I mean not a vacation—"

Damn it, Kristen, you're supposed to be good at this.

"—compared to the difficulties of Syria."

"I survived because there was one safe road that I would take to Beirut every weekend. Beirut has everything—restaurants, clubs, their night life is great!" he said. "Survived" seemed like an interesting choice of words considering that most people in Syria were struggling to *physically* survive every day.

As I looked out the window of my flight leaving Kazakhstan and heading towards the sofa that I currently called my bed, I pondered all the travel I had done over the past decade. Looking back at my career, roaming from continent to continent, from job to job, I did deserve to be at this leadership conference with all these amazing people. I had taken constant risks, had experiences that no one else has had, explored new terrain, and learned so much about people and the world. Travel was this thing that I always said "Yes!" to and it opened a lot of doors for me. What would the next phase of my life be?

The next big leap was not geographic but in trusting in myself. It was also one of recreating a roost in my home country after being away for so long. A new life on the West Coast, pioneering my own path. As they said in China when I ran past on a morning jog, light on my feet, dodging laundry on clothes lines in spindly back alleys: "Jiāyóu!" which means: "Persist! Don't give up! Keep going!"

This I would do.

CHAPTER 21: HONING IN ON HOME

Building My Nest

Three years later, Los Angeles, California, United States—The old mansion was filled with luxury candles. The first serious, non-long-distance partner that I had had since Sam and I perused the Valentine's Day charity event thrown by an A-List celebrity. We were friends of friends of friends of the famous host, so I was basically best friends with her.

"Could you please step forward," a poet, there to write customized poems for party guests, asked. My partner and I sat down before her, her fingers paused over a vintage, robin's egg blue typewriter on a softened wood corner table across the room from the known actress. "I'm writing poems about a place that feels special to you. Could you tell me a little bit about a place and why it's important to you?"

"Like my apartment?" I blurted. Normal people probably said something like "My childhood home" or "Paris," but my apartment was the only extremely important place I could think of.

"Sure," she said.

This made me think. *Why* was it so special to me? It was the first place that I'd designed completely for myself, and L.A. was where I had decided to settle. I was ready to nest, and that apartment was all mine to fill with twigs, feathers, and a bird-eating cat. It felt like more than a physical space.

"Up until this point, I've spent most of my life able to fit everything I own into a suitcase. This is my first real place to call my home," I explained. Tears started to form in my eyes, which was both surprising and embarrassing. I didn't want the celeb to see me cry, should she look over from the other side of the room at this random girl getting a poem written for her. Do you ever have so many good things happen at once that you want to cry? Like you're on that high, but your face wants to melt and contort into the shape of melting pizza cheese and let it all out?

"And what's important about your home?" the poet prodded, her fingers hovering over the keys of the typewriter.

"My cat's there, Nala. She's a gorgeous ginger street kitty I adopted in China. She has four cute fuzzy paws and a wet nose and—"

"The best cat," she typed.

"Exactly!" She really got me.

"Go on." Her fingers twitched. My eyes welled with more tears. Was my period coming? Why was I crying about my apartment?

A year prior, I had moved into my current place. Before that, I had lived with a girl named Karen in Mid-City, L.A. Karen came from Kentucky and had overdone lip injections, stick black hair, and a cosmetically perfect nose. She worked in sales, seemed so cool, spoke with a soft southern accent, and her apartment was this funky, yet breezy vibe. The home was filled with antiques, art deco lamps, glass skulls, and fresh olive branches. In the front there was a balcony, with monsteras elegantly draped over it, as if beckoning for whatever the plant equivalent of Romeo would be, maybe a fiddle leaf fig? It was a dream.

"You have a cat? I grew up with cats! I've always wanted to have one!" Karen cooed. "I guess it's good that Crystal bailed on living with me. She was supposed to live here and signed the lease a week ago, but then abruptly had to move back home." She paused, lacing her fingers together, and sat up straight. "Now, I do want some house rules so we can respect each other in our shared space."

"Of course!"

"Please text me if you ever have a guy sleepover, so I'm not surprised in the morning if there's a strange man in the kitchen or something."

"Sure!"

"Do you have any rules?"

I thought for a moment. "Let's make sure all the doors are closed so my cat doesn't get out, but that's about it!"

"Great. By the way, I know people named Karen are known for being crazy, but that's not me!" she joked. We burst out laughing. We were going to be best friends.

I moved in on January first; it was a new year, new home, new city, new me. I had a gorgeous apartment and a cool roommate for my fur-ocious house lioness and me. After going to an acting audition, I'd come home in the evening, pour myself a glass of wine, put the leash on Nala, and sit out on the porch. One time, while waiting for an audition, another actress vividly described to me hearing her cat get murdered by a coyote outside the window of her home. That was the most successful psychological warfare I had ever experienced. Needless to say, she threw me off my game and I didn't book it. While I sipped on my wine, Nala, in her bright green harness, would peak her head through the Spanish banisters, eagerly watching the squirrels, her eyes darting every time they moved. "You're not rich because you don't work hard enough," someone might say. Excuse me, I'm not rich because I invest all my money into my cat, and she doesn't pay me to be her assistant.

My first week there, I came home to a house full of fresh lavender roses—a color I'd never seen before nor known could exist.

"These are beautiful," I commented as Karen rushed from the back of my house. She'd gone that morning to downtown L.A.'s flower market and brought them home, wrapped in brown parchment paper.

"Oh thanks, my ex is coming over to get some of his stuff," she said. Before me, she had lived in the apartment with her ex—who was also her largest work client—but they'd broken up. At work, her boss was concerned that they would lose all their business due to the breakup and in her personal life, she'd told me she thought he was the one.

"But I ruined it," she said over a glass of two buck chuck. "We had a fight and I said some things and I shoved him. It was over."

"What kind of things?" I asked. I'd never had a fight like that. Of course, I'd had arguments with partners, but none that ever got physical. Then again, I had never lived with a boyfriend.

"The kind of things you can never take back. I did some things, too." She looked off into the distance.

That night, I woke up to the sound of loud thrusting and grunting. She hadn't sent me a text about him coming over, although this was her rule. In the morning, loud, heavy steps sprinted from our apartment followed by the pitter-patter of Karen's feet. Waiting until he left, I tiptoed out of my room for a yogurt. In the kitchen, I found Karen, singing to herself. Hearing me, she turned and looked at me, beaming.

"We hooked up last night," she said.

"Oh," I said, pretending to be shocked, as if I hadn't been traumatized by their loud sex the night before. She looked down, fidgeting with her hands.

"Do you think he and I will get back together?" she asked. She looked up at me, small pools of hope in her soft brown eyes.

"He moved out, so ... no?" *And I'm on the lease now,* I wanted to add. She didn't seem to understand the permanence of someone you lived with for nearly a year deciding to leave. She'd had to deal with getting the lease transferred over to her name, finding roommates, the first one falling through, then us signing the lease at the landlord's house, then me moving all my shit in. Having gone through all that, why did she think that one night of very loud sex would erase him moving out?

The next day, she was on her phone for hours on end. She spoke in a soft voice, threw her head back and giggled in a melodic, high-pitched tone. That night, when I came home from my improv class, she was again talking on the phone. It was like that for the rest of the week; she was constantly on the phone for hours. How could she get any work done? I set up a desk in my room to avoid the noise while I, you know, did things to support myself.

"He lives in Atlanta, but we met on a set, and I don't know. We have such deep conversations, you know?" she said, blushing. The way she looked when she said this was as if she was in love, but maybe it was just the lip injections.

"Is someone whose mother is from Georgia a son of a peach?" I responded. She rolled her eyes and giggled. Nothing could get her down.

"Would it be alright if he visited and stayed with us? He's going to see me and also do an interview with Vice."

"As long as there aren't any distractions during hours when I'm working, that should be fine," I said. After all, we both worked from home, and I had my first freelance tech copywriting client since moving to L.A., who was extremely demanding.

When he showed up at our apartment, he looked like Jeffrey Dahmer. He wore gold-rimmed, clear-glass aviator glasses and a mustache that looked like a caterpillar, and as he traveled about our apartment, he left the scent of a thousand packs of cigarettes. He was short and sort of hunched over, wearing ripped black tees that had faded from a million years of use. Nala hid under my bed whenever he came over, her little eyes peering out in fear. I was not impressed and ... neither was Karen.

"You know, he came here without a credit card, and that's a huge turnoff," she whispered to me while he was in the bathroom.

"Wait, he paid to fly here, but didn't bring a credit card?"

"No, he said he couldn't afford to visit, so I paid for him to fly here, but then he showed up without his credit card! He asked me to buy condoms at a gas station when we were coming back from the airport, and that doesn't get me wet, you know?"

He stayed for a full week, paid for nothing, and they slept next to each other. They didn't have sex at all during his visit. During the day, while I sat in the living room at my computer trying to work, they'd come in and join me and start loudly bickering.

"Do you think I was right, or he was right?" Karen asked me afterward. If only I could've charged a seventy-dollar copay. This was a soap opera with a loud ex, a broke new guy, and that was only in the first month. On my end, I was stretched too thin, trying to build a business, while going out for auditions and taking improv classes and performing in the evenings. Her boy crazy was creating a very tumultuous living situation, one that wasn't the calm I needed to build a foundation and a new life. By then, condoms were burning a hole in her pocket, so she had to find a new guy. A few days later, I came home to her sitting on the sofa with a guy she'd met at a bar the night before. In her role, she could work whenever she wanted, but at that point, she was only working when she was drinking.

By the end of month two, her only working at night while drinking had progressed to pouring herself a full glass of wine on a Tuesday morning. With so much on my own plate, I didn't have the energy or emotional capacity to deal with her drama or drinking. There was only so much time I could spend in my poorly lit room (she refused to let me leave any of the blinds open) and I couldn't close my door since Nala needed to move about as she pleased. Cats hate closed doors. They take it personally.

"You know, you have to pay me. Your cat's ruining my sofa!" She'd started yelling at me in her thick, Southern accent whenever she felt like it. Nala hadn't ripped anything, but she had perforated the sofa when she hopped on top.

To try and solve the situation, I bought leather polish, cat training tape, and even covered it in white blankets, buying hooks to secure the blankets over the entire bare surface of the couch.

"There," I said, pointing to the now completely covered sofa. Nala hopped up on the table.

"What did I tell you? No cat on food surfaces!" she screamed.

"She's a cat. She doesn't know what a 'food surface' is," I replied, not even trying to hide my annoyance.

"I saw someone train a cat on the internet, and you owe me $1000 dollars for that sofa!" she screamed again. It seemed like whatever I attempted to remedy the situation, she was coming up with new, even more unsolvable reasons to be upset with me when she was in a mood.

"Your sofa is secondhand, it's not worth a thousand dollars," I retorted.

"This sofa is very important to me." She paused for dramatic effect. "I bought it with an ex." Translation: an ex bought it for her. She hadn't even spent her own money on it. "And why are the blinds open?" She rushed over to close the blinds on two of the six windows in the living room that I had opened.

"I live here, too. You said that you grew up with cats, so none of this should be a surprise, and I've tried to find solutions. If you care about it that much, put it in the garage."

"You owe me $125 for the mattress in your room," she said.

"What? That wasn't the agreement when I moved in."

"If you are going to use my stuff, you have to pay for it."

"That was not our agreement," I said. If I had known there were additional costs, I wouldn't have signed the lease. I was living off my small savings and only had a single copywriting client for a few hours a week as I was growing my business.

Earlier in my life, I would have been more empathetic, but through my experiences, I knew the signs of a narcissist. Give a narcissist a cookie and they are going to ask for your entire bank account, all your time and attention, and your kidney—not because they need it but simply because they enjoy taking whatever they can. As I watched Karen, I saw her process each thought about how she should react. It was like a five-year-old planning out a tantrum. I was an actor; I knew bad acting!

If I gave her a penny, she'd come up with new excuses to ask for more money. I was only her roommate of two months, not her sugar daddy nor her therapist. While I was constantly dealing with her drama and had to tiptoe around my own home, she couldn't care less about my life. I was working on sticking up for myself, and I wasn't going to let her keep being ridiculous. It was stressful and exhausting, but I was determined to make L.A. my home and she was not going to stop my momentum.

For the next few weeks, every time she saw me, she stomped by dramatically. It was like living in a minefield; I never knew when she'd blow up at me. Luckily, she was heading to a film festival in Paris. We weren't speaking at that point, but I knew that she was alive because of the semi-nude photos she'd started posting on Instagram. Since we weren't on speaking terms, I had no idea how long she'd be gone for or when she'd return. I was simply happy to have peace and quiet in the place where I was struggling to make my home.

"Your shit is everywhere!" Karen screamed from the living room. Asleep, I jumped up from my bed. Apparently, she had returned. I checked my phone, and it was one a.m. I was home alone, and I had a blanket and maybe a dish here or there, but the house wasn't a disaster. I was afraid of the level of rage in her voice. Later, she'd tell me that she had crashed her car on the way home from the airport. The specifics were unclear, but she had to return to get it the next day, which made me wonder if she had been drunk.

The next day, I tiptoed out of the house before she woke, too scared to see her. That evening was my first night working as an unpaid intern at a famous comedy theater in LA. It was my chance to meet other comedians like me. While on my shift, I texted her, *Hey—clearly things aren't working out. I think it's best if I move out. I'll move out by the end of the month, so you have time to find a replacement. We can chat when I'm back.* Normally, I would have that conversation in person, but I was too afraid of how she would react. I assumed she'd be in bed by the time I got home so we could discuss it in the morning when she was sober. I wanted to give her time to cool down.

I got home at 1:00 a.m., exhausted. I was in the bathroom, washing off my makeup, when I heard her bang on the door.

"You're a grown-ass woman; you can't just move out! We've got a contract!" she shrieked at me. I finished washing my face and opened the door.

"Karen, this is clearly not working out. I'm not staying here." *You're unhinged,* I did not add.

"Well, then you have to find a replacement, but they can't tour the apartment because I don't want strangers in my house!"

"That's impossible." I understood why her ex and the girl who had briefly signed a lease before me had chosen not to live with her. I walked out of the bathroom and back to my room. Karen followed me down the hallway, screaming obscenities at me.

She stood in my doorway, blocking me from leaving my own room or trying to avoid the confrontation with her.

"Karen, I am exhausted, I just got off work, and I have work in the morning. I don't want to discuss this right now. Can we resolve this tomorrow?"

She continued to block the doorway. I wasn't sure if she would do anything violent, so I kept a safe distance from her, but I was trapped. My heart pounded. How do you deal with someone drunk, irrational, and volatile? What if she started throwing things at me like she did with her ex? Would *my* skull survive if she threw one of her glass skulls at me? Turning sideways, I hugged the doorway and tried to move past her, although there was nowhere to go. It was the middle of the night, so it was not a good idea to be walking around outside. I didn't want to be in there, but our neighborhood wasn't safe.

As I tried to slip by her without touching her, she started to yell. "Stop hurting me! What are you doing; stop hurting me!"

Perplexed, I stepped back. I hadn't even touched her. I didn't want to, and unlike her, I was dead sober. I wanted to be as far away from her as I could be. Who was this performance for? Herself? Me? Was this something that she screamed every time she got in a fight like this? How many of these fights had she had? She'd mentioned a former roommate banging on her door and it sounded like she had laid her hands on her ex. I wasn't her boyfriend, I was a stranger who had lived with her for under three months. With no idea how to de-escalate the situation, my stress response was to freeze. This behavior was part of a pattern and if I continued to live with her, these types of fights could get even worse. If I called the cops, what would they do, and how would they respond to two tiny girls having a fight? Could they do anything? We were contractually obligated to live together.

"That's it, I'm taking my mattress!" she yelled.

"This was the guest room and you're welcome to use the furniture," she had said with a smile when I had moved in.

She started to struggle to pull the mattress off my bed, so I'd have nothing to sleep on. At first, I stepped back and let her struggle. She couldn't carry it out by herself. Then I decided to help her because I could always sleep on the sofa, and where was she going to take it?

"Here, let me help you," I said, picking up one side. She tilted her head, processing that I wasn't provoked, and put her side down. "Karen, you're drunk; we can talk about this in the morning."

"No, I'm not!"

This went on for another hour until she finally left my doorway. Concerned that Karen would do something to me while I was sleeping, like chopping my hair off or splashing cold water on me, I lodged a chair under the doorknob. Being trapped in my room, I assumed Nala would keep me up all night, but likely sensing something was wrong, she instead glued herself to my side under the covers.

In the morning, I squeezed Nala tight. With hardly any friends or a support network in this new city and my roommate in need of serious help, I had no idea how to handle this situation. My psychiatrist friend said if she did it again, I should have her taken to a mental hospital. That seemed too extreme, but I felt I was in over my head. I didn't feel safe in my own home. In the morning, I explained the situation to the landlord, who spoke to her.

"We've had problems with her before," the landlord said. "I was worried something like this might happen after her boyfriend moved out. I suggested that she ask her mother to co-sign her lease if she didn't want another roommate. She said her mother would refuse, so I think this may have happened before." They were surprisingly understanding, but a heads-up would have been nice.

Under normal circumstances, I would never move out without notifying someone, but when I had tried to, she got drunk and violent. I recognized that sneaking out was fucked up. It was an awful thing to do to someone, but my alternative was living in fear and potentially having to call the police if her harassment turned physical, which it had with the last person who lived with her. I needed to set some boundaries with Karen for my last two weeks there.

"Why would you tell the landlord my business?" They had called her to talk about what had happened.

"Because your behavior is abnormal and not okay. If you ever do that again, I will call the cops," I calmly explained to Karen in the morning.

"Why? I didn't do anything wrong."

"If I ask you to leave my room and you stand in my doorway, screaming at me, that is not okay. This is my house, too, and grabbing my furniture, yelling at me, none of that is normal behavior."

"I didn't scream at you." She denied any wrongdoing on her part.

"You stood in the doorway, your arms across it, saying I couldn't leave unless I paid you for your mattress. Listen, if I'm going to stay here, you need to show me that you're going to change," I said. "If a guy is coming over, text me, the rule you made when I moved in. Please don't leave the doors open, even if you're running down to get the mail, because of the cat."

"Okay," she said with a childish pout.

The next day, the downstairs neighbors brought their cat up "to play with Nala" but when Karen was distracted, one of them followed me into my room and said our other neighbor had heard the screaming.

"She is drinking at all times of the day and screaming at me, I don't know what to do."

"Yeah, she started to come down to complain to us about you, but the stories she told never added up. They didn't make any sense, and we'd poke holes in them. Here's our key if you need it." He handed me a key to their place. Does every apartment complex have that one spicy tenant who only feels at home living in chaos and must spread that to everyone else?

"Thank you." I nodded. This was a nice act from practical strangers.

A few days later, I heard a man's footsteps in the living room—a man who Karen had not texted me about sleeping over. When I went into the living room, I discovered that he had sprinted from her bedroom to the point where the front door was ajar. Nala could have escaped!

My gut instinct was right. Karen was not going to change. We were basically in a two week "probationary" period and even then, she was doing whatever she wanted and not following what we had agreed to.

I knew hardly anyone in the city and no one well enough to ask them to help me move, so I called my distant cousin who had lived in LA his whole life. After explaining my situation, we made a plan for me to sneak out. Slowly, I started to pack. My door had to stay ajar for Nala, so I only left furniture visible in the ten percent of my room that you could see from the hallway. When it was time to move out, we'd only have an hour or two to move everything I owned, so I had to have everything packed and not allow Karen to notice that all my belongings were in boxes. Luckily, she didn't care about me at all.

On my last day in the apartment, Karen turned to me.

"By the way, Nala wanted to go out on the porch, so I let her out."

"Does she have her leash on?"

"No," She smiled at me not-so-innocently. She knew nothing was more purr-ecious to me than my cat.

My heart raced. Nala and I had come a long way to get here. It took ten men and a car jack to pull her out of the engine of a taxi in Shanghai. At that point, she probably thought that that would be the most traumatic event in her life; little did she know she'd be on a thirteen-hour flight with me to move to America, including a snowy layover in Toronto, where slept under a blanket next to me, leashed to a terminal chair. We'd come a long way from an apartment the size of a bathroom in Shanghai to moving to a sunny one in L.A.

I could only imagine what Nala would do. Maybe she'd run to hide and get hit by a car or eaten by a coyote. My first lesson on death was when, as a child, I found Hamsty killed by Meow Meow. I pictured Nala by the side of the road in a similar death, her body hard with two huge coyote teeth marks in her side. My baby girl was adorable, but also dumb as a bag of chips!

I rushed to the balcony. Luckily, I could see her frantic eyes as she scratched at the glass panes of the porch door to be let back in. She only wanted to be with her mum. Picking her up in my arms, I held her close. She was all I had.

"It's so funny. All your dishes are gone!" Karen said from the kitchen, having noticed while making her breakfast. I had packed them all the night before while she was out drinking... I mean *working*. My heart continued to pound.

"Oh, we needed them for the TV show I'm on. Low budget, you know how it is," I lied.

"I thought you were moving out or something," She laughed.

I shrugged.

"I'm going to get a bikini wax," she said, heading out. The moment the door shut, I rang my cousin.

"Ding, dong, the witch is gone."

"For how long?"

"I don't know, she's getting a bikini wax."

"I'll drive over." He was coming from Burbank, a ride that could take up to an hour with traffic. As he drove, I took the boxes and started carrying them down the side hallway, putting them outside. When he arrived, we threw the bags in his car, and with Nala in her carrier on my lap, howling at the top of her lungs, I ducked down as he exited the driveway in case Karen's car came in while we exited. It felt like a really shitty spy movie.

That afternoon, Nala, my cousin, and I put all my belongings in the cheapest hotel room I could find. As I thanked my cousin, Nala pawed at a still-twitching cockroach she'd found in our room. Then, I headed to a night shoot on set for a TV show. I was there for the next twelve hours, and I had to pretend that I had not just escaped my crazy roommate. Scared I'd tag myself somewhere on Instagram and she'd show up and attack me, I blocked her number and on social media. She was the only person I knew personally that I'd ever blocked, but I was genuinely afraid of her. Before moving out, I looked for a new apartment in Koreatown, the only area I could afford. L.A. housing was like: do you want to spend $3K to rent a tin can in the center of town or pay a million dollars to buy a murder house on the outskirts of town?

"It's out of my budget," I told my mom over the phone. "But it's perfect."

"Sometimes you have to believe, and the money will come," she told me. "And without a roommate, you'll be more productive. You can have your own schedule and not have to worry about someone else."

"That sounds amazing," I said, visualizing a light at the end of a tunnel. Since my mom was a painter, I trusted her to know what creatives needed. I signed a yearlong lease that day, but I'd need to move into a hotel for two weeks as they fixed up the apartment. Luckily, my dad was flying in to help me get settled in my new place. I was grateful to my parents for helping out during this time of need.

Two weeks later, I was in my apartment, and my dad and I were sleeping on blown-up mattresses that I'd ordered from Amazon the night before. My new apartment's entire aesthetic was designed around furniture Nala couldn't destroy. Millennial Maximalism? No, it's Caturday Catastrophe. As I filled my closet, it felt weird acquiring and storing things of my own. I wasn't used to having more than a suitcase full of stuff.

As I cleared my schedule of difficult people, something magical happened. Good people started reaching out to hire me. When nearly all my savings were completely gone and I was at the point where I couldn't sleep at night, terrified at how I'd pay my rent, a contact I'd worked with in the past reached out on LinkedIn and hired me to write for their company. On the creative side, I booked more acting gigs and secured more writing bylines. Slowly but surely, L.A. saw I was a hard worker, reliable, and a professional, and it rewarded me.

Flash forward, and all those failed businesses resulted in my successful one as well as learning what makes me truly happy along the way. As someone who spent their twenties traveling the world and doing the exact opposite of what everyone told me I had to do to be successful, I made more money than I ever thought was possible. I thought I had to choose between a life of travel and a career and family, but this binary view was false. When I had money, I realized that it didn't make me happy. Instead, I squirreled it away, living below my means. My financial advisor (I never imagined I'd have one of those) said that I could even retire in my forties, which I visualize as living like a cat: daily naps, getting fed while I lay around, having my nails trimmed regularly, and maybe a little catnip or in my case, wine, when I'm feeling frisky! Come to think of it, that also describes my current life plus my daily work. I was on my way to being my own trust fund, or who knows, maybe I'd spend that money on having kids someday.

My work day ended with Nala howling at my door to walk her around the courtyard on her leash so she could eat grass. Her new life involved training to use the human toilet and her own personal robot to feed her four times a day so she wouldn't overeat. Nala was a true rags-to-riches story: she had upgraded from being a street cat in Shanghai to a diva in LA. On top of the kibble, my partner cooked for us.

"She loves it!" I'd say after giving her a piece of freshly cooked steak.

"Are you saying that my cooking tastes like cat food?" We had a modern relationship: I took him to nice dinners, and he cooked delicious meals. As his sous chef, I predominantly drank wine and said things like, "You know, I think I need a fifth taste test to make sure it's edible." We had romantic, starlit evenings eating boiled crab. Opening a shell, my bright red press-on nail popped off and hit him in the face. He asked if it was crab shell. Who needed Prince Eric? This was what a fairytale romance looked like.

For the first time, our lives were peaceful. My younger self religiously wore thongs because they made me feel sexy. I felt sexiest putting on mascara and sipping on a cocktail in my pajamas alone at home with my cat once I got older. I didn't want to look pretty. I wanted to look comfy. Compliment my fuzzy sweater, my little silk scrunchie, my Crocs. Mistake me for a shag rug; the highest honor a person could achieve. I guess you could say I was a convert.

"But how do you travel with a cat?" You might ask. Easy, I traveled *for* cats. My dream had always been to spend a month a year somewhere else in the world. I didn't want to age well. I wanted to age like I've lived a life naked and unafraid, traveling the world, drinking fine wines, and tasting the most unique of foods.

This past year, I took care of a friend's cat in London while another friend had a writer's retreat in my place with Nala. Nala and I had a little breakdown whenever we were apart, so I got her this calming cat pheromone diffuser, so now we both relied on essential oils to stay chill. While on the tube in London, a child was staring me down, so I blinked at her. This was when I realized that I spent too much time with my cat because I heard cats blink to show they feel safe and happy. Note to self: a real child can't be communicated with the same way as your fur child can.

This past Christmas, I returned to London once again to catsit and spend time with my Shanghai family. Alorec and Juste live there with their two children, Chloe was there visiting her British husband's family, and Ingrid stopped over on her way home to Denmark. My partner and I even popped over to Paris to visit Fabien and his wife ... who—introduced by him—was one of my only friends when I first arrived in Shanghai. As we sat together, reminiscing over our times shared across the globe, their two-year-old son bustled around us, sticking his pinky in his mother's champagne to feel like he was joining in on all the adult fun.

I had set up a life where as long as I got my work done and it was high quality, it didn't matter what time zone I was in. I could live and work wherever, whenever I wanted. My life had everything I had hoped for and more. Even with more success, stability, freedom, knowledge, and experience, what brought me the most joy, every single day, was watching Nala go about her life in the most adorable way.

"What else do you like about your home?" the poet asked as I sat a few yards away from an A-list celebrity. As a Z-list nobody, I had at least made it into the same room without being a nepotism baby. On that note, if anyone famous wants to adopt me, please do. Angelina Jolie, I'm looking at you.

"Each night, Nala and I drink wine on a fake patch of grass I put on the fire escape, watching the sunset and chasing pigeons ... I want to clarify: I drink the wine and Nala chases the pigeons. My place has big French windows, which remind me of when I lived in Paris, and I've used all the feng shui tips I learned in China to bring myself wealth and prosperity."

My Taiwanese partner rolled his eyes at this last comment, finding my obsession with this aspect of his culture bizarre when he didn't believe in it himself. The first time he came over to my apartment he couldn't help but ask why I had a giant, ceramic, gold pig in the northwest corner of my home.

"How am I supposed to attract prosperity into my home without a golden pig?" I'd told him. Wasn't it obvious? That's what Jade taught me in Changzhou!

I continued to explain my home to the poet, "In the morning, I walk a block over to a bodega and get a croissant—like I'm back in Paris—and a coffee with cream and sugar—like I'm in New York."

I started to realize why I was tearing up. In Koreatown—a haven of people from all nationalities and walks of life—I'd created a little place just for me. I'd enjoy dumplings for lunch every day like I did in Shanghai, or, on special occasions, I'd buy black tobiko from H-Mart and eat it in the bathtub, pretending it was caviar. After spending over a decade on the road, I had finally found a home where I could unpack all my bags. I was there to stay. I'd transitioned from a life of traveling the world to a homebody lifestyle in L.A. and was loving it. I had found my nest.

If you liked this book and want to read more, make sure to follow: @Kristen Van Nest and @RAPubCollective
Tag #WheretoNest to share your thoughts on the book and share your next travel adventure!

Acknowledgments

Thank you to my partner David for being by my side during all the highs and lows and calming me like a horse tranquilizer to the neck.

Thank you to my family for supporting me even when it meant reliving old wounds.

Thank you to all my creative friends, who constantly keep me on my grind through every laugh at every social post and every tear shed as I'm moved by one of their books and films. Especially my morning writing accountability group (Jen, Lisa, Natalie, Heloise)—you saw me through writing my proposal, all the rejection letters, the final acceptance jubilation, and the pains and joys of writing this book.

Thank you to Tina, Alex, Miruna, and Kayla at Rising Action Publishing Co. and my agent Mariah Nichols at D4EO Literary Agency for being the best cheerleaders and guides I could ever ask for.

I wouldn't be the creative I am today without the amazing, talented people around me who lift me up and keep me inspired every day.

About the Author

Kristen Van Nest is an American comedian and business owner based in Los Angeles, CA. Having lived in Luxembourg as a Fulbright Scholar followed by 3.5 years living in Shanghai working in the wine industry, she's spent much of her life traveling the world in search of new and exciting ways to eat bread. Her tweets have been featured on Millennial meme accounts including @fearofgoingout, @vodkalana, @Iamthirtyaf, to name a few, and her personal essays and satirical writing can be found on The Rumpus, McSweeney's, SlackJaw, and more. When not traveling, you can find her curled up on the sofa drinking wine with her cat. Kristen is represented by Mariah Nichols at D4EO. *Where to Nest* is her debut memoir.

Notes

1. Apparently our taste buds change on flights, making things like ginger ale taste less sweet.
   Thomson, Lizzie. 2019. "These are the best and worst drinks to order during a flight." https://metro.co.uk/2019/11/09/new-research-reveals-he-best-and-worst-drinks-to-order-during-a-flight-11068267/

2. Apparently, studies show you are statistically more likely to cry on flights due to the altitude and a feeling of not having control.
   Gajanan, Mahita. 2018. "This Is Why You're More Likely to Cry on an Airplane, According to a Psychologist." https://time.com/5274209/airplane-cry-emotion/

3. Vuković, Diane. 2023. "Drinking Urine for Survival – Is it Safe?" https://www.primalsurvivor.net/drinking-urine-survival/

4. Tsjeng, Zing. 2022. "Did Elon Musk Get Rejected From Berghain? An Investigation"https://www.vice.com/en/article/y3vjpb/elon-musk-berghain-refuses-entry

5. Weissman, Jordan. 2012. "U.S. Income Inequality: -It's Worse Today Than it Was in 1774." https://www.theatlantic.com/business/archive/2012/09/us-income-inequality-its-worse-today-than-it-was-in-1774/262537/

6. "Why Most Ski Injuries Happen After 3:30 PM" Health Library Dec 14, 2022. https://healthcare.utah.edu/the-scope/health-library/all/2022/12/why-most-ski-injuries-happen-after-330-pm

7. Fisher, M.F.K. How to Cook a Wolf (New York: Duell, Sloan and Pearce, 1942).

8. Obulutsa, George. 2020. "Westgate attack: Two jailed over Kenyan shopping mall attack." https://www.reuters.com/article/us-keny a-attack-court-idUSKBN27F263

9. Wechsler, Kim. 2015. "Women-led companies perform three times better than the S&P 500."https://fortune.com/2015/03/03/wo men-led-companies-perform-three-times-better-than-the-sp-500/

10. Geffner, Carol. 2023. "Ten Percent Of Fortune 500 Companies Are Now Women-Led: The Changing Face Of Leadership." https://www.forbes.com/sites/forbescoachescouncil/2023/03/17 /ten-percent-of-fortune-500-companies-are-now-women-led-the -changing-face-of-leadership/?sh=4246343d3498

11. Williams, Sarah, Wenfei Xu, Shin Bin Tan, Michael J. Foster, and Changping Chen. November 2019. *Cities*. Nov; Vol. 94. Pp. 275-285. "Ghost cities of China: Identifying urban vacancy through social media data." https://www.sciencedirect.com/scie nce/article/abs/pii/S0264275118307510.

12. Ronghua Ma, Chaolin Gu, Yingxia Pu, and Xiaodong Ma. 2008. *Sensors (Basel)*. Oct; 8(10): 6371–6395. "Mining the Urban Sprawl Pattern: A Case Study on Sunan, China." http://www.ncbi.nlm. nih.gov/pmc/articles/PMC3707455/

13. Prosek James. 2010. "Give Thanks for ... Eel?" http://www.nytim es.com/2010/11/25/opinion/25prosek.html

14. Lockett, Hudson. 2014. "Hukou reform: Beijing abolishes "agricultural" residence class, but rural-urban split remains." http://www.chinaeconomicreview.com/hukou-reform-beijing-abolishes-agricultural-residence-class-rural-urban-split-remains

15. Fourrier, Jacques. 2015. "A Heady Brew." http://www.bjreview.com/Nation/201509/t20150910_800037831.html

16. #Legend. 2017. "Emma Gao of Ningxia Winery Silver Heights is Here to Save the World, One Grape at a Time." https://hashtaglegend.com/culture/emma-gao-ningxia-winery-silver-heights-here-save-world-one-grape-time/

17. Brinded, Lianna. 2015. "These heartbreaking pictures of elderly people lining up outside banks sum up the chaos in Greece right now" http://www.businessinsider.com/photos-of-pensioners-at-atm-machines-in-greece-2015-6?r=UK&IR=T

18. Arnett, George, Ami Sedghi, Achilleas Galatsidas, and Sean Clarke. 2015. "Greek referendum: full results."http://www.theguardian.com/world/ng-interactive/2015/jul/05/live-results-greek-referendum

19. Van Nest, Kristen. 2013. "Be the Death of Me." https://www.edgemedianetwork.com/story/146039 Produced through interviews with death experts by the The Civilians creative team.

20. History.com. 2023. "Ancient Greek Democracy." http://www.history.com/topics/ancient-history/ancient-greece-democracy

21. Thomas Jr., Landon. 2010. "https://www.nytimes.com/2010/0 8/19/business/global/19montenegro.html " https://www.nytim es.com/2010/08/19/business/global/19montenegro.html

22.   Booth,   Robert.   2011. "https://www.theguardian.com/world/2011/jul/08/million-pou nd-bash-nat-rothschild https://www.theguardian.com/world/2011/jul/08/million-poun d-bash-nat-rothschild

23. Bruni L, Albero G, Serrano B, Mena M, Collado JJ, Gómez D, Muñoz J, Bosch FX, de Sanjosé S. ICO/IARC Information Centre on HPV and Cancer (HPV Information Centre). "Human Papillomavirus and Related Diseases in the World." Summary Report 10 March 2023. https://www.hpvcentre.net/statistics/reports/X WX.pdf

24. *Ibid.*

25. https://hpvcentre.net/statistics/reports/CHN.pdf

26. Mirin, A. Arthur. 2021. "Gender Disparity in the Funding of Diseases by the U.S. National Institutes of Health" *J Womens Health (Larchmt).* Jul;30(7):956-963. https://pubmed.ncbi.nlm.nih.go v/33232627/

27. OKR = Objectives and key results. I'm so sorry I taught you this. I wish I went through my life not knowing what this means.

28. Latifi, Fortesa. 2023. "Why So Many Young People are Cutting o Their Parents." https://www.cosmopolitan.com/lifestyle/a44178 122/family-estrangement-cut-off-parents/

29. Ramzy, Austin and Yin Lang. 2008. "Tainted-Baby-Milk Scandal in China." https://content.time.com/time/world/article/0,8599, 1841535,00.html

30. Growth, Aimee. 2012. "You're the Average of the Five People You Sped the Most Time With." https://www.businessinsider.com/jim-rohn-youre-the-av erage-of-the-five-people-you-spend-the-most-time-with-2012-7

31. Cohen, Claire. 2015. "Imposter syndrome: Why do so many women feel like frauds?" https://www.telegraph.co.uk/women/work/imposter-s yndrome-why-do-so-many-women-feel-like-frauds/

32. Palmer, James. 2017. "https://foreignpolicy.com/2017/06/15/kazakhstan-spent-5-billi on-on-a-death-star-and-it-doesnt-even-shoot-lasers/ https://foreignpolicy.com/2017/06/15/kazakhstan-spent-5-billio n-on-a-death-star-and-it-doesnt-even-shoot-lasers/